Philosophy of Sex and Love

Writing for non-specialists and students as well as for fellow philosophers, this book explores some basic issues surrounding sex and love in today's world, among them consent, objectification, nonmonogamy, racial stereotyping, and the need to reconcile contemporary expectations about gender equality with our beliefs about how love works. Author Patricia Marino argues that we cannot fully understand these issues by focusing only on individual desires and choices. Instead, we need to examine the social contexts within which choices are made and acquire their meanings. That perspective, she argues, is especially needed today, when the values of individualism, self-expression, and self-interest permeate our lives. Marino asks how we can fit these values, which govern so many areas of contemporary life, with the generosity, caring, and selflessness we expect in love and sex.

Key Features of *Philosophy of Sex and Love: An Opinionated Introduction*

- Offers a contemporary, problems-based approach to the subject, helping readers better understand and address current issues and controversial questions
- Includes coverage of sex and love as they intersect with topics like disability, race, medicine, and economics
- Considers not only the ethical, but also the broadly social and political dimensions of sex and love
- Includes a helpful introduction and conclusion in each chapter and is written throughout in a clear and straightforward style, with examples and signposts to help guide the student and general reader
- A comprehensive and up-to-date bibliography provides a valuable tool for anyone's further research

Patricia Marino is Professor of Philosophy at the University of Waterloo in Canada, where, in addition to philosophy of sex and love, she works in ethics, epistemology, and philosophy of economics. She served as co-president of the Society for the Philosophy of Sex and Love from 2008 to 2018, and is the author of *Moral Reasoning in a Pluralistic World* (2015).

Philosophy of Sex and Love

An Opinionated Introduction

Patricia Marino

NEW YORK AND LONDON

First published 2019
by Routledge
52 Vanderbilt Avenue, New York, NY 10017

and by Routledge
2 Park Square, Milton Park, Abingdon, Oxon OX14 4RN

Routledge is an imprint of the Taylor & Francis Group, an informa business

© 2019 Taylor & Francis

Library of Congress Cataloging-in-Publication Data
A catalog record for this title has been requested

ISBN: 978-1-138-39099-7 (hbk)
ISBN: 978-1-138-39100-0 (pbk)
ISBN: 978-0-429-42300-0 (ebk)

Typeset in Times New Roman
by Taylor & Francis Books

In memory of Audrey Jennings Marino and Pasquale Marino

Contents

Acknowledgments

Over the years, numerous conversations with friends, students, and colleagues have helped shape my thinking about the issues I discuss here, and it's a pleasure now to express my gratitude; thank you especially to Scott Anderson, Samantha Brennan, Luke Brunning, Ann Cahill, Eric Cave, Justin Clardy, Shannon Dea, Monique Deveaux, Dave DeVidi, Raff Donelson, Carla Fehr, Katy Fulfer, Ann Garry, Julia Hill, Lara Karaian, Penelope Maddy, Shaun Miller, Amy Mullin, A. Y. Odedeyi, Kathleen Rybczynski, Laurie Shrage, and Anita Superson. Helga Varden, Gary Foster, Andrea Westlund, Raja Halwani, Robin Zheng, Shruta Swarup, Michael Perlin, Adrian Walsh, Katrina Monk, Ali Kraushaar, Chris Wass, Andria Bianchi, Isela González Vázquez, and Priscilla Larbi all contributed insightful comments on early drafts of individual chapters. Nathaniel Adam Tobias Coleman brought to my attention texts and ideas that became central to the discussion in Chapter 10. Kevin Mintz and Heather Bone not only read the entire manuscript and provided helpful feedback but also offered much appreciated encouragement. Two anonymous referees wrote substantive, constructive, and comprehensive reviews; my editor, Andy Beck, facilitated the process with philosophical sophistication and good cheer, and Liz Hudson and Stacey Carter provided expert copy-editing and editorial assistance.

I first presented some of the material here in courses and seminars at the University of Waterloo, and my students there have been an ongoing source of novel perspectives and questions. Ongoing conversations with Emma Dewald over the years have shaped my thinking and have been a constant source of inspiration.

This book is dedicated to the memory of my parents, Audrey Jennings Marino and Pasquale Marino, two non-philosophers whose open-mindedness and engagement with the world around them still influence the kinds of philosophy I do. What my partner, Jonathan Dewald, has done for me and for this work is too wide-ranging to be summarized here; without his love, care, and philosophical insight, this book could not have become what it is.

Introduction

At first sight, it might seem that "philosophy" and "sex and love" are an odd fit. Philosophy is often associated with abstraction, reasoning, and big questions about the meaning of life, while sex and love are personal, emotional, and culturally variable. Further, it might seem especially peculiar to use the style of philosophy I use here, sometimes called "anglophone" or "analytic" philosophy, which aims for – some might say "fetishizes" – clarity, precision, and logic. And we might question whether mere thinking, which is so much of what philosophy has to offer, can tell us anything important about such socially embedded activities.

This book seeks to show how philosophical reasoning of this kind can in fact illuminate our twenty-first century disputes about sex and love, in important ways. Theorizing in this domain is often difficult because our thinking is informed by assumptions, some of them explicit, some implicit and unexamined: about what is "normal" and what isn't, about what makes a good life, about the way people should relate to one another, about gender roles, and so on. Our ideas about these matters are deeply informed by background beliefs embedded in particular social and cultural norms and practices. The kind of thinking associated with analytic philosophy prioritizes teasing out implicit assumptions, questioning them from various angles, and asking whether they should be set aside. In this way, the "thinking" of philosophy, especially when combined with observation from ordinary life and analysis from other disciplines, can give us important new insights, and make us question what had previously seemed obvious or self-evident.

Though ancient Greek philosophers discussed sex alongside other matters of everyday life, most philosophers in the Western tradition since had little or nothing to say about sex and love. This lack of attention is striking, since sex and love are of such obvious centrality in our lives. With respect to sex, no other personal activity is simultaneously so important to so many people and yet also so widely moralized about and regulated by social constraints like law and religion. And love pervades our everyday lives, both as an ideal about romantic partnership and in platitudes about how overcoming indifference and hatred will bring about a new social and political order. As we will see in this book, the values we associate with sex and love, such as caring, generosity, and seeing others as special, are different, sometimes radically different, from the values we associate with other interpersonal interactions, which tend to involve self-interest and impartiality. How should we understand these differences? Finally, sex and love are connected to some of the most central topics in philosophy, including those of personal identity and well-being, the relationship between emotion and reason, the nature of autonomy and consent, and the dual nature of persons as individual and social beings.

Many questions in this area have become especially difficult in recent decades, because of changes in how North American and European societies have viewed sex and love. Very roughly, before the twentieth century, these societies framed sexual ethics largely in terms of appropriateness and chastity. Sex between a man and woman who were married was appropriate, other sex was not, and the virtue of "chastity" meant governing one's sexual impulses in a way appropriate to those norms. Marriages were often formed as alliances that would provide solid foundations for familial and social life, leaving "love" on the sidelines. Marriage was thought to unite a man and a woman's wills, with the woman's being largely subsumed into that of the man's; in intimate relationships, men were expected to be decision-makers, women nurturers. These traditional social norms were heteronormative, in the sense that only heterosexual partnerships were socially sanctioned, and sexist, in the sense that gender roles were hierarchical, with a man assuming control and power.

Since the 1960s, for many people the values commonly associated with sex and love have shifted away from this traditional framework, toward a belief in freedom and personal choice. This shift prompted a wave of fruitful philosophizing about sex and love during the 1970s to 1990s, much of which concerned the contrast between traditional norms and newer views dissociating sex from them. In this phase, several topics came to seem particularly salient: the question of "perverted" versus "normal" sex; the ethics of homosexuality, masturbation, abortion, and casual sex; problems concerning rape and sexual harassment, pornography, and prostitution. Partly reflecting trends in philosophy as a discipline, around this time a literature developed in the philosophy of love addressing conceptual and metaphysical questions, such as the difference between different kinds of love, whether love is an emotion or a way of valuing, and whether we have reasons to love.

But even in the short time since, cultural and theoretical frameworks have shifted substantially, and new problems and ideas have come to seem salient while others have come to seem less so. The rise of feminism and queer culture, skepticism about categories like "normal," and new social and political attitudes have sparked changes in which topics are important and how those topics ought to be framed and understood. Taking seriously the idea of sex as a matter of personal choice means that the concept of "perversion" loses its usefulness. It has become widely accepted that people have different preferences; as long as all activities are mutually consensual, the question becomes how to incorporate personal preferences into happy lives and good relationships. Likewise, masturbation – solitary sex for pleasure— no longer seems to raise deep ethical issues. And with respect to love, the idea of analyzing "what love is" from an impartial, objective, and gender-neutral viewpoint now seems naive to many.

One of the most dramatic effects of these shifts has involved attitudes about same-sex and other queer relationships. While there remain people who believe that same-sex or queer sex is wrong, sometimes for religious reasons, I share the widely held opinion that same-sex and queer relationships raise no special moral problems. I write here from the perspective that while there are many interesting philosophical questions about orientations and identities, queer and same-sex partnerships are as ethical as any other relationships, and don't require special defense.

But while questions like these have become less pressing in recent years, other questions and new ways of framing old ones have acquired new importance. If being desired is good, why is sexual objectification wrong? Given the wide range of ways people can be pressured into sex, how should we understand consent? If we can buy and sell everything else, why can't we buy and sell sex? What does it mean to combine the caring of love with respect for fairness and equality? How does love affect the gendered division of caring labor and the resulting wage gap? Are orientations ever a matter of choice, and does it matter? Are racialized dating preferences racist? How should we understand the use of "sexual surrogates" for people with disabilities? What should we make of the increasing involvement of the pharmaceutical industry in our personal lives? Does monogamy have value or is it just old-fashioned? These are the kinds of questions I focus on here.

In doing so, I have tried to integrate existing scholarship with my own views about these contemporary matters, and to explore the complexities associated with adopting new kinds of thinking. As we've seen, while the values associated with sex and love are highly variable and hotly contested, it is now common to prioritize individual autonomy. Individual autonomy means being able to choose for yourself, to act on the desires and preferences that reflect who you really are. Sex is now often seen through the lenses of personal freedom, consent, and the rights a person has to do as they please, as long as they are not harming others. Love is often seen as a domain in which people should express themselves and form the partnerships that work best for them.

This book does not concern itself with defending or arguing for this framework of individual autonomy. Rather, I take for granted its prevalence in our society, and seek to explore some implications of adopting and using it. We'll consider how it fits with our social and ethical understanding of sex and love and the role these play in our lives. While the shifts of values about autonomy in sex and love have been unfolding for some time, I'll argue here that we are still working out what these shifts mean in practice. While prioritizing individual autonomy seems like an answer to the question of how to understand sex and love, as a framework it raises as many questions as it answers. There are questions of what, exactly, autonomy means in social contexts like sex and love, and there are internal tensions between respect for individual autonomy and other values we cherish, like fairness, justice, equality, and generosity. To raise these questions is not to reject or undermine our contemporary emphasis on individual autonomy, but merely to critically examine the complex implications of adopting it.

As we'll see in the course of this book, one dynamic that makes these questions particularly complex is that in a variety of ways, sex and love challenge some basic, though often implicit, assumptions and values of modern, liberal, capitalist societies. Basing values of sex and love on autonomy creates new questions about how these values can be made to fit together. "Liberal" in this context refers not to current political usage, which treats "liberal" as the opposite of "conservative." Rather I use "liberal" in the sense developed by political philosophers, as referring to the idea that, as much as possible, people should be free to do as they please, as long as they are not directly harming anyone else, and that the government should be as neutral as possible with respect to telling people how to live their lives. Understood this way, liberalism is associated with ideas from a range of political viewpoints: social open-mindedness about different ways of life is liberal in this sense, and so also are views in favor of free-markets and against government intervention.

There is debate over the degree to which modern societies are "liberal" in this sense, but there is broad agreement on a fundamental idea that the term is meant to convey: in modern, capitalist societies, social values are individualistic, and in our public interactions, we're encouraged to see ourselves as essentially self-interested, looking out for our own needs and desires and expecting others to do the same – look out for their own needs and desires; when we want or need something from others, we expect to engage in a negotiation or contractual exchange. Liberalism, referring as it does to personal freedom and autonomy, frames us as individuals with rights to our own desires, preferences, and choices. Capitalism encourages a spirit of self-interested negotiation: if we need something from another person, we assume that getting it will be a matter of finding an appropriate, mutually consensual, and thus mutually beneficial exchange. In capitalist democratic societies, then, in our public lives we tend see ourselves as individuals who interact with other individuals, through negotiation, contracts, competition, and free exchange.

It might seem that commitment to individual autonomy in sex and love would fit easily within liberal capitalism of this kind, since it would be a straightforward extension of individualist values to intimate contexts. But as we'll see in the course of this book, there are difficulties. First, the role that sex and love play in our lives, and the way we care about them, often conflict with individualism. Mutuality and generosity are often thought to characterize an ideal or even an essential aspect of sexual interaction and pleasure, in the absence of which sex might seem a sadly contractual or objectifying. Second, love is thought to involve a kind of caring for the other person for their own sake that challenges individualism: if you're in it for yourself, how is that love? Finally, it might be hoped that family life could be a kind of sanctuary from the competition and negotiation that characterize public interaction, a zone in which caring rather self-interested bargaining is the norm; but the individualist approach renders it obscure how love can be theorized to play this role. Many of the contentious questions we'll consider in these chapters have to do with the problems arising from the shift from individualism in public life to individualism everywhere.

In a sense, traditional views of sex and love provided a way of resolving tensions between the values of liberal capitalism and the values of sex and love, and one theme of this book is the surprisingly profound effects of embracing gender equality and variable sex/gender partnerships. Historically, love, sex and family life were protected from the individualism and self-interest of public life because they were thought to be the site of special norms: if sex takes place only in heterosexual marriage, and marriage creates a unity of the wills of two people, then family life creates a context in which negotiation and competition are not required, and caring, love, and generosity can flourish. Self-interest is replaced by a unity of wills; competition and negotiation are replaced by harmony of purpose; contracts are replaced by caring and desire for the good of the other person.

When this unity is achieved through heterosexual paternalism, with a male head of household, and a wife and children who all defer to him, it is possible to see in practical terms how the ideal is achieved. But, as I'll argue in this book, once we see intimate relationships among adults in terms of equal partnership, the idea of love and marriage creating unity or special caring becomes a problem: without individuality, we cannot articulate ideals of fairness and equality, and then the relationship of the individual and their autonomy to the partnership becomes obscure. It is unclear how the love of romance and family life can be a sanctuary after all. Obviously, this is not to recommend a return to sexism and heterosexism. The point is that we may have underestimated the ways that our old frameworks required discriminatory background norms and values. As the traditional model of patriarchal unity recedes and the values of sex and love shift toward autonomy, new problems present themselves.

Furthermore, the extension of individualism and liberty to the realms of sex and love shows new ways that liberty can conflict with values like justice and equality. Individualism in sex and love is profoundly concerned with freedom of choice: whom we love and have sex with, and how, are seen as domains in which our right to choose for ourselves is deeply important. But as we'll see, because of the ways our preferences are informed by social norms – about who is attractive and who is not, who is a sexual being and who is not, who makes a good marriage partner and who does not – people choosing on the basis of otherwise benign preferences can create a social world of injustice and inequality. The resulting patterns can be unequal in the sense that some people – often those thought to be attractive and successful along other dimensions – will have many opportunities for sex and love while others have few. The patterns can be socially unjust in the sense that people who are already targets of social discrimination have worse prospects for experiencing their preferred kinds of sex and love. Sex and love show us another way that, in Isaiah Berlin's (1969) famous phrase, "freedom for the wolves" can mean "death to the sheep" (1969: xlv).

Crucially, to observe that liberty can increase inequality does not mean viewing sex and love as entitlements, and it is not to recommend restricting anyone's liberties. Unfortunately, in contemporary popular discussions, the observation that sex and love are unequally enjoyed is sometimes framed in terms of a male entitlement to sex and linked to a blaming of women; in extreme views, the lack of access to the pleasures of sex and love are used to justify violence. Like other forms of objectification and dehumanization, seeing women as providers of the pleasures of sex and love for men is sexist, misogynistic and wrong. But we can discuss the inequalities and injustices surrounding sex and love while resisting these conceptual links. Indeed, if we are going to include sex and love among the good things in life, we must discuss these inequalities and injustices.

Ultimately, this book will show that understanding philosophical issues related to sex and love requires examining them within their social contexts. That is, we cannot analyze these complex issues by looking at what individuals, in a vacuum, have a right or obligation to do, and we cannot restrict ourselves to looking at the ethical norms that govern sexual and romantic partnerships. Rather, understanding sex and love is always contextual, and the social context is crucial.

Though this book covers a wide range of material, there are many important topics I have had to leave aside. Rather than attempting a cross-cultural analysis, I focus here on North America, and I engage mainly with philosophy in the English-language tradition. To narrow the focus, I discuss love mostly in the sense of romantic love, though there are some discussions of family life and friendship. Likewise, I haven't covered issues like the concept of sexual justice in the current patchwork of laws related to age of consent and sexual offender status, or the relationship between different sex/gender identities such as trans or genderqueer and the particular experiences of sex and love related to these. In the areas I do cover, instead of attempting a broad overview, I have selected a few texts and topics to engage with in detail; this means that in all cases there are many important ideas and excellent pieces of work that haven't been included. Rather than complete coverage, I've tried to present here in some depth a selection of the most important issues in the field, and at the same time to develop a perspective on the field, a set of questions, approaches, and interpretations that can be applied to other situations and issues.

1 Sex, respect, and objectification

Introduction

Why begin a book on sex and love with the problem of sexual objectification? It may seem an odd choice, one that focuses on a problematic and apparently peripheral aspect of sex before we've taken up what may seem like bigger, more profound questions. To be sure, objectification is widespread in most contemporary societies. In North America, we're bombarded with advertisements featuring attractive, scantily-clad women, and pornography dominates the internet; women are regularly whistled or leered at in the street, and men and women alike often feel valued only in terms of their sexual attractiveness, rather than for their other qualities. In our society, sexual objectification is a commonplace and frequently harmful experience, especially for people who are vulnerable in other ways.

So there's no doubt that it's a problem that deserves analysis, but in this chapter and the next, I'll argue that it's also something more: thinking about sexual objectification in fact leads us into some of the most fundamental questions that sex presents us with, and it also raises fundamental questions about how sex relates both to loving relationships and to the other contexts in which sex takes place. Examining sexual objectification forces us to explore what exactly it means to look on another person as a sexual being and interact with them on those terms, and it forces us to think about the ethics of doing so.

Many such interactions seem to dehumanize their targets in ways that are clearly unethical, as when women are evaluated only in terms of their sexual attractiveness. At the same time, being the object of sexual desire and feeling sexy and attractive are often good things. In fact, a lot of sex and sexual attention seem to potentially treat persons as objects in one way or another. Some objectification can be ethical and even quite appealing – as when lovers are so inflamed by passion that they temporarily fail to attend to the complexity and humanity of their partners. A few years ago, the actress Cameron Diaz said "I think every woman does want to be objectified. There's a little part of you at all times that hopes to be somewhat objectified, and I think it's healthy" (Huffington Post 2012). Maybe you've heard men say things like "What's wrong with sexual objectification? I'd *love* to be sexually objectified!" If you desire a person's body because of its beauty and sexiness, and you long to use that body to satisfy your desire, isn't that "objectifying"? Does this mean that all sexuality is somehow suspect? If not, what distinguishes the good from the bad? On the face of it, a certain amount of stripping and flaunting are characteristic both of soft-core pornography and of Pride parades. Is there a difference between these contexts? And if so, what is it?

In this chapter and the next, we'll examine different perspectives on sexual objectification. One way of looking at things is that sex is inherently objectifying, because it is reductive and treats others as bodies. An alternative framework focuses on the sexist ways that women in contemporary society tend to be valued and appreciated for their attractiveness rather than as full human beings. These views seem to lead to the conclusion that sex is always, or generally, a problem. But finding a more nuanced approach is complex. I'll argue here that one common idea – that love and caring mark the essential difference between objectification that is sexy and good and objectification that is degrading and bad – isn't right. In the next chapter, we'll examine the idea that social contexts rather than personal relationships and interactions determine how we ought to evaluate various acts and attitudes of sexual objectification.

Sex as inherently objectifying: the view of Immanuel Kant

To look at the relationship between sex and respect for a person, let's start by looking at the ideas of the philosopher Immanuel Kant. Kant, who lived from 1724 to 1804, was one of the most influential philosophers in the historical Western tradition. He wrote on many subjects including ethics, the nature of reality, theories of knowledge, logic, and religion. His ideas are worth thinking about here both because they have been so influential, and also they're so specific in defining why sex is objectifying and what to do about it.

Broadly speaking, Kant's ethical views are based on respect for individual persons. He is famous for his "formula of humanity," which says that everyone should "act in such a way that you treat humanity, whether in your own person or in the person of any other, never merely as a means to an end, but always at the same time as an end." To treat a person or thing as a "means" to an "end" is to use that person or thing as a tool of your purposes, to get something else. To treat a person or thing as an "end" is to value it as an ultimate goal or object of value. Crucially, Kant's dictum does not rule out using people as means: it just means you can't treat them as a "mere" means, as just a tool of your purposes. For example, if someone makes dinner for you, and you eat it, you are in a sense using that person as a means – to the end of the satisfaction of eating dinner. This is not wrong. What is wrong is using people without, at the same time, valuing them as ends-in-themselves. If you treated someone as being of value only insofar as they can make you dinner, and not because of their whole personhood, if you saw them as just a kind of ticket-to-dining, this would be using them as a mere means and would constitute a moral violation.

For Kant, this distinction between treating a person as a means and as a mere means has to do with respect for autonomy. Autonomy means acting for reasons that are your own, rather than being coerced or deceived or manipulated. Roughly speaking, when you use people in order to achieve your own ends, you must respect their participation in the interaction and in the decision-making process.

The basic idea is simple and intuitive. When Kant tells us to treat people as valuable, as "ends," he means in part respecting their ability to make decisions, for themselves, about the role they will play in an inter-action. It is wrong to manipulate people, to force them, or coerce them, because this treats them as "mere means" – as just tools for one's pur-poses. If a person chooses to make you dinner, perhaps to be nice or in exchange for money or some other benefit, this is fine, because it's their decision how to interact with you and what to agree to. But if you were to force someone to make you dinner, through coercion or threats, that would be morally wrong, because it would be using a person as a "mere means" and not respecting them as an end in themselves. The same applies to deception. If you were to lie to someone and tell them that you have an otherwise fatal illness that can only be cured by a home-cooked meal, and believing you, they made you dinner on those terms, this would also be treating a person as a "mere means" and not an "end in themselves." You prevent them from freely choosing to make you dinner, since you deceive them into doing so.

These dinner examples may seem fanciful, but the preservation of sexual autonomy through avoiding coercion and deception can help us understand what it means to respect people in sex. Later, in Chapter 3, we'll see a range of examples illustrating how sexual interactions can fail to respect the autonomy of another person, and thus fail to be properly consensual: if one person forces or coerces another into sex, or uses the power they have over them to force them to say "yes," or if a person lies – for example about their HIV status – these are some of the most basic ways people wrong one another sexually. These actions fail to respect people as ends-in-themselves: they violate Kant's principle and are therefore morally wrong. Kant's theory of ethics and autonomy gives a straightforward analysis of these cases: they are wrong because they fail to respect someone's personal autonomy.

It might seem that applying Kantian ethics to sex would yield a basic consent-based view: that if you consent to an activity, your choice is being respected, so your interaction is properly respectful and ethical: you're not using or objectifying a person sexually. But Kant held specific views on lust and sex that go beyond concerns over coercion and deception. In a famous passage, Kant writes: "Sexual love makes of the loved person an object of appetite; as soon as the other person is possessed and the appetite sated, they are thrown away, 'as one throws away a lemon that is sucked dry'" (1997: 156). It is a vivid image. Kant is saying while people are in the grip of sexual desire, they are intensely focused on the object of their lust, but once the desire is satisfied – e.g., after orgasm, or after the lustful feeling fades – they suddenly cease to care about the other person. Though Kant, who never married, is widely thought to have had little or no direct experience with sex, this idea is not difficult to understand. Everyone who has experienced lust knows the feeling. When you have it, you have one set of priorities, and when it's gone, those priorities can shift rapidly and dramatically. Kant is saying that sexual desire causes us to have an intense focus on another person, but that focus isn't the right kind: once your thirst is slaked, you cease caring about the other person. You "throw them away."

Kant is also concerned about the way that sex and sexual desire require a focus on the other person's body. In addition to refraining from using others, Kant thought we have some obligation to care about others' interests and reasons, and to help them get what they want and need in life. But when you're caught up in a certain kind of animalistic lust, you can't care about people properly. You're focusing more on the other person's body and not enough on their mind. In sex, a person may not be thinking about what their partner wants and needs, and thinking instead about how to get what they want and need for themselves, from their partner's body. For these reasons, Kant finds that sexual desire and sexual activity are generally a moral problem. In sex we fail to respect other human beings for their full humanity, and sexual desire is therefore dehumanizing.

Though Kant didn't use the language of "objectification," these ideas about dehumanization and using persons as mere means are closely related to what we mean by that term. Sex can be seen as objectifying because it causes us to treat others as tools of our purposes, as bodies, as there to meet our needs; it renders us unable to respect people as full human beings. It's no surprise that sexual desire might cause you to treat a person as a sexual object, as a tool of your purposes, without regard for their humanity. For Kant, this isn't just a possibility. It's what follows from our status as embodied beings. So from his point of view, the moral problem of sex isn't solved simply by all parties being willing and consenting; the sexual appetite, if unrestrained by proper context, always involves using a person in a problematic way. For Kant, even masturbation is morally wrong in this way, because in masturbating, you are treating yourself as a mere means, a means to the end of sexual pleasure.

This is interesting because it illuminates one potential way that sex could be different from dinner. As we said, if you cook dinner for someone, whether from kindness or from self-interest, your autonomy and humanity are being respected. But if you have sex with them, even consensual sex, the act is inherently dehumanizing, because of the nature of the sexual appetite. As we'll see in later sections, in contemporary society people often think that the key to avoiding dehumanization in sex is reciprocity: for healthy relationships and good sex, all partners should ensure that the others are not only consenting but are also experiencing sexual desire, pleasure, and excitement. But for Kant, reciprocity is not generally the kind of thing that makes sex less problematic. Instead, Kant says that our desire to get what we want from others in sex is so intense that we are willing to be dehumanized by them in exchange for being able to dehumanize them. That is, the fact that we reciprocate in sex – giving others pleasure in return for the pleasure they give us – does not transform its ethical quality. From this perspective, it's more like we are willing to be degraded in order to enjoy the base pleasure of degrading another. (For an analysis relating Kant to "kink," see Pascoe 2012.)

Though Kant did not think reciprocity could solve the problem of lust, he did think there was a treatment – not a solution, exactly, but something that would help. His idea involves marriage, and specifically, the nature of marriage as an open-ended and legally protected contract uniting two people. Marriage does not transform lust, but it properly contextualizes it. The Kantian appeal to marriage as a response to the moral problem of lust has puzzled many people over the years. If lust and sex essentially dehumanize, how on earth could a contractual arrangement like marriage solve that problem? It seems the effect would be the opposite, and that the marriage contract would legalize and formalize the unethical violation that sexual desire entails. Marriage would be a contract to dehumanize or disrespect someone.

But as Barbara Herman (1993) and Helga Varden (2006) have explained, there are reasons to think that Kant's appeal to marriage is on to something important. In the lemon quotation, we see the concern that once desire is satisfied, caring ceases. Responding to this, Kant emphasizes the legal standing that marriage gives people with respect to one another. Marriage is a legal institution that mandates taking others' interests into account, at least in some ways. Marriage could make people permanently and formally committed to caring for one another's ends. The law cannot force you to love, but it can force you to do certain things, like share money and decision-making power. At least, you cannot "throw away" the other person.

Marriage, then, is a way of dealing with the degradation and dehumanization associated with sex and sexual desire. Particularly in Kant's society, where divorce was virtually impossible, marriage was a legal way to enforce certain behaviors. In Kant's theory of marriage, personal property becomes jointly owned property, and spouses' common property is subject to their choices as a couple – for instance, one person cannot unilaterally make important spending decisions. So, in this sense, marriage would be a way of ensuring that even if you are, in a sense, using another person for sexual pleasure, your caring for them must at least extend to taking into account their needs and desires. So, if the problem is that with your appetite sated you will desert the other person and fail to care for them, then marriage might mitigate this danger. You cannot simply drain out the savings account, take the kids, and go on your merry way.

To many modern readers, this might seem a bit peculiar, on grounds that most of us want more from our lovers than just rights over someone else's goods and money. We want our lovers to care for us, and you can't legislate love. Yet this is what many people hope for, at least sometimes, when they have sex with people they love: they want to be loved back. As we all know, though it's wonderful when marriage and love do go together, they don't always, and it's certainly possible to be married to someone and obey your legal duties to them without loving them. To Kant, however, what matters is the kind of respect and ongoing care that the marriage institution formalizes. Marriage might not transform sexual desire, but it does provide the proper context for it.

For Kant, then, the problem of sexual dehumanization is universal, in the sense that sex is always in some way dehumanizing; marriage transforms the problem but does not solve it. Kant's analysis is also gender-neutral: the way that sexual desire causes a failure of human full respect applies generally, regardless of the sex and gender identification of the people involved. As we'll see in the next section, these features mark striking differences from the feminist theories of sexual objectification developed in the late twentieth century.

Feminist theories of objectification

Though Kant's perspective is gender-neutral, feminist scholars of the late twentieth century developed the idea that sexual objectification is especially a problem for women: pervasive forces in our society cause us to value women first and foremost not for their qualities as human beings but for their qualities as sex objects. Women are relentlessly judged on their attractiveness rather than their intelligence, accomplishments, or kindness. In addition, cultural expectation of gender roles are such that women are often expected to be passive and submissive – to let themselves be "objectified" – while men are expected to be active and dominant. Feminist scholars found a unifying theme among all these different factors: a tendency to see and treat women as primarily sexual objects, which leads people to dehumanize them and discriminate against them more generally.

In her 1989 book *Feminist Theory of the State*, Catharine MacKinnon says that "All women live in sexual objectification the way fish live in water" (1989: 149). This striking image suggests that objectification not only surrounds women but that it does so in such a way that women must actually derive sustenance from it. A willingness to be objectified is necessary for women to get the things they need to live, and therefore women not only experience objectification, they also participate in it; from this, women may form a positive desire to be objectified.

Let's take a moment to look at how these ideas play out in specifics. In Western societies, our social structures have their roots in a history that was highly patriarchal. It was not that long ago that women's rights to work and even to own and control their own money were severely restricted. Women were not considered to be autonomous individuals, capable of making their own decisions in life. Marriage was thought to create unity between a man and a woman by subsuming the woman's will and rights into those of the man: men would decide things; women, as natural nurturers, would take care of domestic duties.

Today, women can work at lots of different jobs, and obviously they can own their own money and things. But many contemporary feminists think that the patriarchal social relations of the past persist and find new expression in the emphasis on female sexuality and attractiveness over everything else. In contemporary relationships and at work, it's often much more important for women than for men to be sexually appealing in order to be successful. In many industries, women in the workplace are treated as potential dating partners; if they reject the advances of men in positions of power, they may fail to get ahead or even lose their jobs. Studies show that identical work histories can be rated more highly when evaluators believe the applicant is a man, suggesting that people discriminate against women even when they are not aware of it (see, e.g., Moss-Racusin et al. 2012). Practices that are associated with "leadership" in men can be associated with "bossiness" and uncollegiality in women (Butler and Geis 1990).

A simple illustration of the way our society values men and women differently is reflected in the "Bechdel Test" for movies. This test was proposed first in a comic strip by the writer Alison Bechdel in 1985: the idea is that to pass the test a movie must have at least two female characters, and these two characters must talk to one another about something other than a man. In Bechdel's original drawing, the movie that passes the test is the 1979 movie *Alien*, in which two women discuss the monster. The vast majority of movies popular in North America fail. They fail because women are typically depicted in movies as of interest only sexually and romantically, and only in relation to male characters, rather than being depicted – as men are – doing things like catching thieves, solving problems, running for office, playing sports, and so on. This is not to say movies or movie makers are somehow the cause of the problem. Rather, movies fail the test because they reflect something about our culture more generally: we're interested in men doing all sorts of things, and we assume they will, but we think of women as primarily arm-candy.

MacKinnon's fish-in-water metaphor also suggests that when society rewards women primarily for sexual attractiveness, women may then make themselves into sexual objects. That is, women may choose to dress in certain ways and conform to certain beauty norms, despite the fact that this way of dressing or appearing doesn't really reflect who they are as a person. Think about how a person getting ready to give an important speech would dress in order to feel powerful, to feel confident that other people will pay attention to them and listen carefully to what they have to say. A man would likely wear a nice suit. But a woman in a suit is often mocked as ugly or frumpish – indeed, in many contexts, women are accorded respect only if they look, in some sense, "hot." In these circumstances, it is not surprising that women often choose to look as attractive as possible, despite the fact that they might prefer to de-emphasize their sexuality. From the positive attention for sexualizing their appearance, women may develop a desire for a sexualized appearance, and thus come to objectify themselves.

MacKinnon and her colleagues, like feminist legal scholar Andrea Dworkin, say that sexual objectification ties together these various ways women are treated as one-dimensional and less important than men; it therefore forms a root cause of sexism and gender inequality more generally. Pornography, in this view, is a crucial mechanism through which gendered norms are perpetuated. Because so much pornography features scenes in which men are active and dominant and women are passive and responsive, viewing pornography causes us to internalize and eroticize that dynamic. Worse, some pornography depicts violence, and some violent pornography depicts men forcing themselves on women who are protesting or saying "no." Sometimes these women are depicted as welcoming the sex later, suggesting that somehow it is OK to have sex with women against their will. As Rae Langton (2009) says, this "silences" women: when pornography depicts situations where women first resist or say "no," then come to welcome or enjoy the sexual activity that follows, this has the effect of undercutting respect for women's "no" in real life. The dynamics of dominance and submission are sexualized, and this causes men to eroticize power and domination and women to eroticize submission and objectification. In the late twentieth century, before the internet made pornography so widely available, MacKinnon and Dworkin campaigned vigorously for pornography to be outlawed completely, on the grounds that pornography's representation of women causes women's dehumanization and thus harms them.

Like Kant, Dworkin and MacKinnon take as fundamental that people are owed respect and that treating people as objects for your purposes is dehumanizing and wrong. But while Kant understands the problem to be intrinsic to sexual desire itself, Dworkin and MacKinnon trace the difficulties to their social contexts. While Kant's analysis is gender-neutral, for Dworkin and MacKinnon everything has to do with hierarchical and differentiated gender norms, in which men are encouraged to be dominant and active and women are encouraged to be submissive and passive. Finally, while Kant thought the best response to the problem of objectification lay in marriage, for MacKinnon and Dworkin marriage is part of the problem. Because it is rooted in historical contexts in which unity among married people was achieved through the woman subjugating her needs and desires to those of the man and those of household work and childrearing, marriage in their view just makes the problem worse. Still, as with Kant, Dworkin and MacKinnon's analysis suggests that sex is generally a problem: because sexist social structures are so pervasive, there is no escaping the objectifying force of the sexual gaze for women.

Nussbaum on the varying aspects of objectification

Many people want to resist the idea that sex is always a problem. From the perspective that sex is about personal autonomy and freedom of expression, we may find puzzling the idea that sex is radically unlike other activities: as long as we're consenting and not harming anyone, what is the difficulty? From a perspective that sees sexual pleasure as a positive, MacKinnon's and Dworkin's views may seem overstated and over-generalizing: is male sexuality always and unavoidably infused with a drive to dominate and objectify? Nancy Bauer (2007) suggests that it is "soul crushing" for women to be told that having sexual feelings and wanting to be desired is incompatible with self-respect.

Noting that our fantasies, imaginations, and inner life are unruly, Martha Nussbaum (1995) points out that, understood correctly, a kind of sexual objectification might be a wonderful thing, part of what we want out of sex. To understand objectification correctly, Nussbaum says, we have to appreciate first that objectification goes beyond sex, and that objectification is not a unified concept. There are ultimately many different ways to objectify a person. When we're evaluating a case of objectification, things are never straightforward, because a lot depends on context and tone.

For example, suppose a man says to a woman, "Wow, you look hot!" For a couple in an equal and respectful relationship, who value and appreciate one another for the full range of human qualities, this could be a genuine and welcome compliment. But if it's two strangers, and the woman is trying to accomplish something nonsexual, then it could be a way of belittling her, of reminding her that she's really only valuable for her attractiveness. It's not just what you say, it's how and when you say it.

Nussbaum proposes that there are at least seven different ways of treating someone as an object. These are:

1   Instrumentality: the objectifier treats the object as a tool of his or her purposes. (We've discussed this a bit already, though Nussbaum offers her own analysis of what instrumentality means more specifically.)
2   Denial of autonomy: the objectifier treats the object as lacking in autonomy and self-determination. That is, the objectifier ignores the decision-making capacity of the object.

3   Inertness: The objectifier treats the object as lacking in agency, and perhaps also in activity. That is, the objectifier treats the object as passive, not a thing that initiates actions of its own.

4   Fungibility: the objectifier treats the object as (a) interchangeable with other objects of the same type, and/or (b) with objects of other types.

5   Violability: the objectifier treats the object as lacking in bodily integrity, as something that it is permissible to break up, smash, or break into.

6   Ownership: the objectifier treats the object as something that is owned by another, can be bought or sold, and so on.

7   Denial of subjectivity: the objectifier treats the object as something whose experience and feelings (if any) need not be taken into account.

Though these interdependent different forms of objectification often go together, they can also be distinguished. It is generally OK to treat a ballpoint pen in any of these ways – it might be a bit wasteful to destroy it completely, but if you treat it as interchangeable with other pens or just put it in a drawer when you're not using it, no one cares. But a Monet painting is different: it may be inert and owned, but it's not just another painting, and you have to treat it with respect. Enslaved persons are owned, their subjectivity and autonomy are denied, and they are used instrumentally, but crucially, they are not treated as inert or passive, since often their ability to perform labor is crucial to their enslavement. A beloved child may be appropriately denied autonomy without being treated as owned, fungible, or a mere means, because the child isn't old enough to make their own decisions.

This multiplicity shows all the different forms that sexual objectification can take, from violations such as denying respect for autonomy to potentially benign activities like consensually being treated as passive in sex. Evaluation does not depend only on the act, but also on context, the dynamic between the people involved, and whether they respect one another. In some cases, Nussbaum argues, objectification can be a wonderful part of sexual life, and nothing to be feared or shunned. What matters, she says, is whether the people respect one another as full human beings in general.

For example, in the novels of British writer D. H. Lawrence, Nussbaum finds characters who become sexually inflamed by one another partly through a process of objectification: they reduce one another to body parts; they stop seeing one another fully as individuals; they surrender – and ask others to surrender – autonomy, agency, and subjectivity as they are overcome with sexual passion. But far from being sinister, she says, the passion is enlivening, and even wholesome and admirable. In Lawrentian objectification, the characters avoid selfishly using one another, the objectification is symmetrical and mutual, and the interactions happen in a context of respect and rough equality: these factors create sexuality that objectifies and flourishes and does not harm. Nussbaum says, "The surrender of autonomy and even of agency and subjectivity are joyous, a kind of victorious achievement in the prison-house of English respectability" (1995: 275).

But to be used for another's purposes is not like this. Treating another person merely as a means to an end and as nothing more violates them. As an example, Nussbaum cites the kind of objectification depicted in the classic erotic novel *Story of O*. The novel describes O giving herself up into sexual slavery for a male master, Sir Stephen. Though O depicts the experiences as mainly positive ones, Nussbaum classifies the example as one of wrongly using a person as a mere means: O is treated as inert, fungible, and owned, and contextually the relationship between O and Sir Stephen is one of domination, not one of mutual equality and respect. Similar problems arise for pornography. In pornographic depictions, we are invited to respond to another person as merely an object for our arousal, often as an object interchangeable with other objects, and no background relationship of mutual respect provides the appropriate ameliorating context. Pornography makes people into commodities, and there is none of the engagement and mutual respect necessary for objectification to be made into something good.

It's from this viewpoint that Nussbaum finds the view of MacKinnon and Dworkin oversimplifying. Dworkin says that O has been reduced to an object, there for Sir Stephen to use as he sees fit, reflecting an utter failure to respect her as a human being; this is similar to the way women are objectified all the time, especially in their relations with men. Nussbaum says this analysis glosses over important complexities: the real issue is not only that O is treated as inert, owned, and fungible but that these follow from a broader sense of the way that her usefulness to Sir Stephen characterizes their relationship as a whole. It's not that being objectified is always wrong; it's that O is treated always and only as an object in this relationship that makes the problem. In stark contrast to MacKinnon and Dworkin, then, it would not follow that this kind of use must infuse heterosexual relationships in general. Everything would depend on the relationship and context.

We've already seen a similar idea in our discussion of Kant: if someone freely and voluntarily makes you dinner, you are in a sense treating them as a means to dinner, but you are not treating them as a "mere means." Nussbaum's theory introduces a similar distinction between using someone as a means, and using them "merely" or "primarily" as a means. But she characterizes the concepts differently. For Nussbaum, what is crucial isn't so much the consent and autonomous decision-making of the participants but the context of a relationship in which the other person is treated with full respect for their humanity. It is against this backdrop that we may temporarily treat one another as sexual objects. Interestingly, Nussbaum thinks a certain amount of intimacy or closeness with a person is necessary to achieve this mutual respect: if you don't know a person, how can you really engage with and respect their inner thoughts and feelings? So it really matters that people have the right kind of intimate respectful relationship to turn sexual objectification from a bad thing into a good one.

In addition, good objectification should be mutual and symmetrical: it can't always go one way. If two people objectify one another as part of a caring and loving relationship, this can be wonderful. But if one person were always objectifying the other and the other just put up with it, this would be wrongful use. For Nussbaum, this illustrates one problem with pornography and sex work: they are one-sided, with one person being the objectifier and the other the objectified. It might also suggest something wrong with certain kinds of casual sex, such as when one person proposes the activities they like best, and the other person is just consenting or going along with it. In these cases, there is no mutuality or symmetry.

At times, Nussbaum suggests that the kind of "respect" relevant to avoiding using a person as a "mere" means requires some kind of knowledge of them as an individual person. One example involves a novelistic depiction of gay men in the shower room of a gymnasium, appreciating one another's sexuality and engaging in "polyandrous happenings" (1995: 253) – that is, interacting sexually with a range of other men, in a scene of shifting attention and multiple partners, without much regard for who the other men are as individuals. This depiction, she notes, resonates with some theorizing about the positive role that a "fungibility" of sex partners can play in gay sexual culture. Seeing people as interchangeable, one sees them as equal; anonymity and promiscuity can be linked to the virtues of democratic equality (see, e.g., Mohr 1992). But Nussbaum challenges the strength of this connection, noting that the depiction also includes reference to class, race, and penis size. In the absence of "narrative history" with a person, she asks, how can we avoid attending only to the incidental? And attending only to these factors, how can we treat someone with the respect "democratic equality" requires (Nussbaum 1995: 287–288)?

In some ways, Nussbaum's ideas about objectification echo those of MacKinnon and Dworkin. In particular, they all share the idea that objectification is especially wrong in domains like pornography, where we are seemingly invited to depersonalize another human being. But at a deeper level, Nussbaum is really challenging these other views. For one thing, MacKinnon and Dworkin see sexual objectification as being central to objectification and discrimination more broadly. Sex is at the center of things. But Nussbaum disagrees, since people use one another instrumentally all the time, for instance to gain status or money or access, without that fundamental caring attitude she thinks is so important. It's fundamentally objectification of all kinds that's the problem, not sex itself. Also, Nussbaum analyzes objectification in a way that is gender-neutral and goes beyond just the problem of women being objectified in a sexist society. The way she sets it up, the fundamental issues work the same way for men and women and for gay couples and straight ones: in all cases the crucial question is how people relate to one another – and care for one another – in their interpersonal relationships. Finally, while MacKinnon and Dworkin focus on the social and political culture of a society, the key elements of Nussbaum's ideas are quite intimate and personal. They concern how individuals relate to one another, one on one.

Challenges for Nussbaum's theory

In some ways, Nussbaum's analysis fits with many modern, widely shared ideas about sex and love. She says that when people who love and care about one another engage in sex that is objectifying, this can be good – precisely because they love and care about one another. But when people objectify one another in other ways – in pornography, or sex work, or in casual sex where they're just hooking up and getting each other off – then something has gone wrong. This fits with some modern platitudes: sex is OK when it goes along with love but bad when it becomes a part of hook-up culture. But even though it may seem like commonsense, I think this aspect of Nussbaum's theory is mistaken (Marino 2008).

For one thing, I disagree with the importance she assigns to intimacy, symmetry, and mutuality. This is because these factors don't seem to be relevant in the right way. If it's really true that there is something wrong in instrumentally using a person as a means to sexual pleasure, if treating strangers this way is generally a way of mistreating them, then how would intimacy, symmetry, and mutuality help?

Other ways of mistreating people are not made better by these kinds of contextual factors. We know that intentional physical cruelty is a way of mistreating persons. It would be very strange to say that it's acceptable for one person to be intentionally physically cruel to another as long as the second person is intentionally physical cruel back as well. And the same goes for intimacy and respect. How could the fact that one person treats another with respect on most occasions make it acceptable to treat them disrespectfully on others? It seems strange to me to say that objectifying a person is bad when you do it to strangers, or when one person does it to another one-sidedly, but then say that it's OK when there is respect and mutuality.

I would also challenge the idea that mutual respect requires having a certain kind of intimate relationship. In one of her examples, Nussbaum says that if you're lying around and you use your lover's stomach as a pillow, that is OK, as long as it's consensual and you treat your partner as a full human being in the relationship the rest of the time. But if you think about variations on this story, aspects of the "relationship" seem less relevant. If you're the kind of person who just needs a stomach to lie on, there would be nothing wrong with putting an ad up on the internet, offering hourly wages for work as a pillow. It would be strange, but as long as you pay appropriately, respect boundaries, and refrain from acting like a domineering jerk, it doesn't seem wrong. It's not really intimacy or the nature of the relationship that matters.

In fact, I think it's more the other way around: intimacy can make the instrumental use of another person particularly complex and troubling. Imagine, for example, a wife whose husband is affectionate and helpful, and who explains to her, in the most loving way, that what he needs in life is a helpmate, a partner in life, and what he really needs help with in life is typing: he needs someone to transcribe some audio recordings. Imagine this wife is a great typist, but feels the work is beneath her, that it is a poor use of her time. If this happens in the context of a loving relationship, it is easy to imagine that it would feel cold and unloving to say "no" – that one would be almost unable not to say "yes" to such a request. And yet it is easy to imagine that the request might feel manipulative and that the wife would feel herself instrumentally used in a way she did not enjoy or want.

And the same goes for sex. In couples, the things one person likes to do are not always the things the other person likes to do. There are times when what one person finds highly arousing the other person finds boring, disturbing, or even awful. Imagine being asked to do a sexual activity you do not find appealing. If you are asked during a casual or anonymous encounter with a stranger, you could just say "no, I don't want to do that," and walk away. But if it's someone you love, and it really matters to them, it could be much more complicated. It is often easier to say "no" to strangers. This doesn't show Nussbaum is wrong, exactly, since in her examples she says consent is necessary too. But I think it speaks to the way that intimacy can make sexual objectification generally more difficult, risky, or painful than it might be otherwise.

As we'll see in more detail in Chapter 2, part of the problem is the attempt to analyze objectification in terms of how the two individuals are interacting. This mode of analysis shares with the Kantian one the idea that we can look at how sex works and how individuals relate to one another to understand the difference between respect and dehumanization. It thus differs dramatically from Dworkin and MacKinnon's ideas, which focus more on the social context. We'll pursue a different approach to social context in the next chapter.

Conclusion

In this chapter, we've seen several different approaches to objectification: the inherent dehumanization view of Kant, the gendered sociopolitical theory associated with MacKinnon and Dworkin, and the relationship theory of Nussbaum. I've suggested that there are challenges for all three approaches.

This discussion of objectification suggests both the open-endedness of appeals to autonomy and also the importance of considering the social contexts in which autonomy functions for understanding ethical respect in the context of sex. Generally, Kant's theories about valuing people as individuals focus on respecting their individual autonomy, that is, their right to make decisions for themselves on their own terms. But Kant himself finds that sex raises special issues beyond respect for decisions: the sexual appetite causes us to dehumanize others in a particular way, so that valuing people as individuals requires sex to be properly contextualized. MacKinnon's and Dworkin's theory, relating the effects of pornography to eroticized and sexist gender relations, suggests a powerful role for social contextual factors. Nussbaum's analysis suggests that even when it is mutually consensual, sex can be commodifying and objectifying, as in pornography and hook-ups. In the next chapter, we pick up on the importance of context and explore a different social approach to these issues.

2 Objectification, autonomy, and pornography

Introduction

Thinking about objectification, we've seen, leaves us facing some questions. Sex is central to all our lives, and for many people it's one of life's most important pleasures. Yet reflecting on sexual objectification has led some philosophers to raise ethical questions about much or even all sexual activity. Immanuel Kant, we've seen, concluded that sex is always objectifying or dehumanizing in some way. Catharine MacKinnon and Andrea Dworkin view sex as helping prop up sexist social structures, which systematically reduce women to second-class status. Martha Nussbaum and others have responded to these arguments, by suggesting that in the right contexts sexual objectification can be a wonderful part of life. What makes the difference, these philosophers argue, is the relationship between the people involved; in an anonymous sexual encounter, objectification is indeed dehumanizing, but between people who know and care about each other, such as partners in a loving relationship, it doesn't undermine respect for the other person's full humanity. Yet (I've argued), these arguments don't fully resolve the problem. Among other things, partners in intimate relationships may find themselves under especially strong pressure to accept objectifying behavior, precisely because they care about their partners and want to sustain their relationships.

In this chapter, I propose an alternative perspective, one that focuses on sexual actors' places within their society as a whole rather than on their personal relationships. Looking at objectification in this way allows us to make some distinctions that may otherwise seem difficult to justify. Perhaps most important, it allows us to see why objectification has different effects on different social groups and why it might harm some people and not others. I'll start by exploring this approach in theoretical terms, then apply it to the example of pornography, where the issues of sexual objectification seem to present themselves in unusually stark terms.

Objectification and social autonomy

Is there a way to bring together Nussbaum's idea that objectification is nuanced with the idea that it's the social context that matters? I propose that one way to do this is to refocus the problem back to respect for autonomy, but to also build in a dimension of "social autonomy." You can, I will argue, choose to be "used" and thus consent to being objectified. But from this point of view, what matters in objectification isn't so much the nature of the relationship but rather consent and the reasons people have for making the choices that they do. Whether objectification is one-sided, or among strangers, or whatever, what matters is what you choose, and also whether you choose freely. Social factors play an important role in distinguishing choices that are freely made from those that are made in response to pressure or outright coercion.

As we've seen in our discussion of Kantian ethics in Chapter 1, some infringements on autonomy involve coercion and deception: if you are manipulated, threatened, or deceived, you can't choose freely; so respect for autonomy always entails refraining from coercion and deception, in objectification as elsewhere. This means that if you want to objectify someone sexually, you have some responsibility to know the circumstances of the choice and your role in those circumstances and to be honest about the reasons. If A asks B for oral sex in exchange for a place to stay for the night, and the streets outside aren't safe, the request is not in accordance with respect for sexual autonomy, because it's coercive. If A claims to love B but is just using sex with B to get back at C, that is deceptive and not in accordance with respect for autonomy.

But, as MacKinnon's "fish in water" metaphor of the previous chapter suggests, social factors play a huge role in why we do what we do, and this suggests autonomy also has a less direct social dimension. Before we discuss this further, let me explain a bit more about the idea about saying "yes" to objectification. It might seem that there is something paradoxical about consenting to be used or objectified: some philosophers say that if you consent to an activity, your choice is being respected, so by definition you're not being "used" or "objectified" in any meaningful sense (Mappes 1987). But I think Nussbaum's multi-faceted analysis shows this isn't so. There are various forms of objectification, like being treated as passive or fungible, and some of them are definitely possible to choose consensually, as when a person consents to being submissive or consents to being in pornography. I would add that in sex it is possible to go along with an activity where you know your partner is going to be respecting your consent but will also ignore your full range of inner thoughts and feelings. For example, if one person offers to perform unreciprocated oral sex on another, and they accept the offer, this can be fully consensual, but it can also be a case in which they go on to have a very one-sided interaction. The recipient may well be using the one who offers, as a means to sexual pleasure, but consensually.

To illustrate the basic idea that the ethical aspects of objectification have to do more with autonomy and less with individual mutual respect and relationships, consider this anecdote from the advice columnist Dan Savage. In his 2005 book *The Commitment*, Savage describes an encounter he had during a lecture tour with a young man in the audience who had a strong desire for having cake "smashed in his face" as part of a sexual experience. The man had never had cake smashed in his face, he explained during the Q and A, because no one wanted to share this sort of encounter with him: the one girlfriend he told about it dumped him when he did, and he was too scared to bring it up again. After the young man tracked Savage down at the hotel for a personal conversation, and after he interpreted Savage's light-hearted complimentary joke – "I'd smash a cake in your face in a heartbeat" – as a serious offer, Savage agreed to smash some cake in this young man's face. The young man got the cakes, and got undressed; he got into the hotel bathtub, and Savage smashed some cake in his face.

It seems to me that there is nothing ethically troubling in this story, and that certainly the young man did nothing wrong, even though he is objectifying Dan Savage. Though he is acting in accordance with Dan Savage's consent, he is ignoring Dan Savage's particular desires and wishes and he is treating him as interchangeable with others, thus treating him as instrumentally useful and fungible. In Nussbaum's framework, we would consider the context of the relationship and whether the objectification is symmetrical and reciprocated. But there is no context of the relationship, since the two people barely know each another. There is also no symmetry or reciprocity, since the encounter is one-sided from beginning to end. What might we point to for an explanation of what makes this case seem like a nonproblem?

I believe an important part of the answer is that in these particular circumstances, Dan Savage is acting with a great deal of autonomy, and particularly with a kind of social autonomy. Savage goes ahead with the interaction on his own terms; it isn't pushed on him. Savage is a white, American, able-bodied, good-looking man, with a range of sexual experience and a good job that is compatible with such behavior. The world doesn't treat people like him as worthy only of being sexual objects, and he isn't going to get fired for a sexual favor given out freely. Partly because of his situation, and partly because of the unusual nature of the request, people are not going to start denigrating him as "that whore who is willing to smash cake in your face."

This is not to say that Dan Savage has global autonomy in other contexts. Gay people are still subject to serious abuse, harassment, and threats, and these obviously get in the way of their doing what they want to do. But I think in these particular circumstances, Savage is enabled to act with a certain self-determination. Part of the explanation for that has to do with the kinds of options he has in the situation. Whether he participates in the interaction or not he faces few if any costs.

The relative costlessness is absent for many people when they are deciding whether to consent to being objectified, because refusing to go along often comes with serious consequences. A woman who refuses to dress sexily at work might be fired; people who complain about workplace sexual harassment can be vilified and treated as liars or crybabies. There are also more subtle ways that our social environment affects our autonomy, as we'll see in the next section.

Social autonomy and adaptive preferences

What it means to choose autonomously is complicated and variously understood. Kant's specific idea about the nature of autonomy involves respecting people's intentions and decisions, ruling out direct coercion and deception. But what about more subtle forms of pressure, like peer pressure or just facing a terrible choice from among a set of really bad alternatives? We saw early in the previous chapter how people might choose to act or dress a certain way not because they prefer to for themselves but just because it's the only way to get other things they want and need from their social world. Is this kind of choice not "autonomous" because it's the result of social pressure?

There are various ways that autonomy might be related to social and cultural factors. One possibility is that in certain social and political settings it becomes impossible to autonomously consent to being objectified because you can't opt out: you can't choose *not* to be objectified. The most obvious example of this is a society in which people accept being objectified because they do not have a choice in the matter: it is either imposed on them, or it is necessary to survive. In societies in which women are very frequently treated as, and valued primarily as, sexual objects, they cannot freely choose to be objectified because objectification is forced on them; in a sense, they have no choice. As we've seen, in our society, women are frequently evaluated for their attractiveness while they are trying to accomplish something else: the reason this is a problem and not a "compliment" is that it reinforces existing cultural norms that women's value lies primarily in their sexiness rather than their accomplishments or intellect. In a context where this happens often, it becomes impossible for women to choose autonomously to be objectified, because their options are restricted; their social autonomy is therefore compromised.

An inability to opt out is particularly troubling when it comes to sexual objectification because of the particular way that being treated as a sexual object – not by a given individual but by one's cultural and social world – can take over a person's entire life. People who are always treated only or primarily as sexual objects do not have any choice in the matter and are robbed of important elements of a good life in modern society because they aren't taken seriously as citizens, workers, and friends.

A similar problem arises when survival depends on allowing one's self to be objectified. If a person of any sex or gender must accept sexual objectification as a means to live, their choice cannot really be free, because they are being coerced by circumstances. This means that when people consent to appear in pornography or have sex for money, that choice might be a genuine choice in some ways but also coerced in others. So it matters not only that people consent but also why they consent.

These kinds of difficult choices are sometimes discussed using the concept of "adaptive preferences," which refers to the idea that social contexts might cause people to form preferences for what is not really in their best interests. In the twentieth century, Jon Elster (1985) characterized the idea by appeal to the fable of the fox and the grapes. The fable goes this way: "Driven by hunger, a fox tried to reach some grapes hanging high on the vine but was unable to, although he leaped with all his strength. As he went away, the fox remarked 'Oh, you aren't even ripe yet! I don't need any sour grapes.' People who speak disparagingly of things that they cannot attain would do well to apply this story to themselves." In this analysis, people, like the fox, stop preferring things that they know they cannot have; these preferences are "adaptive."

Many people have preferences that are adaptive in this sense. Suppose you are a student who starts out wanting to become a doctor, and then you discover you cannot do well enough in organic chemistry to get accepted to medical school. If you find yourself thinking "Meh, I didn't really want to be a doctor after all," you may have formed an adaptive preference. Likewise, if you cannot engage in some activity because financial considerations prevent it, you may find yourself thinking, "I didn't want to do that anyway." In that case, your preference might be adaptive.

I say "might be" in these examples because it is very difficult to know whether an alteration in your preference is adaptive or not. It's possible that as you learned more at university you genuinely did decide you didn't want to go to medical school after all. This wouldn't be an "adaptive preference" – it would just be changing your mind. The only way to know whether a preference is adaptive is to be presented with the opportunity you thought you'd lost: if you suddenly were granted acceptance to medical school and then you turned it down, this would show your new preference had been genuine and not adaptive. But how often does life present us with the option to suddenly do what we thought was impossible? Unless it does, we can't know for sure whether our preference was adaptive. We can only guess, by imagining different circumstances.

Still, the idea of adaptive preferences might help us understand sexual objectification and autonomy and the way social autonomy plays a role. In a society where women are often evaluated on the basis of their appearance, a woman might find that to be taken seriously in whatever she is doing she must also seem sexually attractive. As we've seen in our discussion of MacKinnon in Chapter 1, this might include self-objectification: dressing a certain way, with girly clothes and heels, wearing a certain hairstyle, developing a gentle and non-threatening demeanor. If a woman doesn't feel like she has a choice about this, she may develop an "adaptive preference" for it: she comes to feel that she wants, and prefers, to do these things. But it isn't really because that is who she is. Instead, it's like the fox and the sour grapes: since she can't have the alternative – dressing in comfortable clothes and sneakers, and still being valued and taken seriously – she comes to prefer the only alternative she has.

These possibilities show how autonomy isn't just a matter of freedom versus coercion but also has social dimensions. The idea of "social autonomy" can illuminate other questions about objectification. In Chapter 1, we talked about *Story of O*, in which O experiences, as positive giving herself up into sexual slavery for a male master. Nussbaum interpreted this story as an example of objectification gone wrong, exemplifying the worst of sexist ideas about men controlling and owning women and treating them as passive and nonpersons. From the autonomy view, this interpretation does not follow so immediately, because instead of the overall relationship we look instead at O's consent and autonomy. We know O chooses "yes," since the novel describes her first-person choices to engage in all of the activities. But does O choose freely and autonomously?

In one sense, the answer to this question seems to be yes as well. The novel presents details undercutting the idea that O is being coerced by circumstances. In the narrative, she is a successful photographer with an apartment, friends, and so on, and she is explicitly invited to break off her enslavement should she wish to. Given that from her point of view she is choosing from among good options, and given that she has good options that involve opting out entirely, she has, in one sense, a high degree of sexual autonomy.

However, we would also have to consider that a preference like O's for being a sexual object is adaptive. In our discussion of MacKinnon's work in Chapter 1, we saw the idea that men and women internalize and eroticize certain modes of interaction of male dominance and female submission. In so far as a woman lives in a society that makes it difficult or impossible for women to opt out of sexual objecthood, her choice may not be autonomous. If women are generally valued for their status as sex objects, then O's choosing one way to be a sex object rather than another may be adaptive in the sense that she cannot opt out of sexual objecthood at all, or in the sense that she does not have options for sexual attention that do not also include being sexually objectified in various ways.

In any case, the idea that autonomy has a social dimension helps us understand why objectification is complex with respect to sex, gender, and other factors. Generally, when women, or people who are racialized in various ways, or other people our society tends to categorize and stereotype, are valued only or primarily for the sexual pleasure they can give to others, their social autonomy is adversely affected. As we'll see later in Chapter 10, "hypersexualization" occurs when people are perceived in ways that place their sexuality at the center of their identity, even when they prefer not to be regarded this way. Hypersexualization negatively affects people's social autonomy because it undermines their freedom to be, and be seen, as who they are. This is one reason why something like whistling at women in the street can be a sinister and serious form of objectification: it is a reminder of the ways in which a women's role in society is still thought of as that of being a provider of sexual pleasure, in a context in which it is impossible to opt out. For white, able-bodied, men, being whistled at in a similar way does not present a relevantly similar situation and thus the ethical aspects are very different. (For an interesting different approach to gender and objectification, see Cahill 2012.)

As we mentioned in the introduction to Chapter 1, sometimes men say "What's wrong with sexual objectification? I'd *love* to be sexually objectified!" The lens of social autonomy helps us understand this response and its implicit challenge. When straight white men talk of their desire to be sexually objectified, it is possible to understand them as expressing an intelligible and unsurprising wish to be the object of sexual desire – to be found attractive, arousing, and so on, and perhaps to be found so because of their bodies and physicality, or as givers and not receivers of sexual pleasure. It is when – and because – these men are typically treated as full persons in other contexts that this choice makes sense for them and does not seem strange or ethically troubling. It follows from this analysis that appreciating and commenting on the physical attractiveness of a person may or may not be objectifying in a problematic way, and much depends on social context.

Similarly, the concept of social autonomy helps explain why women's appearance in soft-core industry pornography aimed at men and their appearance at Pride parades seem different even though they may involve similar kinds of flaunting. Both can involve ogling and regarding others as sexualized objects, and both can involve doing this to strangers – people with whom we have no intimacy or symmetrical relationship. But there is a crucial difference. The pornography reflects and reinforces an existing problem, the same problem MacKinnon and Dworkin started with: that in general, women are treated as valuable for their sexual attractiveness so much more than men are. Women are so often objectified that they can't really opt out, and therefore can't choose autonomously. Pornography often reinforces this, while Pride events, in contrast, are trying to challenge the dominant view in which women are sexual objects and men are sexual subjects. Of course, gay culture also has problems with patterns of objectification, as, for example, when Black gay men are treated differently than white gay men. We'll discuss this issue further below and in Chapter 10.

A social perspective on pornography

These perspectives also help us address the question of pornography. The situation with pornography has changed radically over the past few decades. Until recently, access to pornographic pictures, movies, and stories required substantial effort; you had to go to a store or XXX movie theater, or order things to be shipped to you in suspiciously plain packaging. Now pornography is everywhere. You can watch it on your computer and on your phone; you can watch any of a million different kinds of pornography, and you can use the internet to find exactly the kind you want. Pornography itself has also become massively complex: alongside mainstream industrial pornography, which often features the dynamic of dominant men and submissive or passive women we discussed in Chapter 1, there is a great deal of amateur and homemade pornography that features a wider range of participants, activities, and moods. There is pornography specifically intended to be feminist, pornography meant to challenge standard stories and stereotypes, queer pornography, and pornography for a wide range of specific interests.

In some ways, these contemporary realities complicate any effort to understand pornography in philosophical terms, because for every generalization about its nature and impact you can find a wide array of exceptions and alternatives. Even defining pornography is more difficult than it used to be. When friends send each other intimate photos, they often hope to stimulate sexual arousal, one of pornography's classic functions – but can we analyze these exchanges using the same concepts we bring to thinking about mainstream pornographic productions? At the same time, pornography's immense presence in contemporary life makes the subject even more important today than it was a generation or two ago.

In what follows, I haven't tried to cover all the forms that contemporary pornography takes, or all of its possible effects on viewers. Instead, I focus on some of the main themes in contemporary discussions of these issues. I also try to ask about pornography the question that I've asked throughout this chapter: how do social structures and cultural assumptions affect our assessment of the acts and people we see in pornography? I argue here that thinking in these terms is as important for understanding pornography as it is for understanding other forms of sexual objectification. Instead of proposing a blanket understanding of pornography as good or bad, harmful or empowering, I'll argue that we need to think about the specific messages that the different configurations of pornography can convey.

In the last chapter, we talked about MacKinnon and Dworkin's idea that pornography was at the heart of the problems of sexism and sexual inequality. For them, it's not only in sex that we play out the roles we've learned, it's also in other domains. Their idea is that repeated exposure to the idea of men as active and dominant and women as passive in pornography leads people to see men as naturally dominant and women as naturally passive in other domains, and that this undermines women's ability to live lives of self-determination. Many think the harm argument shows something important ethically about pornography. If pornography depicts women in certain ways – as subject to violent and degrading acts, and even as consenting to or enjoying these acts – this dehumanizes them. As we discussed in Chapter 1, it also silences them, undercutting respect for the importance of consent. Such pornography is therefore disrespectful to women and causes harms to them. Hence, to make or view such pornography would be a serious moral wrong – even if it isn't breaking the law. We also saw that even though Nussbaum rejects this theoretical system as oversimplifying, her theory also implies that pornography is bad. Because it commodifies its subjects, treating them as status symbols or objects to be enjoyed at will, it is dehumanizing and objectifying in a harmful way.

Ann Garry (2002) has developed an insightful response to the idea that pornography is inherently degrading or dehumanizing. She points out that not only does the content of pornography matter, its contexts matter as well; she also suggests that we have limited control over how pornography depictions are perceived. Garry points out that male dominance and hostility to women are not essential to pornography, and that it matters whether women are depicted as being in positions of respect: if women are treated as sexual partners and not always sexual objects, if activities are depicted that women enjoy, and so on. Pornography that shows women and men enjoying sex equally in a give and take differs from pornography that depicts men doing and acting and women passively receiving – or, worse, shown as enjoying plot elements like rape and violence. Imagine a pornographic movie that depicts consent and mutual pleasure, with each person treating the other with respect – maybe like Nussbaum's "Lawrentian" objectification. Why would we think that this disrespects or degrades women?

Garry suggests that if respectful sexual interactions in pornography are seen as disrespectful, especially to women, this might reflect a problem with the kind of respect involved in the first place. Garry says that one reason people associate sex with degradation for women in pornography is that the "respect" people have for women often isn't genuine respect for a person but rather "respect" for women they see as nonsexual, as placed on a kind of pedestal. If people have negative attitudes toward sex, seeing it as dirty or debased, and they divide women mentally into the categories of "good" and "bad," then they will lose respect for women in porn, because those women are seen to be "bad." But this is based on seeing women as "pure, delicate, and fragile" (Garry 2002: 347). This is not a form of respect compatible with equality; instead it singles out women for unequal status. If we weren't being sexist, we'd see that for men and women alike some pornographic depictions can be degrading but others may not be.

Respect is also complicated because it is a socially embedded concept. Whether or not something is "disrespectful" in part depends on whether it causes people to lose respect for you – and this is often beyond your control. The loss of social respect does not affect all people equally. In fact, Garry says, because of sexism, racism, and other forms of discrimination, in our society women and men in historically marginalized groups are more likely to suffer the loss of social respect. Here Garry brings up an interesting point about the way various kinds of stereotyping come into play when it comes to questions of respect. In the case of race, for example, it is common to hear people racialized as nonwhite collectively maligned when individuals racialized that way commit bad actions. Yet white Anglo men as a class do not lose respect from comparable actions – they are seen as individuals. For example, when a white Anglo man commits a crime, you don't often hear people calling for a rethinking of "white culture" or asking "What's wrong with white people anyway?" This is analogous to the way that a woman engaging in a sexualized depiction will be denigrated as a "slut" based on her actions while a man doing the same thing is seen as "manly" or a "stud." This shows how respect for women and non-Anglo men is weaker than respect for Anglo men – people do not respect them as much, and respect is more easily lost.

This means that even if you consent to acting or appearing in pornography, and even if you do not think it degrading or disrespectful, and even if the pornography depicts mutual and respectful sex, you still might be harmed by it, because – especially as a woman, or a person of color, or anyone who is socially oppressed – people might lose respect for you. Consenting to appear in pornography is one thing when your depiction will be received in a respectful way, and something else entirely when viewed by people who think sex is dirty or bad. It's one thing to be sexualized at a Pride parade or similar event, where sex is being celebrated, and another to be sexualized by people who think that a sexualized woman is worthless. For an audience that believes sexual activity wrong for women and incompatible with appropriate female behavior, porn will harm women acting in it, no matter how they are depicted. The audience will in fact lose respect for them. Of course, from Garry's point of view, that is because they had inadequate respect for them as people in the first place.

Garry's idea of pornography as material intended to stimulate sexual excitement leads to the possibility that some kinds of pornography might be a source of pleasure in a harmless or even good way. Perhaps pornography can even serve as a transgressive sort of good, shifting our beliefs toward seeing sexual attractiveness and sexual agency. As Robin Zheng puts it, for oppressed and marginalized groups whose members have been seen as "aesthetically and sexually unappealing," perhaps pornography depicting them as desirable "performs an especially important function in destigmatizing and normalizing such bodies in ways required for genuine social equality" (2017: 188). If people in a marginalized group are seen as sexually unattractive, perhaps pornography is a social good when it presents them as sexually appealing?

In this direction, Mireille Miller-Young's (2013) analysis of Black women in pornography draws attention to the ways that power and control play a complex role in how pornography is produced and received. Miller-Young points out that women of color are "specifically devalued" in the hierarchy associated with sexualized imagery and power: depictions of Black actors tend to involve stories of Black "sexual deviance and pathology," such as narratives of "players and pimps trolling the 'hood for hoes and hookers"; these racialized narratives reflect fetishizing stereotypes, such as those of Black women being hypersexual (Miller-Young 2013: 107).

Miller-Young argues that when they have more control over their labor and the narratives involved, and especially when they direct, Black women in the industry can engage in what she calls "illicit eroticism": engaging with existing racialized tropes like Black hypersexuality to advocate for greater control and for representations that undermine or reimagine the status quo. For example, by emphasizing women's sexual autonomy, or focusing on intimate narratives and the subjectivity of the performers, narratives might subvert mainstream racialized social assumptions, especially those about Black women. This raises the possibility that even if we cannot control audience reception, careful attention to narrative and production can create pornography that shows respect for the people depicted and involved in its creation. Miller-Young argues that in this way Black women's involvement in the pornography can be a powerful feminist force (see also Miller-Young 2014).

As Garry's analysis suggests, distinguishing between "transgressive" pleasures – that reconfigure an existing discriminatory and wrongful status quo – and "regressive" pleasures, that reinforce that status quo, could be difficult. We cannot control how depictions are received and interpreted and what is intended to challenge racial stereotyping and hypersexualization may not be understood that way. For her part, Zheng concludes that pornography can lead to a dilemma: sexualizing women of color in pornography is a problem, but excluding women of color from pornography could be an even worse one, since it would "stigmatize such women as not being sexually desirable" (2017: 192).

The "pornutopia" and pornography's falsity

In contrast, Nancy Bauer (2007) offers a broader critique. She argues that existing philosophical work on pornography comes at the issue the wrong way around, because framing the issue in abstract terms objectification misses the crucial feature: what gives pornography its power to arouse us. Central to that power, she says, is not just seeing people in sexual activities, and not only objectifying them in the simple sense of using them for sexual pleasure. Rather, she says, the objectification we often see in pornography goes beyond this and involves excitement at seeing and experiencing a person being treated as a thing. In this framework, we might say that it's impossible for pornography to both arouse us and exhibit respect for the humanity of the participants. We derive sexual pleasure from the dehumanization itself.

Part of what makes this arousing, Bauer says, is that it turns around the normal relationship between sex and civilization. In normal life, sex has boundaries: there are times and places and ways in which it's appropriate and many more in which it is not. But in pornography, sex is omnipresent. It's there when the plumber comes to fix the sink. It's there when strangers "accidentally" brush against one another's genitals and decide to have sex. It's even there in places like classrooms boardrooms, and parties with your family members. Pornography depicts a world in which sex has broken free from the taboos that normally surround it, to become a part of every aspect of life.

Bauer calls this imagined situation the "pornutopia." Contemporary pornography, she says, depicts a world in which everyone always feels sexual, gets pleasure from every activity, and has orgasms. Even if pornography avoids depicting violence and coercion and shows people as sex "partners" not sex "objects," Bauer says there is still something disturbing about it, because of the way it requires us to subjugate our ordinary multi-faceted humanness to a one-dimensional world in which sex is everywhere and everything. Especially striking, she says, is how this pornutopia functions in a world where women are seen as sexual beings. Before the "sexual revolution," of the 1960s, she points out, the norm was that women were expected to objectify themselves by making themselves visually desirable, but not by participating in sex promiscuously; "look but don't touch" was the basic guideline. Now, she says, women are expected to objectify themselves not only in appearance but also in action, always participating and always interested. The norm of the current pornutopia is "Don't just look – touch!" (2007: 72) But this norm is not really "liberating." Instead of sexual freedom, it's brought about a new set of demands: that women be available for sex, that they be interested, that they be willing to give sexual pleasure even when their prospects of receiving it in turn are narrow.

It's interesting to consider, more generally, why it might be a bad thing, and not a good thing, if pornography depicts everyone as endlessly interested, always eager, and having orgasms at the drop of a hat. I think one answer to this question has to do with the way pornography has come to set the stage for what people expect from sex. Though many people disagree with MacKinnon's and Dworkin's broader ideas about the evils of pornography, many agree with one of their premises: that the kind of pornography you watch can affect how you think and feel about things – both sexual things and nonsexual things. But pornography isn't truthful. It's full of lies.

In pornography, sex is always good and never awkward. Men have big penises and never lose their erections. Women are depicted as enjoying, and orgasming from, activities that are not the ones they would typically enjoy most in real life. For example, in real life, women typically do not have orgasms without direct stimulation of their clitoris. Some women have orgasms from heterosexual intercourse because their clitorises get stimulated in this activity, but many have orgasms only when other things, like hands or vibrators or tongues, are used to touch and stimulate the clitoris directly. Yet much mainstream pornography depicts women as if they almost always have orgasms from intercourse alone. If young women and men learn about sex from pornography, they learn mistaken information that will impair their ability to enjoy sex, since they might have a false understanding. Some women and men believe, mistakenly, that if a woman does not have an orgasm during intercourse there is something wrong with her. Analogously, many men think something is "wrong" with them if they can't get an instant and long-lasting erection at the slightest stimulation. These mistakes could make a big difference in sexual happiness.

Furthermore, pornography creates expectations about what are and are not normal or socially expected sexual activities. If some activity is common in pornography, young people who watch a lot of it come to think it's abnormal not to do it. A recent article in the *New York Times* (Jones 2018) describes teens learning from pornography who had come to believe that male aggression was important for normal straight sex. Adolescent boys thought that because women in pornography responded positively to forceful thrusting, slapping, and so on, that this was what women wanted in sex. Adolescent girls thought that because men in pornography engaged in forceful thrusting, slapping, and so on, this was something men wanted, and women would just have to put up with it. This is a massive failure to communicate.

Especially in a society where people watch a lot of pornography, the activities and narratives depicted there will inform how people think about sex. And the activities and narratives depicted there, at least in mainstream industry porn, are generally not realistic. In this way, the omnipresence suggested by Bauer's idea of a "pornutopia" could have substantive negative effects on our lives, even if the sex is depicted as consensual and mutually desired.

Now that pornography is so easily accessible, young people are watching it more and more, and at earlier ages. At the same time, in many places there is less sex education in schools, and parents often feel awkward talking to their children about sex beyond just giving them the basics. This means that for a lot of people pornography is how they learn about sex. Because of the way pornography typically differs from real life, if pornography is how people are learning about sex, this has huge implications.

Beyond the heterosexual context

Much of this discussion has concerned the ways that heterosexual pornography relates to gender norms, so it is interesting to consider how the theories we've seen would analyze queer pornography or that involving same-sex participants. On the whole, for instance, it seems Bauer's analysis might apply in the same way to gay, lesbian, and other queer porn as it does to straight porn. Some of what she objects to in contemporary porn shows people treating one another as mere means, as always sexual, as always sexualized. She draws particular attention to the falseness of the depiction and how this would affect viewers. If seeing ourselves as always sexualized is a problem, then it's a problem that applies to gay and lesbian pornography as well. Pornography depicting lesbian sex raises especially complex issues because much of it is aimed mostly at straight men and is viewed mostly by them. Here there are definitely issues about falseness: it's often noted that depictions of sex among women aimed at male audiences often depict not what women choose to do sexually when they're together but rather what men enjoy watching them do.

The distinction between hetero- and other pornography seems more directly relevant to Garry's analysis, since her view pays more explicit attention to asymmetries between men and women. Since men are accorded more robust respect in society at large, in Garry's view, there would be less risk involved in gay male pornography, since for men being sexualized does not reduced their respect as easily. But given the way race and other factors can affect how we respect people or fail to respect them, gay pornography could be harmful for the ways it depicts people in certain groups as sexualized. It would follow from Garry's analysis that these groups, because they are not fully respected as persons the way white Anglo men are, might be more harmed by being shown in pornography – respect for them would be more likely to be undermined. As Garry emphasizes, though, one cannot control the attitudes of the audience, least of all now in the age of the internet. So a depiction that treats the participants respectfully – say, by showing Black men having sex with one another as partners – may nonetheless perpetuate a kind of harm, for example, by reinforcing previously existing racial stereotypes. This does not lead to any blanket conclusions, but it does suggest that the issues of power and control that Miller-Young discusses would be just as relevant to same-sex and queer pornography.

Conclusion

In this chapter, we've talked about how, because of social factors, objectifying women and people in other marginalized groups raises special issues: it's not that objectification and pornography are inherently wrong or bad but rather than in a social context that overvalues women's sexual attractiveness at the expense of their other qualities, and hypersexualizes other specific groups, objectification becomes a problem.

This is a useful perspective to apply to pornography because it allows us to draw important distinctions between pornography that depicts male dominance and rape, and is bad, and pornography that depicts mutual respect or more complicated sex and gender dynamics. As Miller-Young says, it matters not only who appears in pornography but also who is making it: for pornography to challenge rather than reinforce racist and discriminatory stereotypes, we need women and people of color in the roles of directors and writers.

As we discussed in the last section, perhaps the most important issue related to pornography is the way mainstream industry pornography misrepresents what sex is like. Increasingly, young people report turning to pornography to learn about sex. If what they encounter shows men being aggressive and dominant, and women enjoying it, then, just as MacKinnon and Dworkin warned us, everyone is at risk of absorbing those ideas and taking them for reality. This suggests that amateur pornography or that outside the mainstream could be crucially different – but only if it presents a range of activities and gender dynamics.

3   Consent and rape law

Introduction

In the contemporary Western world, our beliefs about sex accord enormous importance to individuals' choices. So long as we don't harm others, we believe, we all get to choose the kinds of sex we want to have and the persons we want to have it with; we get to change our minds, about activities and partners alike; we get to engage in nonstandard sexual activities without being punished or shamed for our choices. In turn, the high value we place on personal choice means that we also accord great importance to consent, the process by which individuals agree to pursue a particular form of sexual activity. In this chapter, we'll consider what it means to consent to sex, and we'll consider its negative counterpart, nonconsensual or coercive sex.

These may seem simple and straightforward matters, sufficiently summed up in a few basic principles: just do the things that everyone wants, and don't do other things; don't force others to do the things you want; listen to one another, and don't assume your partner shares your own desires. But, as we'll see, understanding sexual consent and sexual coercion is more difficult than it seems. Some of the difficulties arise from wider societal realities that extend beyond the scope of this book. For instance, the harms that result from sexual assault properly play a large role in our understanding of these issues, but philosophical reflection isn't well suited to understanding the texture of these harms. Likewise, sexual coercion has long been a mechanism for enforcing gender and racial norms and has often been used as a means of intimidation in warfare; gender expectations and racism also frequently inform our judgments about consent and coercion.

In this chapter, our main focus will be on the more abstract problems that surround efforts to define sexual consent and coercion. Making determinations about these proves surprisingly difficult, especially since consent is often understood to be communicated through nonverbal as well as verbal communication and often requires inferences about others' states of mind and emotions. At the same time, much is at stake in understanding these issues as well as possible, for in this domain our abstract beliefs about the ethics of sexual consent overlap extensively with the law and with the regulations governing some of our society's most important institutions, such as universities and corporations. Hence this chapter will also explore some specific questions about of how laws and policies should be crafted to protect victims and punish aggressors, while also protecting everyone's rights. Although sexual coercion can arise in a variety of contexts and involve men and women alike, most cases in fact arise in heterosexual contexts and involve female victims and male aggressors; the discussion here will mainly refer to those situations.

A short history of the law of consent

Since current ethical and legal views of consent are deeply influenced by historical factors, we start by taking a moment to look at the history of rape law and how consent came to play the role that it does. Broadly speaking, in anglophone cultures before the nineteenth century, sexual ethics had little to do with consent. Instead, they centered on norms of "chastity" – a concept that referred not only to virginity but more broadly to the idea that sexual ethics has to do with appropriateness in context. In this framing, sexual activity between a man and woman who were married was appropriate, and sex in virtually any other combination or context – including between members of the same sex – was seen as wrong. This implied that among married people consent was irrelevant because it was thought that a man had a right to have sex with his wife whenever he wanted to. Because women were seen as naturally dependent on men, marriage was thought to join a husband and wife together by subsuming her interests into his. His proper role was to lead and decide, hers was to follow and submit, and this meant that it was impossible for a man to "rape" his wife. So the issue of rape between married people did not arise (Ryan 1995).

Second, in this cultural setting, sex outside of marriage was considered extremely damaging to a woman's reputation. In these societies, because their rights to work or own money were restricted, women were often dependent on marriage for their well-being. A never-married woman who was known to have had sex was virtually unmarriageable. Lawmakers inferred from this that if an unmarried woman did willingly have sex, she would have an enormous incentive to lie about it and say she was raped. That is, the social pressure not to have sex was so immense that it was thought virtually impossible that a woman who had had sex willingly would ever admit it. Partly for this reason, the laws were written so that the crime of rape could only be prosecuted if there were physical evidence of the utmost resistance, fighting almost to the death.

Thus, in eighteenth-century common law, rape was characterized as sex outside marriage "by force and against a woman's will" – and this characterization held roughly until the mid twentieth century (Ryan 1995; Schulhofer 1992). Crucially, this definition requires that to be rape sex has to be both nonconsensual – that is, against a woman's will – and forcible, through physical violence. Women accusing men of rape were expected to show obvious signs of vigorous physical resistance to prove they had been raped.

Into the twentieth century, signs of such resistance were often required for successful prosecution. Even as social norms shifted so that sex outside of marriage became more culturally acceptable, social norms were such that it was assumed that a woman who wanted to have sex would always put up a token resistance and that it was a man's role to overcome this. Because it was thought to be unseemly for a woman to say "yes," she therefore had to say "no," even if she wanted to have sex. The man was expected to keep trying. Again, this meant that to signal that she really meant "no," a woman was expected to fight to her utmost, even to the extent of showing that she had risked her life. Without evidence of such a fight, successful prosecution for rape was nearly impossible. The problems with these laws are obvious: a woman being threatened should not have to risk serious injury or death to establish that she was raped.

A first series of reforms in the mid twentieth century sought to make it easier to prosecute rape, in part by removing the physical resistance requirement. But in some North American jurisdictions, the law continued (and some cases still continues) to include the "force" clause. When the force clause is included, nonconsent is not enough to make sex a crime: even if a woman said "no" and was screaming "Stop!" this would not suffice to show that she had been raped (Schulhofer 1992).

In most places in the US and Canada, there have been changes to this framework: there is no force requirement, and only nonconsent is needed to establish criminality. But even in this context there are many questions and difficulties over the concept of consent itself, and there are many cases in which it is impossible to successfully legally prosecute cases that seem like rape. For one thing, some people still believe that women offer token resistance and that "no" sometimes means that a woman wants a man to keep trying. If a woman says "no" to sex, and a man goes ahead and has sex with her, jurors with these beliefs may find him not guilty, on grounds that her behavior is compatible with consent: she may have said "no," but she may have been offering token resistance. There is also the tricky matter of *mens rea*, which means "guilty mind." In many legal frameworks, intention to commit wrongdoing is necessary for criminal prosecution, so a man who sincerely believed that a woman consented to a sexual encounter can't be seen as having committed a crime. If a man can convince a jury that he believed the woman was consenting, then they may conclude he did not intend to violate consent and thus, without a "guilty mind," could not be found guilty.

We live in a society in which many people continue to think that women should not be sexual, or that if a woman is behaving or dressing in certain ways then she "had it coming." For example, if a woman goes to a certain kind of party, or goes into a man's apartment or dorm room, or is wearing a certain kind of outfit, people will say she is "asking for it": if she didn't intend to have sex, why was she doing these things? These behaviors on their own never constitute consent to sex, but if the law appeals to subjective belief, and a man believes that they indicate consent, then a man can plausibly cite these behaviors as having shown that he did not intend to do anything wrong and thus lacks the requisite "guilty mind." In this case, it would be impossible to convict someone of rape if they had sex under certain circumstances even if the woman did not want to, even if she said "no," and even if she was incapacitated and incapable of consent.

In response to these difficulties, many jurisdictions have not only brought in specific clauses about intoxication, they have also introduced a requirement of "reasonable belief": to legally establish that sex was consensual, a man has to show that his belief in his partner's consent is reasonable. The aim is to be able to successfully prosecute cases where a man cites a subjective, but objectively implausible, belief that the woman consented. So, if a man were to say that a woman's being in his dorm room late at night wearing a short skirt was evidence of consent even though she protested, it would still be possible to convict him – on grounds that his belief is not reasonable.

But even reasonableness criteria can only go so far, because the people making legal judgments – jurors and judges – can be as affected by background social beliefs about sex and social norms as anyone else. So, for example, a jury might judge belief in consent reasonable even if the woman clearly said "no," because they might believe that women like to play hard to get, that women say "no" when they mean "yes" in order to avoid being thought promiscuous or slutty, or that "no" really means "keep trying." They might think that a short skirt or going to back to someone's room really does mean that "she asked for it."

"'No' means no"

One proposal for addressing these difficulties is found in the principle that "'No' means no." The idea here is that if someone says "no," that means stop, and if you don't, you're doing something obviously wrong. In this set-up, there is no force requirement, sex in the absence of consent is rape; and whenever a person says "no," they signal their nonconsent. Proponents of such approaches point out that the principle is simple and that the framework shows respect for a woman's choices and decisions. It doesn't matter what she is wearing or how she is acting; if a woman says no, this is enough. Instead of appealing to a vague idea of what is a "reasonable" belief, subject to interpretation, the "'No' means no" criterion lays down a specific principle that must be followed.

But critics say that "'No' means no" doesn't go far enough in protecting women (Anderson 2005). First, it is documented that fear and mental distress can cause people to "freeze" – a woman who is very frightened or mentally distressed may not be able to say "no," and may be passive or silent. If a woman feels she is being menaced by a man who is being verbally and physically aggressive, she may be silent out of fear that speaking up or saying "no" will cause the man to become angry and hurt her. Second, in other areas of life, we do not think silence means consent. In a vivid analogy illustrating this point, Stephen Schulhofer (1992) asks us to imagine an athlete who has to decide whether to have a risky surgery that might help them but might fail, and who can't make up his mind. Imagine the surgeon is waiting and waiting for consent to operate, and the athlete is quiet, still thinking it through, and the surgeon just loses patience, anesthetizes the athlete, and operates. No one would say the athlete had consented to the operation or that it was appropriate to move forward with it.

Also, what does "No" mean precisely? Presumably it means one must stop moving forward with intended sexual behavior at that moment. But does it also rule out continuing to ask, or asking again later? When? Relatedly, what about a "no" followed by a "yes" later on? Much seems to hang on the intervening activity: there is a difference between badgering, and harassment and a fun evening with conversation and laughs. The "'No' means no" framework doesn't help us analyze this. Sometimes a "no" is followed by a later "yes," and "no" can in some cases be appropriately treated as "not now," but maybe later, perhaps much later, when the relationship has evolved. Sometimes persistent attention is welcome; sometimes persistent attention is aggression and coercion and "not taking no for an answer." The "'No' means no" framework doesn't help with this either (Schulhofer 1992; Anderson 2005).

With respect to this question of a "no" that is followed by a "yes," some questions concern high-pressure tactics – when, for example, a man is unwilling to take "no" for an answer – and the line between appropriately persuading someone to have sex with you and coercion. Lois Pineau (1989) describes one typical kind of problem case: a woman goes out on a date with a guy she may or may not be interested in. They have a couple of drinks. She's not interested in having sex with him, but he starts to pressure her: he tells her how wrong she has been for "leading him on," how his frustration will be painful for him, how deceitful she is. He is interested not in her as a person but rather in a conquest of something he feels entitled to. He uses overbearing physicality while he insists and insists; she judges that not only would it be easier to have sex with him and get it out of the way but that, in addition, in his emotional state, he might be made angry and violent if she resists. She becomes frightened, and she stops resisting. Pineau quotes a rapist, who says:

> "All of my rapes have been involved in a dating situation where I've been out with a woman I know … I wouldn't take no for an answer. I think it had something to do with my acceptance of rejection. I had

low self-esteem and not much self-confidence and when I was rejected for something which I considered to be rightly mine, I became angry and I went ahead anyway. And this was the same in any situation, whether it was rape or it was something else."

(Pineau 1989: 219–220)

Pineau says that these cases should be seen as nonconsensual, even if the woman stops resisting.

There are also questions about coercion and deception. In one case in the United States, a man threatened to send his foster child back to a detention home unless she submitted to sexual intercourse (Schulhofer 1992: 48). In another, a man called a woman who had just had lab tests at a hospital; he told her she had a dangerous and possibly fatal disease, one that could only be treated with expensive surgery or through a serum administered, by him, through sexual intercourse. Some recent high-profile cases of sexual assault and harassment have concerned women who were told, more or less explicitly, that to advance in their careers or just keep the job they had, they had to submit to sex.

If a woman is browbeaten, harassed, coerced or deceived into saying yes, this should not be interpreted as a kind of consent. So how should law and policy be crafted to help address such situations appropriately? Some laws and policies are shifting away from a "'No' means no" framework and toward "affirmative consent": these latter require positive signs of ongoing intention, willingness, or desire. In Canada, consent is defined in the Criminal Code in s. 273.1(1) as the voluntary agreement to engage in the sexual activity in question: sexual touching is only lawful if the person affirmatively communicated their consent, whether through words or conduct. The policy for the SUNY (State University of New York) system says that "Affirmative consent is a knowing, voluntary, and mutual decision among all participants to engage in sexual activity. Consent can be given by words or actions, as long as those words or actions create clear permission regarding willingness to engage in the sexual activity." Some states and many US campuses use frameworks based on affirmative consent, and in 2014, California passed a law that all higher-education campuses had to have affirmative-consent policies.

Often in practice affirmative-consent policies allow for a mix of verbal and nonverbal communication, and they are written in gender-neutral ways to apply to everyone equally. In the next few sections, we'll discuss different ways of understanding affirmative consent, before turning to broader questions about sexual autonomy.

Communicative sexuality and nonverbal consent

Pineau says that a big part of the problem is the way we think about sex as too much like a contract – as if consent to sex is something you get from someone, through pressure if necessary – rather than the result of a mutual and ongoing process. She says the "contract model" of sex leads people to think that a woman, through certain behaviors, commits herself to sex, "asked for it," so that it would wrong for her to not to follow through. She proposes instead a "communicative model" of sexuality, in which sex is like an ongoing conversation, a back-and-forth in which we attend to the other person's desires and moods, and not simply an occasion where one person – usually a man – chooses a sex act and the other person – usually a woman – either acquiesces or objects.

Against the thinking that leads to "she asked for it," Pineau points out that in ordinary life, contracts are nothing like this. High-pressure tactics are particularly frowned on. Suppose you were trying to arrange a mortgage, and imagine the banker took you to dinner where there was drinking and conversation, and then at midnight he started badgering you to sign on the dotted line, saying things like "You'd better sign, you're not going to waste my whole evening with your game-playing!" or "You'd better sign, or I'm going to have to rough you up." That would be wildly inappropriate. What if the surgeon started to harass and menace the athlete, shouting at him for wasting his time and threatening to drop him as a patient unless he came through with consenting to surgery? Not acceptable. The point of fair contracts is that they're supposed to be made freely, in the absence of coercion and pressure. So it is silly to suggest that somehow the contract model means a woman who has behaved in certain ways is obligated to follow through.

In addition, the idea of enforceable contracts in the domain of sex is peculiar. What are you going to do, call the police? Have the courts order one person to have sex with another? Even in regular contract law, the state does not typically compel parties to a contract to keep the exact terms they agreed to. If a particular legal commitment is made, reparations may be required for those who break the commitment, but if you agree to work for Starbucks for one year, the penalty for quitting early isn't jail.

Most importantly, Pineau says that the whole idea of a "contract" is mistaken. In the context of sex, the whole set-up has the air of a protection racket from organized crime. "Say yes – or else!" Why not think of sex more as a mutual, and mutually desired, interaction? Why not see it as "a proper conversation rather than an offer from the Mafia" (1989: 235)? The contract model is embedded in a kind of thinking in which it's appropriate for a man to pressure and threaten a woman to get sex, without concern over whether she wants to be participating or is enjoying it, and which treats sex more like extortion than a mutual and interactive experience. Sexual consent is too much like something you "get" from an otherwise passive partner and makes sex too much like something women concede to rather than actually wanting.

Instead, she says, we should think of sex as involving mutual enjoyment and interest. In her proposal, which she calls "communicative sexuality," people have to pay attention to one another and to whether continued positive interest is ongoing. Specifically, Pineau says,

> if a man wants to be sure that he is not forcing himself on a woman, he has an obligation either to ensure that the encounter really is mutually enjoyable, or to know the reasons why she would want to continue the encounter in spite of her lack of enjoyment.
>
> (1989: 234)

If the legal framework were based on communicative sexuality, then in cross-examination one could demand to know from a man what positive signs he took to indicate ongoing enjoyment, or if there were no such signs, why he thought she wanted to continue. One could ask pointed questions such as whether contraception was discussed, and if not, why not. Or did he ask what kinds of sexual activities she likes most?

Communicative sexuality can be understood as one interpretation of affirmative consent, one in which nonverbal as well as verbal cues are appropriate markers for ongoing interest. A woman might say she is enjoying it. Or she might grab the man and pull him closer, or smile in a way that conveys her pleasure. Obviously, signs that she is not enjoying it are also relevant and show that he ought to desist – if, for example, she is protesting, or frowning, or grimacing in pain, or crying.

Notably, in Pineau's proposal, a woman may have reasons for wanting a man to continue even though she is not enjoying it. There are many such reasons, a common one being hopes of pregnancy. People trying to have children, especially if they're having fertility difficulties, often have sex at particular times – for example, when the woman is ovulating – to maximize the chances that she'll get pregnant, whether or not they feel like having sex at that moment. In other cases, many people in relationships genuinely want to provide pleasure to their partners, and even though they don't quite feel like having sex, they consent, and continue even if they are not enjoying it. Sometimes people have sex they are not enjoying because they know that the first few times with a new partner can be awkward and not that pleasurable, but they know also that as they get to know each other better, the sex will improve. Sometimes people have sex to gain social status or protection or any number of other things. From the perspective of communicative sexuality, these are all appropriate reasons, but there is a requirement of open communication about them. You have to have reason to believe your partner wants to continue; it would seem that you ought to have some understanding of the honest reasons they want to continue.

Some critics say that formally allowing nonverbal cues to communicate consent leads to problems for two reasons. First, it allows for potential misinterpretation, which may be particularly hazardous in the context of sex. As Michelle Anderson puts it, "study after study indicates that men consistently misinterpret women's nonverbal behavior. They impute erotic innuendo and sexual intent where there is none" (2005: 1417). Allowing a facial expression to communicate willingness and enjoyment means running the risk that a warm or welcoming facial expression will be misread to mean "yes" to sex when it's really a result of someone being friendly or nonconfrontational.

Second, because it allows for nonverbal expression, communicative sexuality encourages people to consider responses after and during an activity rather than before. Just because you're enjoying kissing doesn't mean you want to go further – in fact, that you're enjoying any one thing means nothing in terms of whether you've consented to something completely different. Suppose you are enjoying making out but you are determined not to have sexual intercourse or any kind of penetration. As things progress, you may be enjoying yourself more and more, and communicating that enjoyment. From the point of view of communicative sexuality, that would seem a green light to go ahead. But it is wrong to think that your communicating that enjoyment is grounds for thinking you've consented to further acts like penetration (Anderson 2005: 1406).

In support of these criticisms, the authors of a recent study of consent practices among students point out that even asking "Is this OK?" is crucially ambiguous: does it refer to what is already happening, or to some potential escalation or future activity? Suppose a man has a hand on a woman's upper thigh, and he says, "Is this OK?" If she says, "Yes," should this be read as encouragement for other sexual acts like moving the hand toward her vulva? Or does it just mean he can leave the hand where it is (Muehlenhard et al. 2016: 475)? Any reliance on nonverbal communication is going to lead to this difficulty since nonverbal responses are responses, not communications of consent to an activity that is not yet happening. So, you may risk engaging in a new activity that person did not consent to and would not have consented to. As we've seen, contemporary affirmative-consent policies often allow for a mix of verbal and nonverbal cues, so these challenges to nonverbal communication are relevant in practice.

Some discussions of affirmative consent go beyond the importance of communicating positive willingness to indicate that mere consent is not enough: it's not just a "yes" that is needed, but an enthusiastic "yes!" This is usually intended not as part of formal policy but rather as part of rethinking and education. The idea is that a sexual activity should happen only when both people really, really want it, when it's happening out of shared desire and not just because one person is "consenting" to something. This can be part of a project of bringing about change with respect to social norms related to sex. For example, "Project Respect" (2017) says that "positive sexuality begins with enthusiastic consent. This means being as excited and into someone else's enjoyment as we are excited and into our own. Only yes means yes – and yes should come from an engaged and enthusiastic partner." (see also Oklahoma State University 2017). Echoing

Pineau, part of the thinking for talking about shared desire and enthusiasm is to reorient thinking away from the model in which one person, usually a man, proposes something and the other person agrees or acquiesces, and more toward a model in which sex is mutually desired (see also West 2010).

With respect to goals of cultural change and education, proponents point out that thinking in terms of affirmative consent can help us move away from the problematic gender-norm expectations we mentioned above in "A Short History of the Law of Consent." In our society, men are socialized to feel that getting to have sex is "scoring" and that as long as they can get a woman to go along with it they're doing something right. Women are socialized to think that sex is something they either go along with or not but not something they initiate or make decisions about. Against this backdrop, affirmative consent is about changing our attitudes so that it's expected that each partner is paying attention to whether the activity is something both people want.

The goal of reorienting our thinking about sex so as to emphasize women's engagement and pleasure, rather than just her "permission," is of crucial importance. When women have sex with men, their pleasure is sometimes ignored or treated as an afterthought; one large-scale study found that women having sex with men have about one orgasm for every three a man has – something that's been called an "orgasm gap" (Heldman and Wade 2010). But while the aim of mutuality is important, I question a specific emphasis on "enthusiasm," since it implies that sex should only happen when both people really desire the activity. One thing that might complicate this is that sexual desire does always arise spontaneously. As we'll discuss in more detail in Chapter 12, recent empirical research shows that many people – and women especially – are likely to experience desire not so much spontaneously but more "responsively," in response to sexual activity (Basson 2010; see also Cahill 2014). Maybe you've had this experience: you aren't feeling sexy, but you figure you'll go ahead anyway, and once things are under way you get really into it. As Ann Cahill (2014) says, the phenomenon of responsive desire complicates the idea that desire should come before consent. Another issue is that sometimes you don't know what you want sexually because your sexuality is still developing; if you trust the other person, a mood of experimentation and "who knows?" can be just as good as a starting place of specific desire. Women are often told their sexuality should be this way or that; instead, I believe, we shouldn't be too inflexible with the idea that sex is only appropriate when both people already really want some specific activity and want it before starting.

Generally, it's also worth noting that while nonverbal communication is thought to be less awkward and intrusive, in circumstances of ambivalence and uncertainty the requirement that we know the person's reasons could be difficult to meet. In such cases, Pineau's idea entails that each person has an obligation to know the reasons the other might want to continue despite not enjoying it. In a case where two people are trying to have a baby, that would be pretty simple. Both partners know why they are there, even if they are not into it at that moment. But in other cases, it could be difficult. Imagine the first few times with a new partner, and you're not enjoying it much, but you think that with time it is going to get better. Imagine you are therefore a bit quiet or undemonstrative during sex. In communicative sexuality, your partner says, "You're pretty quiet? You're having a good time, right?" And now what? I doubt anyone is recommending lying. So given the norms of communicative sexuality, it would seem that the only acceptable response to this question would be "No, I'm not, but I'm hoping that, with time, and maybe if we have sex more than once, things will improve." This could be an awkward and difficult conversation. Even if people are just nondemonstrative, they may not want to project the kind of enjoyment that communicative sexuality would seem to encourage. As we will see in the next section, sometimes verbal communication is not only clearer, it can also be easier.

The Antioch Policy and verbal consent

In affirmative-consent frameworks that require verbal consent, each person has to ask a specific question and get a verbal "yes" before moving forward. Obviously, this helps with the possible misinterpretation of non-verbal cues, since verbal communication leaves less open to interpretation. It also avoids the problem that enjoying some activities leads to presumed consent for others – like penetration – when this really isn't warranted.

The big question with respect to verbal consent is how often, and for what activities, do you have to ask? Back in the 1990s, Antioch College in the United States tried to craft a proposal that would clarify for students exactly when sex would and wouldn't be considered consensual – a precise and workable procedure to follow. Since any sexual activity is one that should be consented to, verbal consent would seem to require an explicit question and an explicit "yes" for every action that is part of sexual activity (Soble 1997a). The policy had seven principles:

A1. Consent must be obtained verbally before there is any sexual contact or conduct.
A2. Obtaining consent is an ongoing process in any sexual interaction.
A3. If the level of sexual intimacy increases during an interaction ... the people involved need to express their clear verbal consent before moving to that new level.
A4. The request for consent must be specific to each act.
A5. If you have had a particular level of sexual intimacy before with someone, you must still ask each and every time.
A6. If someone has initially consented but then stops consenting during a sexual interaction, she/he should communicate withdrawal verbally

and/or through physical resistance. The other individual(s) must stop immediately.

A7. Don't ever make any assumptions about consent.

As it is stated, this policy is inconsistent with "metaconsent" – that is, with the idea that you could agree with someone ahead of time about what was and was not off limits. With metaconsent, people might lay out in advance what they plan to do; they might decide on a "safe word" – a word that if someone says it means "stop." According to the Antiochian policy, this kind of pre-negotiation is not allowed (Soble 1997a).

As many people have observed since this policy was crafted, it seems that if you took it literally a typical interaction would require a large number of questions. Each person must ask anew, for each new activity. This means every time you touch a new body part you'd have to ask. If you started kissing, then shifted to touching the person's face with your hands, then to touching the person's leg with your hands, it seems you'd each have to ask the other before each shift. In the Antioch policy, the need to ask questions does not depend on how well you know the person or whether you're in a relationship. Even if you've been dating for years and have had sex many times, you still have to ask one another at the start of each new activity every single time you engage in any sexual conduct, from kissing to touching to anything else.

This need for questions at each new stage raises an interesting question. How do we determine what is a "new" act? If you are kissing someone, does kissing in a slightly different way count as a new act? What if you've been kissing and someone's tongue is in your mouth, and the action shifts so that your tongue is in their mouth? If you've been kissing, and then you pause to do something else, does going back to kissing need a new question? Since the wording refers to an increase in the "level" of sexual intimacy but also says consent is "specific to each act," the policy makes it hard to say.

Some critics of verbal affirmative-consent policies question whether asking permission and checking in during sex is compatible with sexual passion. In some studies, young people said they regard verbal consent as "as interfering with spontaneity and the excitement of not knowing what a partner might do next, and as ruining the mood" (Muehlenhard et al. 2016: 475). In response to this idea that having so many questions and constant dialogue during sex would be a downer, some people have suggested that you could kind of work the questions into the sex itself: make the questions sexy and eroticized, and then they won't be getting in the way and might even add texture and passion. But I agree with Soble when he says that taking the questions to be part of the sexiness leads to a crucial problem: if the talk is part of what is sexy, then one would need consent for the talk itself – leading to an infinite regress and other impracticalities (1997a: 28–29). Try to imagine asking for consent to ask someone's consent, and then for consent to ask that question, and then …

This infinite regress problem is more than just a verbal quibble. If part of the problem of consent is that women feel pressure to go along with something, wouldn't they feel pressured to go along with sexy conversation as well? When people enjoy talking during sex as part of the sexual activity, the talking itself gets caught up in whatever dynamic is happening between them: to respond negatively to an erotic question during sex can feel as disruptive as an interjection of "no" or "stop" does. So, if the questions are eroticized, some of the improvement of the asking policy over "'No' means no" would disappear. I think it's essential to the policy that the questions be desexualized. This marks an interesting point of difference from Pineau's communicative sexuality since ongoing signs of enjoyment in her proposal are both part of sex and part of what can count as evidence that the sex is mutually desired. This difference can be traced to the fact that the Antioch policy requires explicit verbal consent for each new action, while communicative sexuality does not.

Alan Soble (1997a) says that the Antioch policy represents a "trade-off": we lose the pleasure of the unexpected, but we avoid the displeasure and harm of interactions that are not expected and not wanted. It is interesting to think of a policy as representing a "trade-off," because sometimes we talk about policies as if once we get the right principle everything will be just right for everyone all the time. But it's possible for policies to be justified on the basis of complex balancing of various considerations: protection from one thing at the cost of another, or protection from harms some people are likely to experience at the cost of pleasures others are likely to experience. These kinds of trade-offs are difficult to judge in ethical terms, because people interpret harms and pleasures differently and also have different opinions about how trade-offs should be made. But it is worth noting here that just because a policy reduces some people's ability to experience some pleasures does not, in itself, make the policy unfair or unjust.

An alternative model based on verbal consent is Michelle Anderson's (2005) "negotiation" model. In this proposal, people would be required to discuss verbally whether they plan to do this or that activity – but only for acts that are penetrative, not for every single sexual act. The idea of "negotiation" includes pre-negotiation: if you don't want to get involved with a lot of questions and answers during sex, you can discuss ahead of time what you're willing to do and what's off limits, and go from there. This is different from the Antioch policy because there are only a small number of acts you have to discuss, and also because it reintroduces metaconsent: you can discuss in advance which things are good to go unless someone says otherwise, so those would be things you don't have to ask about during the interaction. Anderson's proposal is different from communicative sexuality because it requires verbal not nonverbal cues and, again, because it applies to a small number of specific acts. Like those other proposals, though, the negotiation model addresses the problem about silence: because discussion is required, sex with a person who says nothing, perhaps because they are frozen from fear or anxiety, is always off limits. What you think about Anderson's proposal might depend on the extent to which you think penetrative acts should be singled out for special consideration, or whether you think the potential harms of other nonconsensual sexualized forms of touching are similar. This raises the complicated questions of what, exactly, sex is, what counts as sexual touching, and whether a focus on penetration is as appropriate for, say, lesbian sex as for heterosexual sex.

Though nonverbal communication is often thought to be less intrusive than verbal communication, in my opinion it can be more intrusive. As we've seen above, Pineau's proposal seems to require a lot of honest communication, especially when participants may be ambivalent, or uncertain. Even though verbal communication might seem to disrupt the flow of sex more than nonverbal communication, I think the virtues of verbal communication are underrated. As we've seen, nonverbal communication can be tricky: expressing pleasure with what is happening now is not the same as expressing consent for something else that is yet to happen. I think nonverbal communication also helps with the problem of ambivalence or not enjoying it. One virtue of verbal communication is, I believe, the way it allows people who are conflicted, ambivalent, or uncertain to make the decisions they want to make without someone prying into their reasons. For the person who has a mix of feelings but, all things considered, wants to go ahead, all they have to do is say "yes" – they don't have to falsely express enthusiasm or pleasure. In Michelle Anderson's framing, the focus on verbal communication also encourages discussion ahead of time – the "pre-negotiation" – which could be helpful for people who don't feel too demonstrative or expressive during sex.

Affirmative consent, sexual autonomy, and the law

As our discussion suggests, one of the complexities of affirmative consent is that sometimes it is required by law or policy while at others it is intended as educational, as helping to change the sexual culture. When it is incorporated into law or policy, critics have said that it moves perilously close to "guilty until proven innocent": if an accuser claims not to have conveyed affirmative consent, the burden of proof is on the accused to prove that such consent was communicated (Halley 2016: 272). Janet Halley (2016) and others say that establishing, positively, that willingness was communicated will often be impossible in practice, and this makes innocence too difficult to establish. The burdens on those accused, she points out, will fall disproportionately on groups thought to be "sexually dangerous," including "black men, other men of color, men of lower social and economic class than their accusers, and men and women who don't conform to the gender expectations and norms of their accusers" (Halley 2016: 278). Partly because affirmative consent was thought to make innocence too difficult to establish, in 2016 the American Law Institute voted against amending the US Model Penal Code to define sexual consent on an affirmative basis (Richardson 2016).

Policies based on affirmative consent also may not help address broader issues of coercion and pressure, where the issue is not just whether there is a "yes" but also why the person is saying "yes." As we've seen, people say "yes" to sex for many reasons, and some legal scholars argue that the law should do more to protect sexual autonomy. If one person is in a position of power over the other – a teacher, a boss, etc. – they may use that power in an extortionate way, demanding, for example, sex in exchange for grades, promotions, and other benefits. Even where there is no formalized relationship, sexual *quid pro quo* can be wrong: under a widely shared norm that sexual service should never be an appropriate condition of nonsexual employment, a person who offers an employment opportunity with the condition of agreeing to sex has also created a condition in which the sex is improperly coercive.

The contours of coercion are complex, however. Schulhofer suggests that a billionaire who offers marriage to a beautiful young model, but only if she has sex with him, is not acting coercively, because sex is understood to be an appropriate part of marriage and other intimate relationships. Sarah Conly (2004) says that a person who threatens to end a romantic relationship if their partner won't have sex with them has not committed rape even if the threat may be less than admirable; this is partly because one person has a right to break up with another.

Similar considerations apply in the case of deception. The man who deceived a woman into believing that his semen would cure her illness failed to respect her autonomy: she could not make a decision based on her own reasons because she was actively deceived about the facts. But sexual partners need not disclose everything: some information we have a right to keep private. Hugh Lazenby and Iason Gabriel (2018) argue that even when information would be relevant to the decision of our potential partners, we can have a right to be silent about it: a person who has been a victim of a prior sexual assault need not disclose this information to potential partners, even if the potential partners would find it relevant. Judging what is coercive or deceptive in a way that violates sexual autonomy requires using background norms about what is owed to whom and why.

Conclusion

We started this chapter with a consideration of how consent came to play the role that it does in modern sexual ethics. In principle, consent is simple, and it performs what some philosophers call "moral magic": what may be a violation when it happens without consent can be mutual happiness when it happens consensually. But, as we've seen here, specifying how consent should work in practice is always complex, and is made more so by social and cultural norms regarding women and their sexuality.

When we craft laws and policies about consent, we have to specify not only that consent matters but also how we expect consent to be communicated. As we've seen, while "'No' means no" was intended to convey that a woman's "no" is always sufficient to show nonconsent, critics argue that it doesn't go far enough: people may be silent out of fear or anxiety, and their silence should not be interpreted as consent. As we've also seen, the various ways of interpreting the requirements of "affirmative consent" raise difficult questions. Allowing nonverbal communication of consent risks that consent will be assumed for a new act based on the nonverbal positive enjoyment of a previous act. When verbal communication is required, it may be unclear when an act is a new act. According to Halley, adopting affirmative consent as policy risks making innocence too difficult to establish. Finally, we've seen that judgments about whether a sexual interaction is coercive or wrongly deceptive rest on social beliefs about what we owe one another. Expecting sex as part of a marriage or romantic partnership may not be wrongly coercive, but expecting sex in return for a job offer would be, because of social expectations about the role sex plays in our lives. While we have rights to be informed about sexual partners, we also have rights to privacy, and these have to be weighed against one another when we talk about what is wrongly deceptive.

These are among the complexities that lurk within the apparently simple concepts of consenting and refusing to consent to sex. Of course, such complexities do not mean that we should abandon efforts to improve our understanding of consent and our society's practices surrounding consent, what I've here referred to as the culture of consent. On the contrary, understanding the difficulties concerning consent is crucial to establishing effective expectations, policies, and laws about it.

4   Sex work

Introduction

Sex work is the exchange of sexual activities for money or other goods, and in recent years it has raised a series of fundamental, hotly debated questions. Some of these have to do with whether sex work could be like other forms of work. Given the right conditions, could it be an unproblematic or even self-expressive way to make money? Or is there something inherently dehumanizing, unethical, or wrongly commodifying in the exchange itself? Other questions have to do with the relationship between the activities of sex work and the contexts in which they happen. As we'll discuss below, much sex work takes place in circumstances that cause abuse and harm to sex workers. Such rights violations are always wrong, and their frequency means that in practice sex work is often not like other forms of work. However, the philosophical questions about sex work have to do rather with whether, under the right conditions, it could be like other forms of work and how concepts of sex as work fit in with broader social structures and gender norms.

Historically, when sex was understood as appropriate only within heterosexual marriage, the exchange of sex for money was considered not only immoral but also socially destructive. But understanding sex in terms of individual freedom shifts this perspective dramatically. In the absence of coercion and mistreatment, it seems that sex work could be a mutual exchange among consenting adults. It follows that from an autonomy perspective, there is a straightforward answer to the question of whether sex work could be unproblematic. If we grant that people generally have the right to make decisions about their bodies and sexuality, then it would seem to follow that they have the right to buy and sell sex, and the answer would be "yes."

Because this argument in favor of individuals making their own decisions about whether to sell and buy sex is so straightforward, this chapter will focus largely on examining challenges to it. With respect to these challenges, there are two lines of thought. One is that there are ethical problems inherent in the very idea of sex work itself – that there is something essentially wrong about exchanging sex for money or other goods, regardless of the context, because it is damaging to the sex worker or because sex is just not the kind of thing that can be appropriately bought and sold. A second is that there is nothing inherently problematic with sex work, but that in certain cultural contexts, such as societies with hierarchical gender roles, sex work is a problem. We discuss these positions in the sections below.

I'll suggest that these analyses showcase the importance of the question whether the social meaning of sex is or consistent with, or contrary to, the values of the marketplace, and how. Given the wide range of things we buy and sell, is there something special about sex that sets it outside this domain, and if so, what is it? One way of thinking about this question has to do with kind of thing sex is in itself: sex, we might say, should involve attention to the other person as a person, with caring for their sexual feelings and desires, and commercialization destroys that. A different way of thinking attends to context: we live among gendered social norms – that men are naturally dominant, that sex pollutes women, or that sex work is degrading – and the practice of sex work may support and reinforce these, even if we would prefer that they change. I'll also argue that evaluating these arguments, and the fit between sex and work – requires reflection not only on the social meaning of sex, but also on the social meaning of work. If capitalism means that sex work is commodifying and dehumanizing, maybe the problem has to do with the nature of work as well as with the nature of sex. Toward the end of the chapter, we'll touch briefly on the issue of sexual surrogacy, for people with disabilities, to see how that practice challenges our background assumptions about what it means to treat sex as part of work.

Sex work and the law

Though sex work encompasses a range of activities, such as posing for or acting in pornographic representations, agreeing to be a master or slave in a paid dominance or submission interaction, or phone sex, the phrase "sex work" is commonly used to refer to personal, physical, sexual interaction for remuneration, or what might be called "commercialized sex." That is what we'll be focusing on for most of this chapter. The term "sex work" was introduced in the late twentieth century as a way of avoiding the stigma and negative connotations associated with words like "prostitute," and "whore." Though sex workers can be men or women or differently gendered, the vast majority of clients of sex workers are men, and most of them are paying for sex with women. For this reason, much theorizing about sex work deals with considerations particular to the context of men as the buyers and women as the sellers. But men also buy and sell sex with one another, and sex work happens in a range of gender configurations.

Much modern sex work takes place in deplorable conditions. Sex workers can be among the most vulnerable people in a society, and they are often exploited and abused in a range of ways. They may be abused by pimps, who control their activities through threats and violence and take their earnings, and by clients, who may harm them or try to avoid payment. Sometimes women are taken from their home countries under false pretenses of doing other kinds of work, and then their passports are taken away; they may be physically or mentally abused into having sex with clients, and may not receive the money involved. This is how sex work is sometimes associated with human trafficking. Notably, other kinds of workers are trafficked as well, including domestic workers and, in one high-profile case, construction workers building the 2022 World Cup Stadium in Qatar, so human trafficking transcends the domain of sex in particular. These abusive and coercive practices are always wrong, whether sex is involved or not. We are not debating these practices when we "debate" sex work from a philosophical point of view: the only questions with respect to these practices is how best to stop them.

With respect to the wide range of ways that sex workers are harmed in general, there is disagreement over how to reduce this harm and how best to protect sex workers' human rights. In some ways, making the buying and selling of sex illegal can make sex workers more vulnerable, since they can be arrested and cannot call on law enforcement for protection against pimps or abusive clients. To create laws that discourage the practice of commercialized sex while protecting sex workers from harm, some propose a "Nordic model" – used in Norway, Sweden, and some other countries – in which clients, but not sex workers, can be subject to arrest. In 2016, however, Amnesty International released a statement supporting the decriminalization of consensual sex work. Drawing on research from social scientists and input from sex workers themselves, Amnesty concluded that decriminalization was the best way to protect sex workers from human-rights violations and abuses.

In general, movements toward decriminalization have been controversial. Critics say that decriminalization of sex work does nothing to address the power imbalances, especially gendered ones, central to the way the industry functions, and that decriminalization improperly legitimates the idea that women are commodities. But proponents of decriminalization say that even the Nordic model makes sex workers vulnerable: because their client could be arrested, sex workers are extremely reluctant to call the police, even when they are in highly dangerous situation. Melissa Gira Grant (2014) argues that placing sex work outside the "legitimate" economy harms sex workers. This question of what laws and social structures best function to protect sex workers from harm and from violation of their human rights is not a philosophical question, since it's a question of "what works best" – something sex workers, social scientists, and health researchers are best equipped to address.

In the early to middle twentieth century in North America, before the changes associated with the sexual revolution of the 1960s, it was widely assumed that the ethical arguments against sex work were relatively simple. Sex outside of marriage was seen as generally wrong, and sex work would be just an instance of that. In addition, it was often assumed that the existence of a sex-work industry would bring unwelcome societal changes, such as the spread of sexually transmitted diseases, more cheating on spouses, women being coerced into sex work, and women being impossible to reintegrate into society after spending time as sex workers. In the wake of the sexual revolution, however, ethical concerns about sex work became less obvious. If people should be generally able to choose for themselves what to do with others sexually, is there an argument against exchanging sex for money? In what follows, we examine some answers to this question.

Sex work as a free contractual exchange

A first position is that sex work is like other work, reflecting what is sometimes called the "liberal argument." As in the discussion of liberalism in the introduction, the word refers here not to "liberal" as opposed to "conservative" but rather to a more conceptual meaning found in political philosophy: that, as much as possible, people should be free to do as they please, as long as they are not directly harming anyone else. When two people each want to engage in a private transaction, the liberal perspective is that they should be allowed to do so. This is partly because if they both want to engage in the transaction we should assume that the transaction will make each of the people better off, since they are each getting what they want. From the liberal point of view, sex work is just a contractual exchange that happens to involve sex: if the sex worker wants to provide services and the client wants to pay, then each is getting something they want out of the exchange. Of course, many commercial enterprises are regulated to lessen any potential ill effects, and the same could apply to sex work; indeed, in some countries this is how things work: sex workers, for example, might be required to undergo tests for diseases and might receive various protections.

Challenges to the liberal view tend to come from two different perspectives. First, it might be said that there is something inherently wrong in sex work because sex is not the kind of thing it's appropriate to exchange for money or goods. Or, it might be said that while the contractual exchanges of sex work are not inherently a problem, there is something problematic about the way the practice functions in modern society. Next, we consider each of these challenges in detail.

Sex work, commodification, and the specialness of sex

Some people think sex work cannot be understood as a free contractual exchange making everyone better off. Instead, they believe that there is something particular about sex that makes commercialized sex always a problem. For example, it might be thought that sex is so deeply connected to the selfhood of a person, so intimately related to who they are, that to buy and sell it would be wrong. So even if they don't realize it, someone selling sex is harmed by the exchange, because it is selling access to their sexual self, which should be protected from commercialization. In this vein, Carol Pateman (1988) says that in selling sex, a sex worker is literally selling herself, so sex work could never be harmless.

In a 2001 paper, Yolanda Estes develops the idea of sex work as essentially harmful in a particularly original and interesting way. Estes challenges the liberal argument on grounds that it does not reflect the reality of how commercialized sex works, especially when it involves men buying sex from women. The liberal argument seems to say that commercialized sex is a lot like commercialized food: a person goes to a restaurant because they are hungry and desire food. In the exchange, each party gets what they desire, and likewise for a sex worker and client (see also Estes 2008).

But Estes says that this analogy doesn't work, for several reasons. First, she asks, what is it that the client of a sex worker is looking for? In the food case, the client wants to satisfy a simple drive of hunger, a need for food. But that can't be the same for the sex client, because if all the person wanted was to satisfy a need, there would be no point to going to all that trouble of hiring a sex worker. People who want to satisfy a drive for sexual pleasure and orgasm can generally satisfy that aim themselves, by simply masturbating. The fact that they prefer being with a sex worker to masturbating suggests that the need for sexual release is not the whole story.

In response to this, it might be said that the client of a sex worker isn't just trying to rid themselves of a hunger, they're also looking for a special experience: like a gourmet who goes to a five-star restaurant to get a special meal they can't make at home, the client wants have sex with a certain particular type of woman, or one with special skills. But in that case, Estes says, the client could just cultivate sexual relationships with just those types of women, or with women who have those skills. Estes proposes that what male clients are really looking for is a way of avoiding the effort and annoyances associated with real relationships with real people. They want a woman "who ceases to exist when she is not wanted" (2001: 3). This claim about motivations fits with the old quip, used recently by Charlie Sheen when facing a charge of hiring sex workers: "I don't pay them for sex. I pay them to leave." In fact, Estes says, the desire for ease and control goes further: the client wants a woman who will disguise her own subjectivity – her actual needs, wishes, and desires – in order to be the person who will please him.

Looking at the interaction this way, she says, shows that not only does each person not gain something from commercialized sex, in fact both the client and the sex worker lose. The client loses because the subjectivity of the sex worker – their thoughts and feelings – is crucial to what they are seeking, and yet paradoxically is something they cannot access. This means that the client "desires a contradiction": what they want, to experience the subjectivity of another, is just what they cannot have, because of the market aspect of the exchange (Estes 2001: 4).

As in our discussion of pornography, misrepresentations of sex work might also be bad because they risk spreading false ideas, especially about women. It's not hard to imagine that someone who learned about women from seeing sex workers could get mistaken information about women's sexual preferences and anatomy; they might think that whatever it is they like that, magically, women seem to like that too.

In any case, the sex worker loses as well because she must distance herself from her true feelings, and this alienation causes a fragmenting of the self. Echoing Pateman's idea that selling one's sexuality is selling one's self, Estes says that the sex worker must alienate herself from her true sexual self. This is partly because sexual interactions often cause intense emotions and sensations, both positive and negative. It would be dangerous and potentially self-damaging for the sex worker to allow herself to fully feel and experience these. If she is feeling something positive, she risks being attached to her client, who sees her only as a worker he will leave. If she feels something negative, she must repress it to please the client. So she cannot integrate her sexuality into herself, and so she is harmed – and loses – by the interaction as well. The sex worker loses.

It is interesting to consider the ways in which this analysis of the sex-work interaction is or is not gendered. Estes talks about male clients and female sex workers, but we might ask: would her arguments apply in the same way to cases of male sex workers with male clients, or client–worker pairings of other genders? Though much criticism of the sex-work industry comes from feminist perspectives, it seems that Estes' analysis, if correct, would apply in the same way regardless of the gender of the client or worker. Her idea of why the client loses in the interaction has to do with the worker's subjectivity and why payment makes that inaccessible; if correct, this would seems to apply in the same way to people of any gender. Her idea of why the sex worker loses has to do with repressing their authentic reactions to please the client; this, too, seems to apply in the same way across the board. On the face of it, this seems reason to think her analysis would apply generally and would extend as well to women buying sex from men and people of any gender buying and selling sex.

Is Estes' broad conclusion justified? Estes attributes to the client a particular kind of motive: to experience the subjectivity of a person who will disappear, and thus to have sex in a way that does not require a relationship. One way to challenge this assumption might be to point out that some clients say they visit sex workers to experience novelty or to experience specific kinds of sex acts that they cannot find others to enjoy with them. Some people in long-term relationships seek out sex workers because they want to experience having sex with a person who is not their partner. Some people who have specific interests – like wanting to be dominated, or fetishes about feet or other body parts, might be willing to pay to be able to enjoy these with another person. In these cases, the motive might not have to do with avoiding intimacy and the struggles of being with a real person. Estes suggests that people with these desires could cultivate relationships, but there are many people whose sexual and romantic interest in others is not reciprocated. They may not be able to cultivate such relationships, and may seek out sex workers for that reason.

We might also challenge Estes' point about the client losing because they can't access the sex workers' subjectivity. On the one hand, this may well be so, on grounds that even the person motivated by novelty might want to experience sex with a real person, and the payment might make interacting with the sex worker's honest subjectivity impossible. On the other hand, maybe the client can enjoy the experience even while knowing that it is, in part, fake. Most movies are fiction, and this does not count against our enjoyment of them. Maybe a client can enjoy the performance of a sex worker even while knowing that what it represents is not her genuine inner thoughts, feelings, and desires. Similarly, with respect to alienation, we may note that many jobs in modern society require us to distance ourselves from our true feelings. Working in retail or in the food service industry requires being cheerful with customers even when you don't feel like it. Even skilled workers, like therapists and teachers, might have to seem patient and caring when they are feeling frustrated and annoyed.

It's also worth remembering that people differ with respect to how they experience their sexuality. For some people, sex might be something they expect to share only with one or a few people, something connected to selfhood, so that the alienation Estes describes would feel horribly damaging to them. But other people might have different relationships with their sexuality, experiencing it as more variable, or as something they can feel in different ways (see Satz 1995: 71). For these people, perhaps sex work may not be very different from other kinds of work – such as nursing or childcare – that involves touching other people and taking care of their emotional and physical needs and desires.

Given the wide range of work that we have come to see as acceptably part of market-based transactions, a central issue for this line of thought is whether sex is somehow special. Is there something about sex that explains why it should not be subject to market forces the way so many other interactions are? One way to answer this question would be to ask whether there are things that ought to be valued in a certain way, so that valuing them through market norms would be to make a fundamental moral mistake. Some things, like cupcakes and computers, are perfectly acceptable to buy and sell. Other things, like friendship, are not. If you tried to buy friends, you would simply fail: friends aren't the kind of thing you can buy and sell. And if you took your existing friends and started pawning them off to others for fees, you'd be valuing them wrongly: you'd be valuing them for what they can get you, instead of valuing them for who they are.

We saw a similar argument about sex in Chapter 1 when we talked about the idea of commodification: that some practices inappropriately apply market norms where others kinds of valuing are appropriate. In her discussion of *Playboy*, Martha Nussbaum (1995) described the wrongful objectification of pornography partly in terms of commodification. When we commodify people, we approach them asking only "What's in it for me?" We fail to think of ourselves in a caring and joint relationship. We also reduce the person to a commodity: something with particular qualities we evaluate with respect to our own feelings and desires. This is because the idea of a market exchange, where people buy and sell commodities, is typically one where each person is looking out for themselves and hoping to get the most of what they want in a product at the least cost to themselves.

An interesting example of how market forces can shape our interactions is found in Chester Brown's 2011 graphic memoir *Paying for It*, which focuses on his experience as an ongoing client of sex workers over a period of years. Overall, Brown is a thoughtful guy who puts care and attention into his interactions. He carefully avoids exploitation, and the book shows his earnest efforts at treating the workers with kindness and respect. It's a good example of how a person can be paying a sex worker and also treating the sex worker as a fellow human being.

But reading the book with commodification in mind, it's interesting to see how as time goes on Brown begins to narrow his demands, to seek out more and more the exact specific set of qualities he wants, and to become a bit peevish when those specific qualities are not provided. In one striking scene, he becomes annoyed by a sex worker who gives him an intense oral-sex experience, then covers her face during intercourse. He conjectures that she was trying to get him to have an orgasm during the oral sex in order to avoid having intercourse itself (Brown 2011: 137). If you were with a friend or partner, outside a commercial exchange, you might interpret such behavior in a different, more generous spirit, talking over different options. The two of you would have goals that coincided. In the commercialized case, the goals of the two people become very different. One is there to get as much as possible of the things they want, the other to get money and limit the emotional, physical, and labor costs involved. It's worth noting, too, that Brown's story opens with an explanation of his motives, and they are like the ones Estes describes: he wants to be able to have sex with women without the difficulties and annoyances of having a relationship.

If the problem with commodification is that it gives people license to dehumanize other people, I wonder if the problem is as much about modern notions of work as it is about the social meaning of sex. In modern capitalism, we sometimes think that once we've hired a person to do something for us, anything – as long as it's legal – is on the table. This encourages employers to think in terms of squeezing out of their workers as much as they possibly can at as little cost to themselves as possible. In modern business practice, even profitable companies are criticized for raising workers' wages, on grounds that the expense cuts into shareholder profits. Treating someone as a worker doesn't necessarily mean treating them this way, but increasingly in our society such employer–worker relationships have come to seem normal. If clients of sex workers feel entitled to treat them, as beings they can get as much out of at as little cost to themselves, and not simultaneously as people with thoughts and feelings, then the problem of commodification might be partly about the norms that modern capitalism sanctions when it comes to paying someone to do something for you, and not just about sex specifically.

This discussion highlights several specific complexities of theorizing sex through free choice in contexts of liberal capitalism. Once we move away from the framework in which sex takes place only in heterosexual marriage, and toward sex as a matter of individual expression, it might seem that buying and selling sex is the same as choosing sex for any other reason. But not all goods are appropriately understood through the values of market exchanges, and there is debate over whether sex belongs in the market category or whether there is some way that an appropriate generosity or sexual caring for the other person, for their own sake, is incompatible with commercialization.

Commercialized sex in context

Estes' argument concerns the inherent contradictions and harms associated with buying and selling sex, but a different way of approaching the issue considers sex work in context. Even if sex work is not inherently wrong, it may be a problem because of the way it props up gender norms, or beliefs that sex is dirty or polluting for women. Laurie Shrage points out that although we think of sex work as an obvious, straightforward thing, it has been different in other times and places. In some societies, some sex workers were seen as providing a useful, and even sacred, service, embedded in spiritual values (Shrage 1989: 349–350). A woman could be a sex worker for part of her life, then move onto a different phase with no stigma attached. This is very different from seeing sex work as a degraded or inferior kind of work.

As this variation suggests, acts have different social meanings depending on context. For example, consider what it would mean for a person in our society to start eating cats and dogs. This would be extremely upsetting to many people. But the reason wouldn't be because of biological issues to do with health, or matters concerning whether dogs and cats are biologically special beings. Instead, it has to do with the meanings cats and dogs have as pets in our society. When we say that the social meaning of the act depends on context, that doesn't mean that actions are wrong only because people think they are wrong. It's just that an action takes on a different kind of significance in various contexts.

And so, Shrage says, the meaning of sex work is affected by its context. In our society, what matters is less the inherent values at play in buying and selling sex and more how the practice of sex work functions socially. In our society, she says, the practice of men buying sex from women reinforces problematic assumptions about sexuality, gender, and sex roles: that men have a constant "need" for sex, that they are naturally dominant, that sexual contact "pollutes" women, and that our sexual practices tell the world who we "really" are.

Let's look at these ideas in more detail. Remember how Estes said that the liberal view was that buying sex and buying food were basically the same thing? Some advocates of commercialized sex say that because men have a biological "drive" – like the drive to eat – there will always be commercialized sex (see Ericsson 1980). Shrage, though, says it works the other way: the practice of sex work helps prop up the false assumption that there is such a drive. She points out that there are cultures in which long periods of abstinence are considered normal. Scientists have also challenged the idea of a male "need" for sex, pointing out that without food, we will die, but no one dies from not having sex. The point is that if we think there is a constant need for sex, that is partly because we live in a world in which this is a basic belief not because it is an ahistorical cross-cultural absolute truth, and the sex-work industry functions to make that belief seem true.

The second cultural assumption is the natural dominance of men. As we've seen, most sex workers are women, and almost all sex clients are men. Shrage says that implicit in this division of labor is the cultural principle that men are naturally dominant in their relation to others. In exchanges where the man is the client and the woman is the worker, the man – as the client – dictates which activities will take place and how; he assumes a dominating role while the worker has to obey. This fits with and helps reinforce broader social ideas that men ought to play a dominating role. Even when a woman is being paid to be "dominant," she is being paid to do what the man wants her to do; if she does not do it as he likes, presumably he will not come back.

We've touched already on the idea that contemporary gender norms are such that women are expected to be more passive and submissive while men are expected to be more active and dominant. As we saw in Chapter 1, some research confirms the thought that these assumptions are at play in a broad array of contexts, sometimes in ways we're not even aware of. Subconscious beliefs about how people ought to act because of their sex, race, orientation, and so on are called "implicit stereotypes," and studies in this area confirm that both men and women associate qualities like "strength" and "leadership" with men and qualities like weakness with women. In so far as we do have implicit associations of women with passivity and submission and men with being naturally dominant, the practice of sex work, in which men are seen as dominant and women seen as serving them, could serve to reinforce and heighten these.

The third problematic assumption is that sexual contact pollutes women. It's often pointed out that there is a double standard at play when it comes to gender and sexual experience. When a man has a lot of sex partners, he is a "player," or a "stud"; when a woman does she is a "slut" or "whore." This is an area where social norms vary a lot and things are changing quickly. In some social groups, people don't expect women to refrain from casual sex on a first date or ensure they don't have "too many" sex partners. But it's not hard to find this attitude prevalent on the internet, where articles and comments frequently reinforce the idea that a woman's eagerness to have sex or her promiscuity would be reasons not to have a serious relationship with her. Think about how unlikely it would be in our society for someone to boast to friends about how much sexual experience their new girlfriend has. This is a social and cultural attitude. It doesn't have to be this way. We might live instead in a society that prizes sexual experience, in which experience means know-how and expertise, in which a woman who has had a lot of sex with a lot of different people might be judged positively for that quality.

The way the practice of sex work functions in our society fits with, rather than challenges, this set of assumptions. People work as sex workers are often treated as damaged goods. Imagine if you had a new girlfriend and you introduced her to family and friends by saying, "My new friend here is a sex worker!" In our current cultural climate, I expect people would respond very negatively and would try to talk you out of the relationship. This aspect of sex work reflects social expectations about sexual experience polluting women, making them into damaged goods, but also serves to reinforce those same expectations: the way sex workers are denigrated in our society goes hand in hand with the way other sexually experienced women are denigrated as well.

The fourth relevant cultural assumption involves the reification of sexual practice. As we'll discuss further in Chapter 8, this refers to the idea that whatever people do in sex tends to get them labeled as if they are a certain kind of person. If you have sex with a same-sex partner you're "gay." If you do it too much you're a "slut." If you sell sexual services, you're a "prostitute" or "whore." There's no reason that the kind of thing you do has to be a reflection of the kind of person you are, but when it comes to sex we tend to think about it this way, as if the act of selling sex and the quality of being a certain kind of person were inextricably linked. Again, this way of thinking about sex workers is informed by, but also reinforces, our social ideas.

Overall, Shrage says, sex work is problematic because of the ways it reinforces and fits with these problematic and deeply held cultural beliefs. There's nothing inherently wrong with buying and selling sex, but the social meaning of sex work makes it a problem. This means that it's impossible to evaluate the sex-work industry by looking at individual people or specific cases, or by asking whether a person is inherently misused by paying for sex. Even if there is nothing essentially bad about it, its social meaning can be bad – not because of the kind of act it is but because of the social meaning it takes on in our society.

Could things change? Could we live in a society in which people could buy and sell sexual services and there would be no problem? Maybe. If men and women were seen as equal, if sexual experience were not seen as a negative for women, if there were no ideas of men as naturally dominant – in a society like this, sex work would have a completely different social meaning and would function in a radically different way. The sex worker would be seen as a skilled professional, providing a service. Visiting a sex worker might be more like visiting a counselor or a massage therapist or taking a class with a professor. You'd be having an experience that you could have with anyone – talking, learning something, being massaged – but that you're going to get a great version of, because of the person's expertise and ability. Family and friends would be happy to see their loved one marry a sex worker because the person with experience will be great to have sex with. The social meaning of sex work would be completely different.

Seeing sex work in social context raises other questions about the ways in which sex work fits into what we think of as appropriate employment demands. Scott Anderson (2002) argues that because of the role sexuality plays in our lives, taking sex work to be the same as other forms of work would frustrate, rather than enhance, our personal sexual autonomy. For example, if sex work is just another form of work, it would seem an employer could require sexual activities as part of your job, or the government could demand you accept a position as a sex worker in communities where accepting work is necessary for gaining benefits. If you worked for a large corporation providing sexual services, you might be subject to non-discrimination clauses, reducing your ability to have a say in who your clients are and what services you will provide them with. Anderson says that because of what sex means to us, these demands would interfere with our ability to live our sexual lives as we see fit. That is, somewhat paradoxically, having rules restricting our ability to engage in sex work would increase, rather than decrease, our personal sexual autonomy.

As in our discussion above, this shows how the values we use to contextualize employment are just as relevant to thinking about sex work as the values we use to conceptualize sex. Should an employer have the right to demand any type of service from an employee? If workplace requirements to have sex violate our sexual autonomy, does this mean other workplace requirements violate our autonomy more generally? Why would sex be in a protected category, while other activities are not?

This discussion of the contextuality of sex work highlights in a new way the complexities of framing sexuality in terms of free choice in liberal capitalist contexts. Liberalism puts our individuality front and center, but, as Shrage points out, choices take on different social meanings against different cultural backgrounds; our choices can support, or challenge, widely shared social assumptions. In the case of sex work, those assumptions are gendered and often hierarchical: that sex is polluting for women, that men are sexually dominant, or that sex work is demeaning. And Anderson's discussion shows how we already have background assumptions about what work is and what it should be, and putting sex into that category may or may not be a good fit.

Sexual surrogacy

In the analyses above, there is special attention to the questions of whether honesty and mutuality, which may seem important to sexuality, are problems when sex is commercialized, and whether sex work could be a respected and skilled profession rather than stigmatized. These questions are too large and complex to address fully here, but it is interesting in this context to consider the practice of sexual surrogacy, which is where a therapist helps a person with sex. The therapy can take a wide range of forms. As we'll discuss in more depth in Chapter 11, some sexual surrogacy is for people who have psychological issues with sex: the client might meet for talk therapy with one person, then meet with a sex surrogate to learn to experience healthy intimacy and sex by engaging in it physically. Other sexual surrogacy is for people with disabilities who might find it difficult to have sex on their own.

In 1990, Mark O'Brien, a journalist, poet, and advocate for the disabled, wrote an article about seeing a sexual surrogate that was later made into a movie called *The Sessions*. O'Brien had contracted polio as a child and spent most of his time in an iron lung. Polio can lead to muscle weakness and paralysis, and it was much more widespread before a vaccine was developed in the 1950s. Before then, children who got polio were sometimes affected in ways that made them almost immobile, and, in advanced stages, muscular paralysis left them unable to breath and they would die. In the late 1920s, the iron lung was invented: basically, this is a long airtight tube that a person lies in that uses vacuum pressure to raise and lower the rib cage so air gets in and out of the lungs. For a long time, people with polio had to stay in iron lungs all the time – twenty-four hours a day, seven days a week – until modern ventilators were invented that could push air in and out of the lungs. But for some people, ventilators aren't sufficient on their own. As an adult, O'Brien spent most of his time in an iron lung, and attended the University of California, Berkeley in one. At the time that he saw the surrogate, in his thirties, he was able to spend short periods outside the iron lung using a mobile ventilator.

His 1990 article, "On Seeing a Sex Surrogate," is a fascinating read. O'Brien writes movingly about being ashamed of his pale and bent-over body and of the way his parents discouraged him from seeing himself as a sexual person. He describes the panic and fear he felt as he was deciding to seek out a sex surrogate and the immense practical problems to be solved with respect to finding a private place and a way to get there and so on. He ends up working with a surrogate named Cheryl Cohen-Greene, who works to help him overcome both psychological and physical difficulties. They end up seeing one another several times and eventually they have sexual intercourse.

It's interesting to consider O'Brien's experience in light of the ideas in this chapter. O'Brien points out that surrogates "deal mostly with a client's poor self-image and lack of self-esteem, not just the act of sex itself." They are "trained in the psychology and physiology of sex so they can help people resolve serious sexual difficulties" (O'Brien 1990). This calls to mind the question of whether sex workers can be seen as kinds of therapists. This could be an example of someone who is both a sex worker and a therapist being seen, as Shrage thought they might be seen, as a trained professional with special skills and knowledge.

At one point early on, O'Brien touches and kisses the surrogate's breast. He writes, "She said she liked that. I knew she was helping me to feel more relaxed, but that didn't make her encouragements seem less true" (O'Brien 1990). This is interesting for the way it speaks to the issue of honesty. He knows this is said to encourage him and not necessarily as a spontaneous expression of pleasure. But even knowing this he is able to experience it for its positive aspects. This suggests an interesting emotional perspective: that one need not take the surrogate's statements as literally true in order to appreciate a positive intent behind them.

At one point, the honesty question becomes more pressing, as they decide to have sex. He writes, "'Was I inside of you?' I asked. 'Just for a second,' she said. 'Did you come, too?' She raised herself and lay beside me, 'No, Mark, I didn't. But we can try some other time if you want'" (O'Brien 1990). This conversation has an aspect very different from what we stereotypically associate with sex workers. The client wants to please as well as be pleased, but, more importantly, the therapist feels compelled to say, honestly, the ways in which the attempt to please succeeds and the ways in which it doesn't. We'll discuss O'Brien's experience and reflections, and the broader issues of sexual surrogacy, in detail in Chapter 11.

Conclusion

In this chapter, we've seen various perspectives on the normative aspects of commercialized sex: that sex work is just another kind of work; that sex work is inherently bad and damaging to the sex worker; that sex work is only a problem because of certain contingent aspects of our culture. I've argued that evaluating these arguments requires reflecting on the social meaning and values we associate with sex.

I've also suggested that seeing sex as subject to market forces and sex work as work forces us to think about commodification and work in modern capitalism. If commodification is bad partly because it encourages us to focus solely on our own good and put aside the good of others, then perhaps the problem is that commodification has itself been taken to extremes. Taking account of our own interests is compatible with looking out for other people's interests at the same time, but the competitive forces of modern capitalism make this balancing act difficult. If sex as part of work means our sexual autonomy is reduced, then maybe the problem is as much with the demands of modern work as it is with sex itself. We'll discuss the tensions between self-interest and caring further in Chapters 5–7, when we turn our discussion to love.

Finally, I've suggested that the practice of sex surrogacy, in which sex is just one part of a complex therapeutic job, challenges our assumptions about how jobs involving sex might work. In this context, having sex as part of work can be part of a mutually respectful, caring, and honest relationship. In Chapter 11, we'll consider whether the kind of sex involved in surrogacy raises the same normative issues that sex work is typically thought to involve.

5 Union theories of love

Introduction

What is love? Especially when it comes to romantic love, I've always thought this an awkward question for a philosophical answer. Is love really the kind of thing you can have a "theory" about? After all, love, even more than sex, is a socially embedded and variable phenomenon. People in different societies understand love and its relations to culture in a wide variety of different ways. In some communities, marriage is about forming appropriate formal partnerships, and love – if things go well – may come along later. In others, love is thought to be essential to marriage from the start. Some people associate love with passion; some think that maturity in love is calmer and quieter. Love is thus perceived, understood, and contextualized in all kinds of ways.

When you first think about it, love might seem to be mostly a certain kind of emotion, feeling a certain way toward a person. But many people find this view of love inadequate on its own. For one thing, it doesn't help us understand whether, or how, love might be different from other positive emotions like liking or caring or how it might be different from friendship. Does "love" mean something special? For another, it doesn't seem to capture the special sense in which love seems to entail a certain commitment to, or caring about, the well-being of one's beloved. Normally we think of love as involving essentially "other-regarding" attitudes: love might feel good to you, but to love means caring about the other person for their own sake.

In the next three chapters, we discuss two theories of love, starting with the question of why love is a concept to theorize about. There are many other theories of love, but I focus just on two, to engage with details of the views and they fit with the role that love plays in our lives. When it comes to a desire for a theory of love, I'll propose that one set of motivations has to do with the disconnect between our self-image as rational, autonomous individuals and the attitudes and commitment love seems to require. For many in the twenty-first-century West, those attitudes and commitments derive from ideas about love as a "union" or "merger:" love involves the melding together selves or at least the mutual adoption of desires and interests of the other. From this point of view, the tension between individuality and the demands of love is partly that love creates a new individual, formed through the merger of the people in love.

It's worth noting in this context to notice that historically in Western culture the formal institution of marriage was defined in terms of "uniting" two people into one specifically through the woman's rights being subsumed into those of the man. The woman took on the burden of obedience, and the man took on the burden of protection. As we saw in Chapter 3, the idea of marriage as union was part of the justification for saying that a man couldn't rape his wife, since they were seen as essentially united wills. This way of interpreting the merger of potentially conflicting individuals simply demotes the woman's individual interests.

One important question for union views, then, is whether the idea of union can work in contexts of equality. After exploring the question of "why a theory of love," we'll consider various aspects of, and challenges to, the union theory. Many of these have to do with the possibility of conflicting interests. Surely what is good for one person is not always what is good for another, but if love involves a merger, the distinctions between people are blurred, so how can we say that this is so? This suggests that the individuals must somehow exist alongside the union of selves, raising difficult questions about the relationship between the individual selves and the unity between them.

Ultimately, I'll argue in this chapter that for reasons related to fairness these questions have no satisfactory answers. While union may have been workable in a past context of distinct gender roles, gender hierarchy, and strictly heterosexual marriage, equal selves cannot be both merged and distinct. Furthermore, when it comes to questions of individual autonomy and rationality, the conceptualization of love as union leads back to self-interest in surprising ways. After examining a different theory of love, we'll return to issues of rationality, autonomy and individualism and the social and political implications of love further in Chapter 7.

Why a theory of love?

One of the more interesting questions in the philosophy of love is why, exactly, love is the kind of thing we want a theory of. We'll return to this matter several times over the course of our discussion, but let's start by looking at a few reasons. One reason to think theoretically about love is that it might help us examine some popular ideas about love more critically. For example, sometimes people say that love means seeing the other person's well-being as identical with your own so that their wishes and desires become your wishes and desires. Or they say that love means caring for the other person and making their needs and desires a priority. These ideas sound appealing. But what happens when we take them to their logical conclusions?

For example, sometimes when you love someone you encounter various obstacles. Maybe the two of you want to do different and incompatible things – like one of you wants to have children while the other does not. Or maybe the person you love changes, and you find yourself daydreaming about other people. Or maybe the person you love ends up requiring an enormous amount of physical or emotional care, and you become over-whelmed. What happens then? Does love require you to step up indefi-nitely – to forgo your own interests in favor of a shared identity, to stick with the person you love no matter what, to give them whatever care they need regardless of what that means for yourself? Theories of love might help us address these questions, by being more precise about vague concepts like "sharing desires and interests" or "prioritizing the other person."

Also, a theory of love might help us address specific questions about love. It's sometimes thought that love and marriage, in so far as they entail forms of commitment, reduce a person's individual freedom or autonomy. A theory of love might help us understand whether this is so, and if it is, how. Love has also been seen as a challenge to rationality, since it requires us to forgo personal advantages for the sake of our loved one, or because we might fall in love with a person who is unworthy. Is love fundamentally irrational? Later in the book we'll be talking about whether you can pro-mise to love another person, or whether that makes no sense because love is, essentially, not under our control. We'll also be examining economic models of love, in which love can be caring but also self-interested, and about polyamory, in which one can love several people the way one loves a single romantic partner or spouse. As we'll see in future chapters, a theory of love can help us think through these matters.

Finally, love seems to challenge some of the implicit elements of the way people relate to one another in liberal, capitalist societies. Part of the way we conceptualize social relations in these societies is to see people as self-inter-ested rational maximizers of their own well-being; this way of seeing people implicitly justifies the contractual exchanges and negotiations that structure most of public life. But love is often thought to be deeply incompatible with self-interest: if your action is all about trying to get something for yourself, can you really call it a loving one? Also, it might just seem wrong – or intol-erable – that the contracts and negotiations of public life should be carried into our most intimate exchanges. If it is, we need an explanation of why the modes of life thought fit for public interaction are not appropriate for domestic life and love. After we see two theories of love in detail in this chapter and the next, we return to these topics in Chapter 7.

The union theory and its difficulties

This chapter focuses on the "union view" – the idea that love involves a kind of fusion of selves into one shared identity. This idea of love as fusion is baked into popular culture and elements of it inflect many of our ordinary life discussions, even if the specifics remain unstated. It also is an idea with a long history in Western culture. Famously, in a speech in Plato's *Symposium*, Aristophanes tells a story in which long ago the world was populated by beings with two heads, four arms, and four legs. Some had two sets of male genitalia, some two sets of female genitalia, and some were mixed. These beings angered the gods, and as punishment the gods cut them in half. Since then, we are all walking around searching to reunite with our lost other halves, and this is the yearning of love. Even though it is so old, it's a metaphor that resonates with us today – people are attracted to the idea that love means finding "the one" – their "other half" or "soul mate" – and that loving another person involves a kind of binding together or fusion.

Less metaphorically, the idea of a "union" between people is that love means merging, and thus sharing, interests, burdens, and cares. What happens to one of you happens to both; what is good or bad for one of you is good or bad for both. In some ways, this idea of love as merging and sharing sounds great: when you fall in love, you expect to share things, both good and bad.

In a widely cited 1989 article, the political philosopher Robert Nozick developed this commonplace intuition into a full-blown union theory of love, based on the idea of a "we": a new entity that is formed from the union of the two individuals. Nozick says that when people fall in romantic love, they feel a desire to form a union with another person. As we all know all too well, sometimes when you fall in love with someone, they don't love you back! Unreciprocated romantic love is one of the worst feelings in the world. So initially, Nozick says, love is just the "desire" to form a union with the other person, and this starts with a kind of infatuation. If the person doesn't love you back, that initial infatuation will fade. But if they do love you back, Nozick says that the relationship will move forward into the stage where the lovers unite, or merge, to form a "we."

What does it mean to form a "we"? Nozick focuses first on the fact that merging means that lovers "pool" their well-being. This means that when bad things happen or good things happen, they happen to both of you: love places you at risk, but also makes bad things not so bad. It places you at risk because if something bad happens to the person you love, it means something bad has happened to you as well. But it makes the bad things that happen to you less bad because the badness is shared. For example, suppose Cameron and Devin are in a loving relationship, and Devin gets sick. In the union view, the illness is something that happens to both of you, to the "we" – not in the sense that Cameron and Devin each get half-sick, obviously, but in the sense that the badness of Devin's being sick is spread to Cameron and Devin equally. In this sense, love places a person at risk: Cameron now risks bad things happening to them because they happen to Devin. On the other hand, Devin's getting sick is not so bad for Devin as it would have been had they been alone. The badness is spread around.

But there's an immediate puzzle about this idea of union, namely: what about conflicting interests? Depending on how it is interpreted, the union view seems to imply that what is bad for one person is bad for the other and what is good for one person is good for the other. But surely it's possible in love for something good for one person to be bad for another. What if one person wants to have children, and the other does not? Or what if people disagree about other life plans? For example, suppose Morgan and Nico are in love, and Morgan wants very much to stay in their current home where they are close to family and friends, and Nico gets a fantastic job offer in a distant city. (In all of these examples, names have been chosen to be gender-neutral.) The way Nozick expresses it, this idea of union seems to imply that Nico's good fortune is Morgan's good fortune. Yet it seems Nico's good fortune might also be, in another sense, bad for Morgan. If they do move, Morgan might be happy for Nico but might also be much less happy with their own life. If the move makes Nico better off and Morgan worse off, this does not seem to imply that Morgan and Nico do not love one another sufficiently, and yet the union theory seems to imply that it does.

In addition to pooling their well-being, Nozick says that people in romantic love "limit or curtail their own decision-making power and rights" (1989: 71). They cannot make unilateral decisions. In the case of Morgan and Nico, it means Nico cannot simply say to Morgan: "I am taking a new job and we are moving far from here." But we might wonder: how is this "reasoning together" supposed to work? Suppose Morgan articulates their reasons for wanting to stay, and Nico acknowledges those reasons as reasons that bear on them as a couple. And then suppose Nico articulates their reasons for wanting to go, and Morgan acknowledges those reasons as bearing on the couple. And then they deliberate about what would best overall. How is the idea of union going to help this deliberation move forward? It would seem the central matters would concern how weighty the various reasons are, and who has done what for whom in the past, and who will suffer more if they go along with the other person's plans. But these considerations all reflect the point of view of the individual persons and what is best for them. It's almost the opposite of the "union" idea.

Nozick seems to suggest that *all* decisions must be based on a kind of mutuality, acknowledging that this would entail that even the decision to end the relationship cannot be made unilaterally (1989: 71). A person who wants to break up may not simply announce their intentions or leave: union means that those who love must give the other person a chance to have their say in the matter. To many readers, I expect this ban on walking out will seem extreme and bizarre. Surely in certain cases, there is a right to end a relationship unilaterally – that is, without consultation? In her wide-ranging book on love, bell hooks (2000) discusses the problem of abusive intimate relationships, arguing that love should be understood as incompatible with harm: you cannot truly claim to love people if you are hurting or abusing them. If one person in a "we" becomes abusive to another, it seems obvious that the target of that abuse has the right to walk away, and need not ask the other person for their input on the matter.

But the "right to break up" may well go even further. Even when there has been no abuse, a person is within their rights to make decisions about their own romantic life. Particularly if the people are unmarried and have never formally promised to stay together – can't one person simply leave the other? Sure, you might want to do it politely, and not with an email or text message. But you don't have to invite deliberation. If one person wants children and their spouse is determined not to have any, they can just decide to leave, to try to find someone to have children with. In the case of Morgan and Nico, where one person gets an excellent job far away and the other does not want to leave, there may be no way to make a joint decision. If both want to stay together but neither is willing to capitulate, eventually one might decide to just do what they want, even if it means the relationship will end. One may decide to do this in the absence of consultation. In Chapter 9 we'll see other examples where it seems one person has a unilateral right to leave.

At one point, Nozick seems to suggest that the "unitive" aspects of sexual experience "mirror" and "aid" the "we", and thus fit well with the idea of love as merging of identities. As we've seen in our discussions of objectification and pornography, while it can be true that sex can create intense mutual desire and pleasure, it is also true that often what creates pleasure and orgasm for one person is not what creates pleasure and orgasm for another. Because people's tastes and preferred activities in sex may be different, we again confront the problem of conflicting interests. What if Quinn really likes to receive oral sex, and Robin really likes penetrative or genital–genital sex? It seems reasonable that they might compromise: to do one thing one time, and another, another. But from the "union" point of view, compromise is hard to understand. If the two people have merged into a new entity, it's hard to see how there could be a compromise, because it is hard to see how something could be good for one person and not for the other. If Quinn and Robin have merged, it would seem there's just one set of things good for the "we." The whole idea of different preferred activities in sex seems to require an individuality that is outside the union of the two people.

In fact, if we think of Quinn and Robin as a fully merged "we," we might get the strange result that it would be just as good for a couple to have sex in which one person experiences all the pleasure as it would be to spread it around. Imagine that Robin doesn't love to perform oral sex but does like to make Quinn happy by giving them pleasure. If the two people have formed a "we," then it would seem to follow that a sex life consisting mostly of Quinn receiving oral sex and Robin giving it would constitute a good set of activities. This is because in a "we," what is good for one person is good for another – so that when Quinn experiences pleasure through receiving oral sex, this is a good for both of them in the same way that anything else would be a good for both of them.

These kinds of difficulties – about unilateral decision-making, about the possibility of competing interests, and about the possibility of one-sided-ness – suggest that any "union" of individuals cannot replace the individuals who make up the union. Individuals must continue to persist alongside the "we," so their interests can be represented. Even if they form interconnections that function like a union, they do so partly as individuals and are thus not fully merged together. If love truly means forming a new entity with the other person, it is obscure how one person could unilaterally break it off, or how we could talk about one person's interests and pleasures as opposed to another's, given that there would be, in a sense, no individual or "one person and another" in the first place. These questions and challenges suggest that when selves are united, the unity cannot replace the individuals, or erase them; to make sense of conflicting interests, we have to say that the individuals coexist with the union somehow. In the next section we consider how.

The relationship of self and "we"

It seems clear, then, that forming a "we" does not supplant the individuals involved; they continue to exist. At some points, Nozick, too, suggests that the idea of union makes the most sense when the "we" exists in addition to, instead of in place of, individuals. But if the individuals persist alongside the "we," this raises further questions. What is the relationship between the selves and the "we"? How does the merger of the "we" happen if the selves continue to exist? What does it mean to say that the interests of individuals are merged if their identities are maintained?

First, let's look at the question of the relationship between the individuals and the "we." As Nozick explains, we have essentially two choices for each person, leading to three possible outcomes. The two choices are that the self can be part of the "we," or the "we" can be part of the self. So either both people have the self as part of the "we," or both people have the "we" as part of the self, or one has one and one has the other. As a product of his place and time – he was born in the United States in 1938 – Nozick reflects gendered assumptions of his culture, that loving relationships unite men with women, and that women's lives are mostly about relationships, while men's lives are mostly about other things. He concludes that perhaps for women, the self is part of the "we," and for men, the "we" is part of the self. While it's not the same, this echoes the idea of marriage we saw at the start: that union is achieved by women giving up their individuality and becoming a part of something larger, while men retain their individuality. But leaving aside for the moment this gendered aspect of the discussion, let's look in more depth at the various possibilities.

In one way of putting this all together, both people might have the "we" as part of the self. In this way of interpreting union, it is only a part of the two selves that changes identity and becomes fused in the "we." In a second, alternative way, it might be that for both people, the self is part of the "we." If each of the two people in a couple experienced love this way, it would be like each individual is fully subsumed into the merged union. Yet a third would be the asymmetrical case, in which in which one person is part of the "we" and the other has the "we" as part of the self; then we have to imagine two identities, where one is subsumed into the "we" and the other has a "we" as only part of it. Which of these interpretations of self and seems to offer a better way of understanding love? Is it better for the self to be part of the "we" or the "we" to be part of the self?

First, let's consider the symmetrical cases, where each person is experiencing the same relation between self and "we." On the one hand, it might seem best to take the "we" as only part of the self. If the selves are part of the "we," it is hard to see how individuals can keep their own individuality, and as we've seen, keeping our own individuality is important. In our examples where only one person wants children, or where Nico wants to take a new job and move, or where Quinn gets most pleasure from some particular sexual activity that Robin is not so enthusiastic about, the loss of the individual self seems to eliminate the idea that there is something wrong in a relationship in which one person's desires always get satisfied at the expense of another's. If we take literally the idea of the selves being part of the "we," there seems to be no way to articulate even of unfairness in a relationship, the idea that one person's desires could be satisfied at the expense of another – instead, desires are always shared.

So maybe it makes more sense for both people to take the "we" as part of the self? But as the philosopher Alan Soble (1997b) has argued, if we take the "we" to be part of the self, this just pushes the problems one step back. Which aspects of the self, or interests, remain tied to individuals, and which are part of the "we"? If a couple has different attitudes about children, or moving, or sex, are they supposed to try to see these as somehow included in the "we," or as somehow outside it? How would they decide? If they're in the "we," we get the problems we've already discussed, of not enough individuality. If they're outside, the concept of "union" doesn't seem to play any important role at all.

Furthermore, once there are individuals back in the picture, it's difficult to see how the union view accomplishes what it's intended to do. The idea of union was supposed to involve merger, in part to explain how love changes a person so that they take the other into consideration in a deep way. But if the "we" is part of the self, then it seems that just a small part of the self could be devoted to the other person, while a significant part of the self would bear no relation to the "we" at all. Suppose Nico were to say to Morgan, "I realize you don't want to move to a new place, but the question of moving just happens to be part of my non-'we'-self. So I'm just going to go ahead, whether you like it or not." This would be in violation of everything the union view is supposed to be about.

Now consider the third option, in which for one person the self is part of the "we" and for the other the "we" is part of the self. Here, it would seem that only one person retains a robust individually identifiable identity outside of the relationship. Though Nozick describes this in the gendered terms of his era, it needn't be gendered; we can imagine couples of any sex/gender combination in which one person has their whole life and identity wrapped up in the couple and the other person has a strong identity that goes beyond the life of the couple.

But this seems the most dangerous and pernicious option, because it seems too much like one person being subsumed into another, making themselves subordinate, and also too much at risk if the relationship sours. Suppose Nico is the person who has the "we" as part of the self, and thus has an identity outside the relationship, while Morgan's self is contained in the relationship. When we talk about something being "good for" Morgan or Nico, it is easy to see how something can be "good for Nico" even if it doesn't benefit the couple, since Nico has an identity beyond the relationship. But we can't even say something is "good for Morgan," since Morgan is inside the "we"; things are only "good for Morgan" if they are good for the couple. So when Nico gets the job offer, we can say that moving would be "good for Nico" even if it doesn't benefit the couple overall, while we can't even identify the sense that moving would be specifically "bad for Morgan." Furthermore, in this interpretation, if the relationship ends, Morgan's identity would profoundly affected, while Nico's would be only partially so.

The imbalances of the asymmetrical framework are particularly salient given the possibility that in a heterosexual relationship a man would be seen as having the "we" as part of the self while a woman has the self as part of a "we." It's not hard to see why Nozick was led to this interpretation, because he accepted gendered social norms about how love and caring function differently for men and women. He expected men to support the family financially and women to take on more family responsibilities. As we've seen, historically this division was formally codified, where in marriage, women's individual identity would become part of the union while the man would continue to have an identity beyond the marriage. The complexities emerging in this discussion of self and "we" illustrate how once we give up on the idea that all romantic love will concern heterosexual relationships in which it's the woman who subsumes her identity and the man who does not, it becomes very difficult to say exactly how "unity" or "union" of persons should work.

The "we" as a merger of ends and desires

Maybe we can avoid some of the awkward difficulties raised in the previous section by thinking of "union" in a more nuanced way: not as a merger of selves but simply as a merger of ends or desires. Noël Merino

(2004) proposes that this is at the heart of what "union" theorists really have in mind: it's not that the people merge, but just that the what one person needs and wants should become merged with what the other person needs and wants. It's like a new basket of needs and wants reflecting the interests of the two people, showing how love requires taking the other person into consideration in a deep way.

Again, there are several ways to interpret this metaphorical basket of needs and wants. The first interpretation of union that Merino considers is "replacement": that the union of shared interests replaces the individuals' set of interests. That is, the pooled interests stand in for, and replace, the set of interests of the two people. Of course, merging ends and desires can't mean that people literally take on the same ends and desires. If Kerry wants to read all the Harry Potter books, and become a doctor, and Kerry and Lane love one another, then replacement would mean that Kerry and Lane have an interest in reading all the Harry Potter books and becoming a doctor. But it would be silly to interpret this as meaning that Lane then has to develop these interests – as if love meant always wanting to do the same things. If Quinn loves to experience oral sex, it would be bizarre to suggest that for Robin to love Quinn, Robin also must also develop an interest in experiencing oral sex.

Instead, we should say something like: for Lane and Kerry to merge in love means that Kerry and Lane both have an interest in Kerry reading all the Harry Potter books and becoming a doctor, and that for Robin to love Quinn would mean for Robin and Quinn to each have an interest in Quinn's experiencing oral sex. The interests are, in a sense, tagged to the individual to whom they are relevant, and love means wanting the other person to get the things they want for themselves. That is, each of the two people, while staying separate, adopts a collection of ends and desires that are each tied to the individuals. In this interpretation, Morgan and Nico would merge their interests into one big basket, and then Morgan and Nico would adopt all these interests. So, we would say that it is in the interests of Morgan and Nico both that Morgan gets their desires met and that Nico gets their desires met; i.e. it is in the interests of Morgan and Nico that they move and also in the joint interest of Morgan and Nico that they stay put. Again, to say this requires retention of individuality. Even if the "we" takes on each person's interests and goals, those interests and goals still track the individual people.

The problem, though, is that now we can't even articulate that there is a conflict between the two of them. Now there is one set of conflicting desires, one basket of interests, which contains an interest in doing one thing (moving) and an interest in doing the opposite (staying put). This means that from the point of view of what they want to do, the couple is like a single entity that has conflicting desires, and we lose the sense that this is a conflict in which there will be a person who comes out better off and another who comes out worse off, no matter what the decision is. In this interpretation, Morgan and Nico are like a single person who wants to do two different things.

When a single person has conflicting interests or desires, we usually think of that as "ambivalence." Ambivalence of this type is when you want to do one thing and you want to do another thing and you can't do both. In ordinary life, when a person wants to do two different things, often they sort it out by trying to figure out which thing they want more. For example, if one person was ambivalent because they wanted to take a new job far from home but also wanted to stay close to family and friends, they might realize on reflection that while they wanted both, their desire to take the new job was stronger – that it outweighed the desire to stay put. In that case, it would make sense for the person to simply move, even if they might also feel regret at leaving family and friends.

If we use this reasoning in context of the "ambivalence" of Morgan and Nico, though, we get some strange outcomes because it means that the person with the stronger feeling or opinion would always get their way. Suppose Nico feels very strongly about moving and Morgan wants to stay, but not so strongly as Nico, being the kind of person who adapts easily to whatever comes along. In that case, the ambivalence interpretation of merger would mean that Nico's desire to move would simply outweigh Morgan's desire to stay, and they would decide to move. Maybe in the case of one move that seems OK. But what if Nico is just generally the kind of person who has a really strong personality – everything they want to do, it's like a matter of life and death to get their way. And suppose Morgan is just more laid back in general. Then when Morgan and Nico merge their desires, Nico's will always outweigh Morgan's, so that doing what Nico wants will always be the right, rational, sensible thing to do. But that seems wrong and unfair to Morgan, because Morgan would never get their way.

As Merino points out, another strange thing about this interpretation of union is that it eliminates the possibility of self-sacrifice. Referring to Soble's (1997b) discussion, she points out that if the ends and desires of the two people are taken on by each in equal terms, then what is in the interest of one person and what is in the interest of the other are always the same: all interests are in one basket. But this means that when one person does something *for* the other, it's not self-sacrifice, and it's not even doing something for them. Doing something for the other person means you're doing something for yourself (Merino 2004: 127; Soble 1997b: 83).

For example, suppose, after much discussion, Morgan decides to go along with Nico's plan to take the new job and move, and thus lose the proximity to family and friends that means so much to them. In the basket of interests interpretation of union, the decision to move would *not* be a sacrifice for Morgan: Morgan's ends would include the end of Nico getting what they want, prioritized equally to Morgan getting what Morgan wants for themselves. So, paradoxically, it comes out as good for Morgan when they acquiesce to Nico's desire to move. As we'll discuss further in Chapter 7, this problem might be a general one for unity views. If two identities become one, then it is impossible to articulate a sense in which one person does something for another. If the people or their interests are merged, there's not enough distinction between them to make sense of the possibility of self-sacrifice or even generosity.

An analogy to illustrate this might be found in the case of couples who share bank accounts, and who want to buy one another expensive birthday presents. Suppose Kerry and Lane have only one bank account into which they put all their joint earnings and out of which they pay all their expenses. Then imagine Kerry wants to do something really dramatic and generous for Lane's birthday: to go out to an expensive dinner and buy an expensive gift. If the payment for this dinner and gift come out of their joint account, then it's not really like Kerry did something *for* Lane. Instead, they are paying equally. Lane might well be discontented at the expenditure, having preferred to save the money or spend it on something else. If Kerry and Lane had separate finances that problem wouldn't arise: Kerry could then spend money for Lane, without it affecting Lane in a negative way at all. Just as it seems difficult for Kerry to do something financial for Lane, analogously it's hard, in the union view, for any action to be by one person for another: their ends are shared, so their interests are furthered or frustrated only in tandem.

Is eliminating the possibility of self-sacrifice a problem for union theories? A defender of the union view might challenge the preconception that self-sacrifice has something important to do with love. They might see this as a holdover from an excessively romantic notion, and they might point out that love in which there is no possibility of self-sacrifice, because lovers have merged together, is a deeper or truer love than one in which self-sacrifice is meaningful or important. Imagine Morgan and Nico and Quinn and Robin feel themselves so deeply intertwined with their beloveds that they've lost the sense of one person doing something for another because what makes one person happy just makes the other happy. A union theorist might posit this as a kind of ideal of love.

Against this, however, we might say that the kindness and generosity of love ought to involve doing things for others even at a cost to ourselves. If Kerry wants to do something lovingly generous for Lane, they should find a way to do it that doesn't involve spending joint savings. Maybe Kerry could use their time off to cook one of Lane's favorite meals, or maybe do an activity Kerry usually finds dull that Lane enjoys. In the case of Quinn and Robin, where Quinn loves to experience oral sex, it might feel like a generous and giving act when Robin gives Quinn oral sex. Under the shared-ends interpretation, though, all of Kerry's cooking and doing things for Lane and all of Robin's giving of oral sex would not be "giving" activities at all, since in satisfying Lane's and Quinn's interests, Kerry and Robin are, in effect, satisfying their own interests as well. This is a challenge to the union idea of love in so far as we think the ability to really do something for someone else at a cost to yourself is important.

It's also worth remembering here the very real possibility that mergers are formed not because of mutual oneness but rather because one person sublimates their interest and identity to that of another. If Morgan and Nico always do what Nico wants, because Nico has stronger desires and these always trump Morgan's in the merger of interests, then the elimination of self-sacrifice means not only that Nico always gets their way but also that Morgan's going along with it counts not as generosity or self-sacrifice but as a kind of self-interest. As we'll discuss in Chapter 7, given that mutuality and fairness in relationships requires some tracking of who is doing what for whom, union could lead to one person's will being sublimated into that of the other, just as the gendered model of unity in heterosexual marriage used to involve – a decidedly unattractive prospect.

Love and irrationality

As we discussed above, one reason to theorize about love is that the selflessness or caring of love seems an ill fit with the self-interested way people are thought to relate to one another in the public life of liberal, capitalist societies. As we will see in more depth in our discussion of economics in Chapter 13, part of the latter conception is an individualistic theory of rationality in which to be rational involves efficiently getting what is best for oneself.

The union theory has implications for two specific ways that love might be thought a challenge to this individualistic view of rationality. First, the choices we make involving love are radically unlike the choices we make when shopping: love should be incompatible with a willingness to "trade up" – that is, to dump one's partner just because another person with preferable qualities becomes available. Second, given that love involves curtailing our own decision-making and requires us to take on the burdens and cares of another person, what makes it rational to fall in love – why form a "we" in the first place? Let's discuss these in turn.

Love does seem incompatible with an attitude of trading up. Suppose you had a friend who said they were madly in love with their partner, partly because of how their partner was so funny, smart, kind and attractive. Now imagine your friend started talking about how they were always on the lookout, at parties, on the internet, wherever, for someone the same but a bit better – someone who was just a bit funnier, smarter, more kind, and more attractive – so they could jump ship as soon as they found the upgrade. This wouldn't seem like love at all.

This is interesting, because in other domains of life, an unwillingness to trade up can seem irrational and peculiar. If you live in one home, and another home becomes available for the same cost, and the new one has a better location, more room, nicer floors, a more pleasing layout, and so on, it might seem irrational not to move. If you were to say to someone, "That new place fits my needs much better than my current one, and I would like to live there, and it's affordable ... but I'm not going to move," people might wonder what was up. They'd ask if you had some sentimental attachment to the house, or some phobia about moving. But no one would challenge you about why you don't trade up to a nicer spouse or partner.

Nozick says that a theory of love should be able to explain why a failure to trade up in love is not irrational – that is, what makes love unlike commodities and contractual exchanges. His answer is that from the point of view of the union theory, trading up means destroying the "we," which essentially means destroying yourself. Because love involves forming a "we," you cannot trade up without destroying that "we" altogether. But this would be to harm yourself. So, unless you felt you had to destroy the "we" for other reasons anyway – that is, unless your current relationship is already gone bad for other reasons – it would make no sense to trade up. Love is special because in love when you trade up you hurt yourself. Strikingly, this is an individualist answer and not one that has to do with what is good for the beloved. If trading up is wrong, this is because it's not ultimately in your self-interest after all.

The answer to why it is rational to form a "we" in the first place is similar. Why should we form a "we," when forming a "we" means curtailing our own individual decision-making? The answer is that this is where the idea of the "we" as "pooling" really comes into its own. As we discussed above, in the union theory, when bad things happen to you they're not so bad, because they're shared. If you get sick, the badness happens to the two of you, and therefore is less bad for you as an individual. Nozick says that love therefore places a "floor" under your well-being, "providing insurance in the face of fate's blows" (1989: 71).

Love is thus a kind of "risk pool," a concept that comes from the insurance industry. The idea is that when a lot of people share a risk they can buffer themselves against the risk of bad things happening. If everyone buys flood insurance, it just costs a bit for each person; then, if you experience a flood, you can make a claim on the insurance, and you won't be as badly off as you would have been otherwise. Analogously, when you form a "we" with someone, bad things that happen to you are not so bad, since the badness is spread around to two of you instead of one.

I think this idea of love as an insurance policy is peculiar along several dimensions. For one thing, once you get beyond metaphors, the idea of love as risk pooling doesn't really make sense. Recall the example of Cameron and Devin who love each other and Devin gets sick. It's true that this might be less bad for Devin than if Devin were all alone. But that's mostly because Devin would have someone there to care for them, spend time with them cheering them up, and that sort of thing. A good friend could do the same things; it's not necessary to have merged into union to get these benefits. And it's not that the mere existence of Cameron makes it somehow less bad, or that Cameron's taking on some of the suffering makes Devin's suffering less. It's only if Cameron does loving actions or has caring attitudes that things are less bad for Devin. So the badness isn't really spread around; it's more that lovers care for you emotionally and in other ways. Risk pooling makes sense as a theory of insurance but not as a theory of love.

Also, what about the problem of loving someone who is, themselves, a bad person? People do sometimes fall in love with people who are cruel, or dishonest. Is this more irrational than loving someone good? With the idea of love as a personal risk pool, it almost seems like you're looking out for yourself, so as long as the other persons' gains are your gains, you don't have to worry. What happens if the person you form a "we" with becomes a bad person? Do you, then, become a bad person as well, just because you are in a union with them? That seems strange. While it's true that people in partnerships often take on the qualities of one another, the sheer fact of being in the partnership shouldn't be enough to condemn you.

Most importantly, the idea of love as an insurance policy means that the seeming caring or other-regardingness of love is a bit of a sham: it's still fundamentally about looking out for yourself. This is because if love is an insurance policy, rationality would require you to size up the potential costs and benefits of the person you might fall in love with. Imagine you meet someone to whom you know bad things are going to happen. Maybe you meet someone who is already ill – who has what the US insurance industry calls a "preexisting condition." Maybe you meet someone who is poor, or likely to be a target of hate or discrimination. Maybe you meet someone committed to an unpopular political cause. From Nozick's way of approaching these issues, it would seem like it would make no sense to get attached to them, since any "risk pooling" will almost certainly make you worse off than you were before. If love is insurance, you're really not in it for the other person any more.

Ultimately, the union theory fits love into individualistic rationality by showing how love can be, ultimately, a kind of self-interest. The "we" has reason to look out for itself, and so has self-interest of its own. The individuals have reason to become part of the "we," and stay part of the "we," because it is in their own, individual self-interest. We'll examine further implications of this relationship between caring and rational self-interest in Chapters 6 and 7.

Conclusion

I said at the start of this chapter that there are various reasons to be interested in a "theory" of love, and that one of them was to test how far various ideas can be taken. It's common to hear people talk about love as a merging of souls or selves and to use that idea to motivate and understand the caring or selflessness of love. We've seen in this chapter various problems with taking that idea literally. Once we move away from the gendered idea that a woman's self will be subsumed into that of man, all kinds of difficulties arise. The union theory faces problems in contexts of conflicting interests: we must retain some sense of individuality, but then the relationship of the individuals and the selves becomes obscure. When interests are shared, the person with stronger interests can dominate their loved one. And we cannot explain the sense that one person has acted for another. These challenges to the union view are particularly salient to our contemporary situation in which an equal love between two adults is the paradigm case we're trying to understand.

As we discussed at the start, one question about love has to do with how with how loving commitment fits in with the common social framing of people as self-interested individuals, looking out for themselves, relating to one another through negotiation and contractual exchange. As explained in the Introduction to this book, this social framing is implicit in many liberal, capitalist political systems and seeps into our social fabric as well.

The union theory of love suggests several responses to the question of how the caring and selflessness of love fits with the individualist model of people in public life. Most basically, the idea of love as union constructs our relationships of love as radically different from other relationships like friendship or the fondness and caring we may feel for relative strangers. Furthermore, the union theory creates a new individual – the "we" – with its own needs and desires and thus a self-interest of its own, though, as we've seen, the relationship between that self and our individual selves is difficult to understand. Finally, the reasons to join a "we" and stay with that particular "we" are ultimately self-interested: the "we" is a risk pool, and in destroying it you harm yourself. Given these limitations, we need to consider some of the alternative theories of love, starting with the idea of love as caring.

6 Concern theories of love

Introduction

As we saw in the previous chapter, viewing love as the union of two individuals raises serious problems, partly because this view seems to erase the distinctions between individuals. When we talk about loving someone, we often mean something about how we relate to them – and to *relate* to someone, you have to see them as separate and distinct from yourself. In contrast, the concern theory of love leaves intact the lovers' individuality and focuses instead on the specific caring attitudes and actions thought to characterize love. In concern theories, to love someone is to have a particular attitude toward them: wanting what is good for them, caring for them for their own sake. On this view, love affects a person's reasons and motivations in a deep way, so that when they act for the other person, they are acting for their own reasons. This means that even though love compels a person to perform caring actions, those actions are free, autonomous, and rational: in these actions, the person who loves expresses who they are in the deepest sense, and does what they have most reason to do from their own point of view.

As we'll see in this chapter, though, concern theories of love also raise difficulties. One has to do with the question of whether love requires caring for the other exclusively for their own sake, or whether wanting something for yourself out of love can be a good thing. The concern theory is also potentially one-sided: it seems to imply that love can be unreciprocated and still be romantic love. Finally, just like the union theory, the concern approach raises difficult questions about cases in which what is good for one person is not what is good for another. In these cases, love seems to elide the distinction between one's own good and the other person's. For example, if we cannot distinguish between what is good for one person and what is good for the other, we cannot judge when mutual decisions give appropriate weight to the interests of both.

A special manifestation of this problem arises in cases of deference, where one person prioritizes, perhaps excessively, the needs and interests of the other. Since gendered social norms push women to be more deferential than men, this challenge is particularly acute when it comes to theorizing equality and fairness in heterosexual relationships between deferential women and self-directed men. To understand deference and its relation to autonomy, we will briefly return to the union theory to compare the way the two views interpret these concepts.

Ultimately, I'll argue that the concern theory, at least when taken to its logical conclusion, has no satisfactory way of dealing with these challenges. It's been suggested that in focusing on caring feelings and caring actions, the concern theory patterns romantic love on parental love. The resulting theory fits well with some aspects of love, and especially with the way love seems to require a set of attitudes and actions that are directed toward another person. But because it requires us to say that what is good for the loved one is good for the lover, the concern theory is ill suited to understanding fairness in relationships among equals.

Love as caring concern

Though there are several ways to develop the details of love as concern, we'll focus here on the work of Harry Frankfurt (1999, 2004). At the heart of Frankfurt's theory is the idea that love is "volitional," by which he means it has to do with "the will" – that is, with our intentions, motivations, and actions. This means love isn't fundamentally a matter of what you believe about someone (that they are particularly good or worthy or attractive or lovable) or a matter of what you feel emotionally about them (fond feelings, warmth, desire) but rather about what you do and what you have reason to do *for* the other person. Love goes beyond emotions and has to do with deeper and more stable attitudes, the ones that make a person who they are. Love has to do with your ongoing motivations: not the ones that are fleeting or superficial but the ones that reflect your identity. When you love someone, your motivations must be caring and other-regarding: love means you want to do, and you have reason to do, things that will bring about and increase the well-being of the beloved.

In his theory of selfhood, autonomy, and the will, Frankfurt distinguishes between simple "desires," and the special desires that we endorse or stand behind, which he calls "second-order desires." Those second-order desires that we want to ultimately move us to act are "second-order volitions," or, as I'll just say here, "volitions." Desires are just ordinary wanting to do things: to eat a sandwich, or play tennis, or whatever. Volitions, though, are the desires we take a positive point of view on: they have to do with what we endorse or stand behind. For example, if you were angry you might temporarily experience a desire to shout at or harm someone. But you might hate that you feel this: you do not stand behind or endorse it, you think shouting at and harming people are not only wrong but that they do not reflect the kind of person you are or want to be, a person who is calm and kind. In this case, your desire might be to harm, but your volition would be against this: the desire to be calm and kind is the one you stand behind and endorse, the one you take to reflect who you really are (Frankfurt 1971).

When Frankfurt says that love is "volitional," he means that it has to do with your volitions and the actions that result from them. To really love someone is to have the volition to act in ways that reflect caring concern: that is, to act in ways that bring about the well-being of the beloved precisely because you care about their well-being. In the simplest kind of example, if Harper loves Indiana, then Harper will be eager to perform acts that bring about Indiana's well-being and unwilling to perform acts that undermine their well-being or hurt them. Moreover, these feelings of eagerness or unwillingness will stem from ongoing, stable motivations directly related to the other person. You want to help and not hurt them, precisely because you care about them for their own sake.

Just as in the anger example, this doesn't necessarily mean that Harper will never act badly, or want to act badly, toward Indiana. Just as you may value calm kindness but sometimes break down and shout, you might love someone and sometimes act unlovingly. If Harper feels an unloving or destructive desire but doesn't act on it, Harper acts appropriately and in accordance with their own volitional structures. But if Harper is overcome with anger or bad feelings and acts badly toward Indiana, then Harper isn't acting according to their own sense of self. Instead, Harper allows their actions to be determined by the wrong force: by the non-endorsed desire rather than the endorsed volition. Frankfurt thinks that when a person's desires take over in this way, as when Harper acts cruelly to Indiana even though Harper loves Indiana, that that person was taken over by a force from outside themselves. That is, just as we say of a person in a state of high emotion, "I know she did that, but she wasn't really herself at the time," Frankfurt thinks that when we act on desires that are not our volitions, we aren't really being ourselves at all. So if Harper loves Indiana then hurts them, Harper is not being themselves: it's like they are overcome by an emotion foreign to who they really are.

In the concern theory, to love is to have a stable ongoing caring for the well-being of the beloved. This will motivate the lover to do things for the beloved: to act caringly, to do things that foster the beloved's well-being. In this picture, a lot has to do with how the potential lover regards their own feelings and actions. One who loves must regard unloving actions as "volitional failures" – as not reflecting the true self. If a person repeatedly regards with approval their own angry feelings or cruel emotions toward another, we would then conclude that the person didn't really love.

Notably, Frankfurt's way of thinking about our desires and our stance toward them associates a person's true or real self with the self that thinks and reflects. When your desires conflict with the conclusions you come to about those desires, it is the latter that reflects who you really are. In some ways, when it comes to love, this focus on reflective endorsement might seem apt. Suppose, for example, that you promised to love and be monogamous with one person but found yourself with a powerful desire to have sex with someone else. Your thoughts tell you that you made a promise of exclusivity and that you're not the kind of person who breaks a promise. In this case, the idea that your truer self is your thinking, reflecting self seems to give a pleasing analysis of your situation: your true self is the one who keeps a commitment, and this self is being assailed by an outside force, the yearning to break it.

It's easy to think of examples that challenge the idea the idea that reflective thought reveals a truer self. What if you're an LGBTQ+ person raised in a homophobic family or society? If you are raised to believe desires for same-sex sex are wrong, you may well come to wish you were the kind of person who does not have such desires. You might find yourself constantly experiencing sexual desires that conflict with what your thoughts judge to be best. But if you find a supportive community, come out to yourself and others, and start living a life in accordance with your desires, to say that you're defying your "true self" seems deeply mistaken. It's much more like you're discovering and identifying with your true self.

Likewise, if a person continues to act badly toward another, it strains credulity to say that the aggression doesn't reflect who the person really is, even if they do not endorse or stand behind their actions. In Chapter 5 we discussed bell hooks' (2000) idea that love is incompatible with harm or abuse. In one way, the caring concern theory might seem to support and explain hooks' idea: to love someone means having your identity bound up with reasons to promote their well-being and never to hurt them. The volitions of the person who loves is essentially that of someone committed to bringing about good for the loved person, and it would follow axiomatically that the person who hurts another does not really love them. On the other hand, what if a person is abusive but does not "stand behind" or endorse their harmful actions? They might claim to love, on grounds that their "volitions" are pure, even as their actions violate that love. With Frankfurt's theory of selfhood, we would attribute to them a true loving self, but this doesn't seem right. A person who repeatedly violates what they claim to care about, and does nothing about it, can hardly be said to be genuine in their caring.

There is no easy answer to the question of whether simple desires or reflectively endorsed volitions better represent a person's self. From a psychological view, some recent research suggests that when we make judgments about when people are really acting as their "true selves" and when they are not, our judgments more often track our evaluative and moral judgments than anything else: we ascribe "true self" to the desires we approve of and externality to those we don't (Newman et al. 2014). If we associate love with reflective endorsement, maybe that's partly because we regard love as good and admirable.

Disinterestedness and reciprocity

One of the most striking aspects of Frankfurt's theory of love is his idea that love has to be "disinterested" (2004: 79–80) "Disinterested" in this context does not mean "uninterested"; instead, the word has its more traditional meaning of "unbiased" or "detached." It contrasts not with "interest" in the sense of caring but rather with "interest" in the sense of personal advantage or "self-interest." For Frankfurt, real love means caring for the person for their own sake and not because of anything you expect to get out of it for yourself.

It's easy to see how caring actions might fail to be disinterested because they're self-interested instead. For example, if you bought flowers or chocolate for the person you love, and you did it in the hopes and anticipation of having your gift reciprocated, this would be an act that is "for" the other person in one sense but really for yourself in a deeper sense because your ultimate aim would be your own good. Or if you made dinner for the person you love but you did it because you were hoping to seduce them into having sex with you, this would be more self-interested than disinterested. In these examples, a person does caring acts but the ultimate motivation is to get something for themselves. Frankfurt says that real love cannot be self-interested in this way. Drawing on the example of a parent's love for a child, he says that instead the acts one does out of love must be done selflessly. The loving "volitions," that is the motivations, must be all on the side of acting for the other person and not for yourself.

It follows from this that people can be mistaken about whether they love someone. Sometimes we might not know our true motivations – we may not even know whether we're acting ultimately for the sake of the other person or ultimately to get something for ourselves. Actions can seem loving on the surface but actually be motivated by self-interest, and from Frankfurt's point of view these are not loving at all. One way to be mistaken about whether you love somebody is by thinking that your motivations are for their well-being when in fact they are selfish. Maybe you enjoy being loved back. Maybe you like the appreciation and attention. Maybe it makes you feel like a good person to do nice things for someone. All of these motivations, because they ultimately refer to yourself, are self-interested and not disinterested in the right way. So, whether you love or not is a fact about you, and it's a fact independent of whether you believe it to be true or want it to be true.

Frankfurt doesn't say much about why, exactly, he thinks disinterestedness is so important for love, but maybe it has to do with the widely shared idea that true love has to be "other-regarding" – oriented around the loved one. After all, if you are ultimately acting purely out of self-interest, it's less like love and more like using another person to get what you want, like a kind of manipulation. Not only does it show disrespect for them as a person, it's often deceitful, since the other person may well assume you are acting lovingly because you actually care about them. Imagine if Harper told Indiana over and over that they were madly in love and wanted to be together forever, that Indiana's well-being was the only thing that mattered. Imagine that hearing these things made Indiana very happy. But imagine if Harper was saying these things only to get Indiana to have sex with them. Suppose that after succeeding, Harper dumped Indiana suddenly and completely. Harper's actions couldn't be seen as loving even if they did make Indiana happy momentarily. This supports the idea that love can't be 100 percent self-interested.

But the way Frankfurt develops the idea of "disinterestedness" is surprising because he says that not only does love have to be motivated by concern for the other, it has to be motivated *wholly* by concern for the other. This means a longing for reciprocity, for returned love, or even for just closeness to the loved one would be incompatible with true love. It's been observed that for Frankfurt the paradigm case of love is that of a parent for a child, and that his view treats romantic love as a somewhat debased form of love (Foster 2009: 154). Thinking about disinterestedness, we can see why people say this: romantic love is often of such a nature as to include a yearning for the other person that is anything but disinterested while parenting might seem more plausibly consistent with the idea that you have to be all for the other person and not for yourself.

A more fundamental objection to Frankfurt's claims about disinterest, however, is that single-minded focus on the other's well-being could in fact seem very unloving. Imagine Harper loves Indiana and wants good things for them but that Harper doesn't need to spend time with Indiana, never cares whether Indiana reciprocates their attention, and isn't interested in whether Indiana cares back for Harper or wants to spend time with them. This seems more like worship from afar than love. We often expect love to involve not only caring but also a desire to be with the other person.

This conclusion is supported by reflection on the example from the previous chapter of Morgan and Nico, where Nico gets the job offer far from home and Morgan doesn't want to move. Imagine that instead of a job where Morgan and Nico could move together, Nico's opportunity requires that they go alone. Perhaps Nico has a long-dreamed-of opportunity to be a war correspondent for a news organization, or a physician with Doctors Without Borders, and they finally get a chance. For Nico, the opportunity is wonderful – just what they wanted to do – but it will mean Morgan and Nico have to be apart a lot, spending only brief periods of time together over the next few years. Frankfurt's theory seems to require that Morgan's love requires greeting this news with pure happiness and no regret, which seems an odd conclusion.

Monique Wonderly (2017) says this problem arises because concern theories don't recognize the way attachment is an important part of love. In romantic love, we want to be valued but we also want to be *needed*. Love involves not only caring but also attachment: we want to be with our loved ones; we seek them out as safe havens in times of distress; they provide comfort and security for us as well as other things. This attachment creates its own kind of intimacy. It would be unloving to say, "I hope my spouse recovers from this illness quickly. Where else will I find hot food and good sex?" but not to say "I hope my spouse recovers from this illness quickly. Without them I feel lost and sad!" Both fail the disinterested standard, but the second one feels loving regardless.

It might seem that radical disinterestedness fits parental love better, but even for parental love excessive disinterestedness could feel unloving. Suppose your parents always wanted what was best for you and always did what they could for your well-being but never expressed an emotional desire to see you, to have you visit, to be near you and spend time with you. Imagine that after making sure you were eating enough vegetables and doing well at your job, they were immediately eager to get off the phone and never expressed a desire for you to call or visit. This would feel less loving than a parent who not only looks after your welfare but also demands that you visit and call, on grounds that they can't be happy without your presence.

Disinterestedness is also incompatible with certain kinds of infatuation and passion. Sometimes infatuated people daydream about bad things befalling the loved one – that they will be caught in a desperate situation, or that they will be rendered vulnerable – in hopes that the lover may rescue them or become more central to their happiness. It is a cliché of a certain kind of romantic obsession that the lover imagines the love object in a dangerous situation and needing rescue. From Frankfurt's point of view, such imaginings are inconsistent with real love. I leave you to judge for yourself whether Frankfurt seems right about this or whether these infatuated daydreamers are loving after all.

In a discussion of Frankfurt's view, Gary Foster (2009) says that, contrary to Frankfurt's focus on the one-sided concern that one person feels for another, reciprocity is essential to romantic love. Without it, what you have is not really love but rather an illusion. There does seem to be a sense in which love, and even friendship, require some reciprocity. If someone told you they were "friends with" some celebrity because they stalked the places that person would show up, sent them messages on social media all the time, and thought about them constantly, they'd be using "friends with" in a non-standard way. You can't be friends with someone that way. It's a relationship between two people not a way one person relates to another. Maybe the same is true about romantic love. If the person you're crazy about doesn't know you exist, maybe you could say you're infatuated with them, but could you really claim to have a loving relationship with them?

Love and autonomy in the union and concern theories

Love and commitment are often thought to reduce a person's individual freedom to do as they please, so let's take a look at the relationship between love and autonomy. In this section we'll consider the concern theory alongside the union theory so we can compare them. In the concern theory, when Frankfurt says that love is volitional, he means partly that the person who loves is compelled to act in a certain way: their love demands that they act to bring about the well-being of the person they love, and they don't really have a choice in the matter. It may seem that this kind of love undercuts one's personal autonomy or freedom to do as one pleases. The person who is unattached can deliberate, contemplate options, decide how to spend their time and energy. But the person who loves has some decisions taken away from them, since they must act lovingly. You're compelled to do caring things for the other person.

But Frankfurt emphasizes that the compulsion of love does *not* curtail one's personal autonomy. This is because in his framework autonomy – acting for one's self – is compatible with having no choice about what to do. As we discussed in Chapter 2, there's a sense in which autonomy seems to require choosing among options. If you went to school and the only option was for you to study medicine, and you wanted to study mathematics instead, it would be natural to say: they made me study medicine; I wasn't free to decide for my own reasons. In the "social autonomy" framework described there, the availability of desirable options is essential to autonomy: in choosing from among a range of reasonably good options, you exercise your personal freedom.

But some philosophers see freedom and necessity as compatible and even linked together, so that the availability of options doesn't have anything to do with it. As we've seen, Frankfurt thinks you are being yourself, and thus acting freely and autonomously, when you are acting in accordance with your volitions in the right way. So what matters isn't the existence of options, exactly, but rather how your volitions relate to what you end up choosing to do. What if you went to school, and the only option was to study medicine, but all you ever wanted to study was medicine? Imagine you'd come to school with a "second-order volition" to become a doctor; your sense of self is that being a doctor would be the best outcome for you; you feel deeply committed to caring for people's health. In that case, being told it was the only option would be no problem at all. You'd be autonomous in your choice because your choice reflected accurately your sense of who you are and what matters to you. Having other options is irrelevant. So if you act to foster the well-being of the person you love, and you feel compelled to do so out of love, you are expressing exactly who you are at the deepest level; so your personal freedom and autonomy are enhanced, not undermined.

Let's compare this to the union theory. When it comes to the relationship between love and autonomy in the union theory, Nozick's specific formulation makes this question difficult to answer. On the one hand, he does say that being part of a "we" requires people to "limit or curtail their own decision-making power and rights" (1989: 71). So yes: this does seem to limit one's personal autonomy. We can't make unilateral decisions. But, on the other hand, once you become part of a "we," the whole idea of individual autonomy changes because a union of two people has its own ends and desires and thus its own reasons for acting. When two people pursue these ends, they are essentially enacting, not curtailing, their own "decision-making power and rights." In the example of Kerry and Lane, where Kerry wants to read all the Harry Potter books and become a doctor, if Lane and Kerry decide to set aside time in the evenings when Kerry can read and study, they are acting on good shared reasons. As a couple, they are autonomous because the "we" is doing what brings about the shared, merged, interests.

As in our discussion of conflicting interests in Chapter 5, however, how union is compatible with individual autonomy is less clear. As we saw above, if Morgan and Nico merge their interests, and Nico's interest in moving for the new job is very strong, the union will have an overriding interest in moving and the couple will be rational to act on that interest and move. In that case, has Morgan's individual autonomy been respected or undermined? It would seem like the answer to this question depends partly on how the decision unfolds and on the context of their relationship. If Nico pressures Morgan into moving, or implies that they will be angry and resentful for a long time if they have to decline the offer, this seems to undermine Morgan's individual autonomy. And yet if we take union to enhance autonomy through the "we" as in the example of Kerry and Lane above, this would be impossible to explain, since Morgan's and Nico's interests and well-being would be merged.

As we saw in Chapter 5, in response to these kinds of challenges, the union theorist may point out that individuals persist alongside the "we" and are not fully merged. When it comes to autonomy, Nozick emphasizes this point, explaining that however we understand the union it need not "consume" an individual self or it leave it without individual autonomy of its own. In fact, in a striking passage, he says that only a partner who has, and expresses, an appropriate individual sense of autonomy can be an "apt" partner. Excessive subservience or deference creates a bad relationship. The next section explores this idea and the relationship between autonomy and deference in theories of love.

Love, autonomy, and deference

These discussions of autonomy help us to understand a special manifestation of the problem of conflicting interests, arising from a form of deference sometimes called "self-abnegating deference." Imagine a couple in which one person, Taylor, is self-directed as an individual and the other person, Sydney, is deferential, in the sense that Sydney prioritizes Taylor's interests. Sydney buys what Taylor prefers, spends time with the friends Taylor likes best, has sex with Taylor when Taylor feels like it. Imagine Taylor has a job, and activities they enjoy with others; but Sydney spends their time taking care of things at home so that Taylor doesn't have to worry about them. If Taylor were offered a new job far from home, Sydney would willingly move and would consider their own relationships and geographical preferences insignificant (cf. Hill, 1973). As Andrea Westlund (2003) describes it, it's not that Sydney defers to Taylor in certain areas of life as a trade-off for Taylor's consideration in other areas; rather, Sydney tends not to form their own "interests, values, and ideals," and when they do they count them as less important than Taylor's. Feminist theorists of autonomy have pointed out that women are often socialized to be deferential to men in this self-abnegating sense, so deference is particularly interesting in the case of women's deference in relationships with men. But anyone, of any sex/gender and in any kind of relationship, could be deferential in this way.

There are several reasons that one-sided deference in relationships could be seen as a problem. First, it may make the relationship seem more like assimilation than love. If Sydney takes on Taylor's perspective on life and gives up their own, this makes Taylor seem more like a borg than someone who loves Sydney for who they are. Second, when one person in a relationship is deferential in the self-abnegating sense, this could be bad for both people. In Sydney and Taylor's case, not only would Sydney suffer from the loss of sense of self, but Taylor may well suffer as well. Imagine how dull and strange it would be to have someone constantly agreeing with you no matter what you said. What if every time you pronounced an opinion or preference, your partner said "Oh yes, me too"? I don't know about you, but I would find that disturbing.

It's also been suggested that self-abnegating deference might be bad from an ethical point of view. Marilyn Friedman (1985) says that being an ethical person requires us all to be non-deferential, partly because the people we love sometimes get into doing bad things. If the person you love is tempted to hurt someone or steal or be cruel, a deferential person may just go along with it. But an ethical person shouldn't just go along with it.

When it comes to the problems of excessive deference, neither the union view nor the concern view helps us address the issue; in fact both obscure it. As in the discussion of self-sacrifice in Chapter 5, the union theory makes deference difficult to even describe properly. In the union theory, Sydney's deferential preferences become merged with Taylor's more selfish ones; acting on the merged interests will result in Taylor's selfish interests always being satisfied, as if this is an ideal outcome. Again, suppose Morgan has been raised to be a very deferential person, and so when Nico is offered the job far from home, Morgan immediately agrees to put aside their own ends and desires to make sure Nico gets what they want and need. If Morgan and Nico love one another, the union theory makes it hard to even articulate the idea that Morgan has acted deferentially, because as long as the action emerges out of the merged identities, it would follow that Morgan has acted in their own "self-interest" – in the interest of the "we." So Morgan isn't really deferential at all. This seems the wrong conclusion. And if we can't even describe deference, we can't raise the question of when deference is or isn't appropriate or when deference is excessive. With the person who wants to menace their cow-orker, the union view seems to suggest that menacing is in the joint inter-ests of the "we," and it would then make no sense to object.

Concern theories like Frankfurt's have a similar problem. We've seen how Frankfurt says that love enhances, one's individual autonomy rather than diminishing it because when you act to bring about the well-being of the loved one, you are acting on motivations that are deeply your own. The one who loves is really themselves when they are acting lovingly. Andrea Westlund (2008) points out that this way of framing love collapses the distinction between self-interested and other-regarding attitudes because when you act to satisfy the other person's needs and desires you are acting to satisfy your own at the same time. Sydney's love for Taylor means that Sydney wants to act to benefit Taylor, so in satisfying Taylor's needs and wants, Sydney is doing what they, themselves, most want do to. As before, suppose Morgan has been raised to be deferential so that when they learn about the job they immediately go along with whatever Nico wants. From the point of view of the concern theory, Morgan isn't acting "deferentially" to Nico at all – in fact, they're acting autonomously and doing the action that best expresses who they are as a person. But this seems, again, the wrong answer; and if we cannot theoretically distinguish deferential preferences and choices, we cannot analyze when deference is proble-matic or excessive.

The one way the concern theory might be better than the union theory is when it comes to deference and ethically questionable beha-vior. This is because the concern theory requires care for the other person's objective well-being rather than care for their preferences. This is a subtle distinction, but the idea is that sometimes people prefer what is actually bad for them – people smoke, or drink too much, or destroy relationships, even when doing those things makes them much worse off. In the union theory, it seems that each person must consider the other person's preferences and desires. But in Frankfurt's concern theory, it's the actual well-being of the other person you have to con-sider: you have to try to get them to stop smoking and take care of themselves and so on. In the moral cases, if acting badly is in some sense self-destructive, then caring for well-being might mean telling your partner when they are doing the wrong thing. This raises difficult questions about the nature of morality and its relationship to personal well-being.

Still, the concern theory, like the union theory, erases the distinction between deferential and non-deferential behavior. Excessive deference can be bad, but both theories leave us unable to explicate or analyze this. We discuss this further in the next chapter.

Love and rationality revisited: appraisal and bestowal

In Chapter 5, we saw how Nozick analyzed the question of love's rationality. Love involves a "risk pool": bad things aren't as bad when there is someone there who loves you. I mentioned two criticisms of this view: it seems to imply that falling in love with people who were sick or poor would be a mistake; relatedly, in fashioning love as a kind of insurance policy, it ultimately grounds love in self-interest.

Frankfurt is also interested in the question of how love can be rational. As we saw in our discussion of deference, once you are in love, things are relatively straightforward: when you act lovingly to bring about the well-being of the other person, you are acting rationally to satisfy your own interests as well. But do we have reasons to love in the first place? And is it better to love one person rather than another? Frankfurt's answer is that love involves "bestowal" and not "appraisal" of the other person's value. In appraisal views of love, love is thought to essentially involve some judgment or recognition of value – that a person is, somehow, worth loving. In bestowal views of love, love gives you reasons to see the other person as a source of value – that is, as someone worth loving and doing things for.

On the one hand, it might seem odd to think that love would involve "appraising" or judging someone since we often think of love as essentially nonjudgmental. You're supposed to love a person for themselves, and not for some particular set of qualities they have. What if you love them because they're smart and clever but then they develop dementia and they're no longer smart and clever? This suggests something wrong with the appraisal view.

On the other hand, if someone we care about loves someone who is cruel or unkind to them, it's common to say something like "You shouldn't love that person – they're not nice to you!" This way of saying "shouldn't" means we do evaluate who earns our love and who does not. Also, people often list "qualities" they're looking for in someone to love. Some dating sites and matchmaking services are organized around the idea that we can figure out in advance what qualities we want or would be a good fit for us, and then use those qualities to narrow down our search for love. Since they rest on the idea that qualities are essential to love, these facts suggest something wrong with the "bestowal" view.

In his defense of the bestowal view, Frankfurt points out that to think that something is valuable entails nothing specific about how we feel about that thing, or whether we care about it at all. But the essence of love, as we know, is caring. So for Frankfurt, it's not that we recognize value and then come to experience love – it's rather that we experience love, and because of our love, we regard the object of our love as especially valuable. Caring about something is not a matter of making judgments about it. Instead, it is a kind of immediate and unjudging commitment. In the appraisal view, you would have to see certain qualities in a person – kindness, goodness, whatever – and judge that for those reasons the person is worthy of your love. Frankfurt rejects the idea that qualities can give you reasons for love. As Foster says, for this reason Frankfurt's view has been called a "no-reasons" view. The "no-reasons" view is contrasted to a "quality theory," in which the qualities of a person show them to be worth loving.

The "no-reasons" view would seem to entail that there can be no "shoulds" about whom to love and whom not to love. When people say one person "shouldn't" love another, because of that person's bad qualities, or when we use qualities to figure out who might be a good candidate for love, from Frankfurt's perspective we're making a kind of mistake. This way of thinking leads Frankfurt give his own answer to the "trading up" problem. We saw in Chapter 5 the question of why it would seem wrong to "trade up" in love: to drop a person just because someone smarter, funnier, and nicer came along. And we saw how Nozick's answer to this question had to do with the way union meant that trading up would mean, essentially, destroying a part of yourself. But Frankfurt has a different answer, which is that love has nothing to do with qualities in the first place. Because love has nothing to do with qualities, the question doesn't even arise. If "smart," "funny" and "nice" aren't relevant in the first place, then "smarter," "funnier" and "nicer" don't make any difference. Love is a direct relationship between one individual person and another. It is unavoidably personal: a caring attitude one person has for another person, for themselves, for who they are, and not for their qualities. Love just attaches to a person, so you cannot shift it; indeed, it seems you would have no reasons to stop loving once you'd started – unless, perhaps, someone changes so much that they're not even the same person anymore.

In certain ways, the bestowal view of love is an attractive one. Often we love people not because of specific qualities but more for something about them that is hard to describe. And, notoriously, people are capable of falling for the "wrong person": someone who isn't good or nice but who seems irresistible. But in other ways, to say that love has nothing to do with qualities is a very weird idea. In addition to the idea that we often say one person "should" or "shouldn't" love another, Foster (2009) points out that bestowal makes love into a kind of mysterious phenomenon. If it's not in virtue of someone's qualities that we love them, what is it exactly? It would be a strange theory of love that posited that love could come to attach to any person, regardless of what that person was like. It makes love seem almost random.

Maybe there is something to this when it comes to parents' love for children. Parents often do become tied by powerful attachments to their children, regardless of what their children are like. In some ways, this is one of the most distinctive aspects of parental love: that it is not only unconditional but nonjudgmental. But, as a general theory of love, there's a big problem when we extrapolate to the cases in which, unlike parenting, you are coming to love one person rather than another, or possibly falling out of love with one person or other. Surely, we should be able to explain why a person should try to foster their feelings of love when the love object is a good kind suitable mate and to smother those feelings with the love object is cruel, unkind, or indifferent. The bestowal theory has no resources to explain why we come to love some people rather than others, or why we think it makes more sense to love certain people rather than others, or how it could make sense to say that we "should" love a person less or more.

Limitless care and the problem of paternalism

As we saw at the start, Frankfurt takes to an extreme the idea that love has to be other-regarding. This means there is no room for self-interest in the form of a desire for reciprocity or a limit to deference. One implication of this is that it's hard to see how there is a limit to the caring actions that people have to do. It's like each person has to make the other person's well-being an absolute priority all the time. In cases like Morgan's and Nico's, we've seen how implausible it is to think that moving is as much in Morgan's interest as it is Nico's. But if we try to keep their interests separate, then the concern theory runs into a different problem, since it entails that each of Morgan and Nico must try as much as possible to do what would be good for the other. Love means having reasons always to further the well-being of the beloved, so it seems Morgan must put aside their own views entirely and should push for the couple to make the choice to move.

In reciprocal love, this is extra confusing. Would Nico have to push for the couple to make the choice to stay? In addition to a potential infinite regress, the difficulty here is that the person who loves has no room for selfishness at all. The concern theory makes the demands of caring unlimited. This "limitless" aspect might be especially confusing in the context of sex. Remember the example from Chapter 5 of Quinn, who loves to receive oral sex, and Robin, doesn't love to perform oral sex, but does like to make Quinn happy by giving them pleasure. From the point of view of the concern theory, it seems there is no limit to the amount of oral sex Robin must provide, as long as it continues to make Quinn happy. But surely Robin gets to say, sometimes, that they just don't feel like it – regardless of how that makes Quinn feel? Does love require making yourself into a doormat?

The "limitless" aspect is also particularly problematic when it comes to the possibility of two people who have dramatically different needs for caring. Remember Cameron and Devin, who are in a loving relationship when Devin gets sick? Of course Cameron ought to help Devin, but if we take the concern theory at its word, there are there no limits to the extent to which Cameron must sacrifice their own interests and pleasures and goals to perform these caring acts. From the point of view of Frankfurt's theory, it is difficult to say how there could be any such limits – love, essentially, involving taking the other's well-being as valuable. But does love really require extraordinary self-sacrifice to be love? Couldn't it be acceptable for Cameron to be there only some of the time, and to bring in extra help from nurses and other paid caregivers? Even if it's just so Cameron can go hang out with friends occasionally? The concern theory seems to require unlimited care for the other person.

There are also questions concerning Frankfurt's idea of fostering "well-being." As Westlund (2008) says, doing things "for" another person without consulting them can be a form of disrespect – more the way you'd treat a pet than a person. Explaining this, Kyla Ebels-Duggan (2008) points out that Frankfurt's theory of love treats the lover more as a "benefactor" than as a participant in a shared relationship. What if Morgan wants to stay put but Nico decides that moving would really be in Morgan's best interest, even if Morgan doesn't know this themselves. From the point of view of the concern theory, Nico may be justified in making plans without consulting Morgan about their feelings, on grounds this would be a form of caring for Morgan. But this absence of deliberation, and listening to the other person, seems wrong. The concern view leaves little room for the role of interaction in love.

In this sense, a view like Frankfurt's can seem dangerously paternalistic. Paternalism is when one person or group makes judgments regarding the behavior of others that is supposed to be in the other's best interests, even if it's not what they say they want. For example, when parents tell children they can't eat all their Halloween candy at once, this is paternalistic, since it's making a judgment about what's best for the children that ignores what the children themselves have to say about it. In that kind of case, the paternalism is justified, since part of parenting is making rules for children so they stay happy and healthy. But adults are supposed to be able to make their own decisions.

Conclusion

Unlike union theories, which seem to risk collapsing identities into one, concern theories focus on the relationship between two distinct people. But because they require limitless disinterested care for the other's well-being, and because they entail that the person who loves must act to further the well-being of the loved one, concern theories encounter difficulties that echo those of the union view. Both theories have trouble identifying excessively deferential behavior or explaining why it is bad. And both theories have difficulty with the idea that some forms of individual self-interestedness can be healthy for relationships.

As with love as union, concern theories have resources to address the seeming conflict between the individualistic autonomy and rationality we ascribe to people as citizens in public life and the caring and selflessness of love. Here, the caring concern theory has one essential answer. Because love has to do with our volitions, it profoundly affects our sense of self, and the person who acts lovingly toward another is, in a sense, acting autonomously and rationally for themselves. Like the union theory, the concern theory thus ultimately elides the distinction between the lover and the one who is loved. As we've seen here, however, this elision leads to problems. To say that love means taking the other person's well-being as your own might sound good, but when you take it literally, the idea doesn't work very well. Taking parental love as paradigmatic, the theory fails to fit the kind of situation we're most interested in today: how to understand love so that it is compatible with both equality and mutual individuality.

7 Love, fairness, and equality

Introduction

In the past two chapters, I've examined two prominent theories of love, and I've argued that they face a common problem: both have difficulty in dealing with individuals' competing interests. In the union theory of love, the union threatens to swallow up the individual lovers altogether, leaving us unable even to formulate the idea that they might have different and possibly conflicting interests. In caring-concern theories, the demand that each lover feel disinterested concern for their partner's well-being threatens to crowd out the lovers' other desires and needs, and to render self-assertion impossible.

Objections like these suggest a somewhat different way of looking at these theories of love. Perhaps the problem is not so much that they're wrong as that they go too far, presenting extreme versions of views that might be workable if formulated in more moderate terms. Perhaps these theories could incorporate ideas about balancing and shared egalitarian deliberation and thus allow a place for the individual lovers to assert their own needs and interests.

In this chapter, I'll consider this possibility by exploring what moderate versions of these theories would entail. I'll argue, however, that addressing the relevant difficulties would mean letting go of the idea that love and other forms of caring are distinct; the resulting approaches are not really theories of love at all, because they emphasize the continuity between loving caring and other forms of caring. When the theories are not modified, though, they obscure questions of fairness and equality in decision-making; this is especially significant in contexts in which gendered social norms affect how we form and express our preferences.

As we've discussed, one reason to pursue a theory of love may be to understand the seeming conflict between the individualism and self-interest that play such an outsize role in the public life of liberal capitalist societies and the caring that seems characteristic of love. The union and concern theories we've considered each lead to their own responses to this conflict. But I'll argue that while these resolutions may have functioned well in contexts of gender hierarchy, such as North America in the 1950s, considerations of fairness and equality show that they don't work well in modern contexts of equality. In the end, we may simply have to relinquish the idea that love is fundamentally different from other forms of interaction.

Union theories and balancing

One way of rendering the idea of union more moderate is to say that instead of fully merging our interests and desires we should aim for a balance between taking on the needs and interests of another person and preserving the distinctness of our own needs and interests. Noël Merino (2004), for example, proposes that what we want out of love isn't to be subsumed into a new entity but rather to occupy a space of both individuality and relatedness. From a practical point of view, it would follow that sometimes you look out for the other person and sometimes you look out for yourself, in some appropriate way. Could the idea of balancing be an interpretation of the union concept that allows us to avoid some of the challenges we've discussed?

Generally, the metaphor of "balancing" means finding a way to incorporate different considerations into a decision in a way that respects the proper weight of each. In this context, it means seeing ourselves as having individual identities that are distinct from those of our partner, while also seeing ourselves as enmeshed with our partner's interests, then finding a way to appropriately prioritize the resulting concerns. We aim to respect the individual and the union, and to find a way to incorporate their interests and well-being into decision-making.

This framing raises the question of what it means to balance "appropriately" or to respect the "proper" weight of things. Saying that "balancing" is what you need tells you nothing about how to do it, or when to prioritize the other person's interests and when to prioritize your own.

When it comes to love, one way to frame the answer appeals to the idea of different "domains." The idea is that there are some domains especially suited to merging interests, some especially suited to individuality, and some where you need to work out a mix of things. For example, in thinking about the tension between merging and individuality in love, Neil Delaney (1996) points out that while we might desire to merge in love, we also want to be loved for our individuality, so we might resolve this tension by carving out domains of sharing and domains of separateness. It might be, for instance, that interests to do with childcare might be "fully collaborative and communal," and interests to do with careers or personal projects might be private and individual. Other domains, like entertainment, might be a mix.

While interpreting the idea of balancing through domains might give us a good way of understanding the importance of being loved for our individuality, I don't think it helps with the challenges we've seen in Chapters

5 and 6, about competing interests. For one thing, interests can conflict across categories. Some of the most difficult problems in modern life have to do with conflicts between domains like work and domains like child-care. In working couples who have children, there are many competing interests that arise: maybe the kid gets sick on a day when both people can't miss work, or maybe both adults come home exhausted and don't feel like putting in the effort of cooking dinner. If love means merging childcare interests and keeping work interests relatively separate, the difficulties we discussed, of merging in the case of conflicting interests, persist.

For example, if the interests in the domain of childcare are shared, then the couple has a merged set of interests relevant to childcare that don't distinguish between them as individuals. Those interests might include items like "child gets to doctor's appointment on time." As we saw in Chapter 5, if these interests are merged, it's in the couple's interest when they get satisfied. If one parent ends up doing all the childcare work, the union theory delivers the strange result that in doing so they are benefiting themselves just as much as they are benefiting the other person – because they are working to satisfy the joint interests and benefit the union. Furthermore, if the work interests are in another domain, we then face the question of how to balance each individual's work-related interests with the union's childcare-related interests. The question of how to balance across domains is left unsolved.

More significantly, there are conflicts within domains, and these inherit the difficulties we've already seen. The examples of Chapters 5 and 6 are of this kind: Morgan and Nico can't decide whether to move, and Quinn and Robin want different things out of sex. Domestic arrangements and sexual activity would seem good candidates for shared domains. But if they are, then taking interests in that domain to be merged means we encounter again the problems we've already seen: we can't say that one course of action is better for one person than for another, we can't say that one person's action is done for another, or at a sacrifice to themselves, and we can't distinguish deferential from non-deferential actions.

For these reasons, I don't think the idea of domains helps the union theory out of its troubles with divergent and competing interests. The idea of balancing is apt, but it works better without the idea of domains. Instead of balancing shared interests and individual ones, we can just frame the matter as one of balancing your own interests and your partner's interests. This way of balancing would mean respecting your individual needs and desires and also your partner's needs and desires in a way that shows appropriate care for the significance of each. For example, remember Cameron and Devin, who are in a loving relationship when Devin gets sick. Suppose this happens at a time when Cameron is especially busy with work and other things. Cameron might find there are small things they can do to make Devin more comfortable – like making Devin's favorite food, maybe something Cameron themselves doesn't really like – that involve only a small sacrifice on Cameron's part. There might be other, much more intensive things that Cameron could do that would make Devin more comfortable, like staying home with Devin all day. That would be a much bigger sacrifice on Cameron's part and only a small help to Devin. In this kind of situation, the idea of balancing means giving things proper weight: maybe for Cameron to go to their job is more important than Devin having company for TV-watching, but for Cameron to make special meals might be a small thing Cameron could do to make Devin feel better – and feel loved.

Balancing in this way is obviously subjective: it relies on judgments about how much things matter and what can and cannot be given up. It is also complicated. To balance, people must make a wide range of judgments about significance and the appropriate trade-offs in life. These judgments are, of course, things people can and do have disagreements about – sometimes huge, relationship-ending disagreements. But this doesn't mean there's something wrong with the idea of balancing. Making judgments is an inevitable part of human life and of all relationships. And balancing provides an apt metaphor for the kind of activity we commonly use in trying to resolve such agreements: we try to impress upon others our own sense of how important things are, so they'll come to share our sense of what would be an appropriate action, compromise, or overall way of doing things.

For example, in the case where you have two adults with children and conflicting interests over who does most of the childcare, the parents would have to work out how to "appropriately" compromise, perhaps appealing to questions like whose workplace issues should take precedence and when, perhaps appealing to an idea that the burdens should be spread equally. In a case like that of Quinn and Robin, balancing means finding a way to do some of the things that each person likes best, perhaps on different occasions. In a case like that of Morgan and Nico, balancing interests might be difficult and complicated, because in this case each person has a strong interest in doing the thing they want most, so there are two conflicting interests that are each very important. And when you're talking about moving or staying put, it's not easy to find a compromise position. Nonetheless, Morgan and Nico might try to find a way that whoever wins out this time can make it up to the other person another time.

Crucially, though, the idea of "merger" or union plays no real role in this form of balancing at all. In fact, merger would get in the way. Figuring out how to appropriately honor each person's needs and interests requires, most fundamentally, recognizing that people have different needs and interests that are individually theirs. As the childcare example shows, even when two people "share" an interest – in the sense of both having it in the same way – we have to preserve the distinctness of individuals in order to make sense of appropriate compromises that take into account the interests of both people.

As Merino says, once you get into balancing, what you've got is not really a union view of love, because friendships and other caring relationships work on the same principles (2004: 130). If people are friends, they often do things to help one another, taking into account both their own and their friends' needs and interests. If the person you love is sick you might make their favorite food for them, but if your friend is sick you might very well do the same thing. In fact, balancing your own needs and interests with those of others is not special to romantic love. It is what we do with family, friends, casual acquaintances, and sometimes even strangers. It is characteristic of a sensible approach to life in general.

Balancing interests is great for understanding interpersonal relationships, but it's an awkward fit as part of a union theory. This means that the problem isn't that "union" has been taken too far. The problem is seeing love as a special and distinct thing, unlike other caring relationships, needing a theory of its own. We return to this topic below.

Concern theories and deliberation

Similar conclusions apply in the case of concern theories. In Chapter 6, we saw that some concern theories collapse the distinction between self-interest and caring, because when one person does something for another, the theory interprets them as doing it for themselves. Among other things, this has the peculiar implication that the loving and deferential person, who is always taking care of everyone else's needs first, can be interpreted as satisfying their own interests. Love as caring concern can obscure the difference between selfishness and self-sacrifice, and collapse the distinction between deference and self-directedness. Concern theories also face the challenge of requiring unlimited care.

As a corrective to some of these, Andrea Westlund (2008) proposes shared egalitarian deliberation, a practical perspective in which each person should take on the point of view of the other. Joint deliberation, she says, "requires each party to be open to guidance by the perspective of the other, which in turn requires each to be open to guidance by her own perspective, which in turn requires each to be open to guidance by the perspective of the other, and so on" (Westlund 2008: 568). This results in a kind of "argumentative" picture of what love is like: requiring not only sharing but also interpersonal communication about difference. It's important to take into account the interests of others, but it's also important to assert your own. When each person takes into account the perspective of the other, the result is an "egalitarian" deliberation: because it is reciprocal, it is also equal.

Perhaps the deliberation model could provide a moderate interpretation of concern theories. Shared deliberation helps us avoid the peculiar one-sidedness that results when love requires adopting the other's needs and interests as your own. One person no longer has to adopt the volition of acting always to bring about the well-being of the other. And, importantly, this approach avoids the problem of paternalism we saw in Chapter 6: instead of one person trying to bring about the other person's well-being, the two people try to work together, bringing their own and possibly different perspectives to decision-making.

While the egalitarian aspect of shared deliberation ensures that each person takes up the perspective of the other, it does not dissolve the problems we've been discussing, about divergent and competing interests. What if the perspectives are incompatible? For example, in the case in which two people take care of children and there are conflicts between work and childcare responsibilities, shared deliberation requires us to see the issue from the other person's point of view. But in this case, it might be the perspective of each person is that it's the other person who ought to sacrifice; each might believe that their own personal interests, conflicting with the childcare responsibilities, are the most pressing. In the case of Morgan and Nico, does shared deliberation mean simply that Morgan and Nico have to listen to one another's reasons? What if they judge those reasons differently? It's possible that Morgan and Nico will each see why the other person feels as they do, but it's also possible that one would think the other is overreacting or getting upset over nothing. Maybe Morgan can't see why this new job is so important to Nico. Maybe Nico thinks Morgan is just afraid of new experiences and should conquer their fear. In the case of Quinn and Robin, what if Robin finds that giving oral sex to Quinn feels uncomfortable or degrading, but Quinn thinks Robin is being just being silly, or difficult? How does shared deliberation work when, as so often, there is a difference of opinion about what counts as a good reason?

While shared egalitarian deliberation does not give answers to these questions, it does give a framework for decision-making when interests conflict. As with balancing, much will depend on what the individuals judge to be reasons and what they take to be appropriate respect for those reasons; these judgments will inform what does, and does not, seem like a fair compromise. When we experience difficult conflicts with the people we love, we have to listen to and engage with their perspectives, and shared egalitarian deliberation reminds us that in love, this must be done reciprocally.

Crucial to these ideas of reciprocity and compromise, however, is acknowledging that conflicting or incompatible interests are, in fact, in conflict. For this, each person must be able to represent their own well-being in terms of their own interests, so a self-oriented perspective is necessary. We must be able to engage in a process of negotiation, in which we represent ourselves; this is incompatible with the complete disinterestedness required at least by Frankfurt's theory of love as caring concern. While shared egalitarian deliberation is a good model for preserving mutuality and individuality in love, it is best understood on its own terms and not as a modest interpretation of a caring-concern theory.

That is, as with union theories, the modification that makes the theory less extreme also destroys it as a distinctive theory of love. Once we change the wholeheartedly caring and distinterested love of the concern theory to shared joint deliberation, it is – as Westlund says – no longer a model for love only but rather something shared by most people who care about one another, including friends. If you are friends with someone, of course you will try to take up their perspective: assertion of individuality is important in friendship as well as love, and when friends do things together they try to make decisions together about how. Again, the modifications create a view in which love is a lot like other relationships. This discussion suggests that the problem with theories of love isn't about being extreme but rather about trying to be distinctive – in taking love to be the kind of thing you can have a theory about.

Equality and fairness

As we've been discussing, some of the most persistent and difficult problems in modern loving relationships have to do with decision-making when interests conflict. We've seen the importance of maintaining individuality in relationships. We've seen how the importance of individuality means that we have to balance concern for ourselves with concern for the couple or the other person. We've seen how coming to a perspective on shared decision-making requires being willing to take up the other person's perspective and finding appropriate ways of honoring both people's needs and interests. But people who love one another face a further question: what does it mean for the resulting decisions to be fair and equal?

How much must we sacrifice our time and energy to mutuality when doing so means we can't satisfy our own interests and desires? When is it unloving to insist on doing things our own way and when does love require us to give up what we would otherwise want? What does it mean to have fairness and equality in the way we resolve our competing interests? In the case of the couple who have jobs and children and share a desire for the kids to be well cared for, how do we decide what is an equal and fair division of household labor? Does it matter what the two different jobs are? Does it matter if one of them enjoys childcare more? What if one person just complains about it a lot? If Morgan and Nico both insist it's their way or the highway, that seems wrong. But if Morgan almost always does what is best for Nico, that seems wrong too. Quinn and Robin, who like different things in sex, should try to do different activities so everyone is happy. But how often should people have sexual activities they don't like that much, just to please another person? Or forgo what they do enjoy? Occasionally? A lot? Does it matter what the activity is? These are the questions of fair compromise.

Balancing and shared egalitarian deliberation on their own do not answer these questions, but they do provide frameworks for discussing them: balancing means making judgment calls about how strong various reasons are and how individuality should be prioritized alongside a shared perspective; shared egalitarian deliberation means listening to the other person's perspective about why those reasons are as they are. These frameworks invite us to consider what is a fair and equal way of taking a complex range of reasons into consideration, showing immediately why these questions of fair compromise are so important and providing a starting point for thinking about them.

The union and concern theories we've considered actively obscure these difficult questions. It's not just that these theories of love don't solve the problems of equality and fairness. It's that they block our ability to conceptualize them, to articulate what it would mean to have a pattern of decision-making about areas of mutual concern that is fair and takes each person's needs, interests, and well-being into consideration equally.

With the union view, we've seen the problems in Chapter 5. First, if the two individuals lose their identities, then we can't even say whose desires and interests are being met. So questions of fairness and equality among individuals cannot even be framed. But even if individuals persist alongside the union, then the pooling of interests means the stronger one wins out, and this makes fairness and equality obscure as well. For example, if Nico's desire to move is very strong and Morgan's desire to say is only moderate, then when Morgan and Nico take on the collected and merged interests, that collection will include a stronger desire to move. And generally, in cases of conflict the stronger desire will win out; this might mean one person always gets their way. If Morgan then goes along with Nico, from the union view we can't even say that this was in Nico's particular interest or an act of kindness and generosity on Morgan's part. So there would be no sense in which equality and fairness require that this kindness or generosity ought to reciprocated in ways that prioritize Morgan's needs and interests.

In the shared-ends interpretation of the union view, since Morgan would be acting in the interests of both together when Morgan says they can go, Morgan hasn't sacrificed their own interests, and so there wouldn't be this sense that Nico has to give something back. The identity replacement view of union entails that each person is supposed to take the other's ends and desires into account equally to their own – that is, take them as their own. Either way, it's impossible to articulate a sense in which an action could have been good for one person and not good for another, or even more good for one person and less good for another. So adopting this framework prevents us from articulating and addressing the crucial question: when are one person's interests unfairly dominating another's?

With respect to concern theories, in Chapter 6 we showed how Frankfurt's theory renders it difficult to distinguish deferential actions from non-deferential ones. As we discussed, this leads to a problem right away, since excessive deference can be bad, for people and for relationships. But, in addition, eliding this distinction makes it difficult to pose the question of what constitutes a fair distribution of caring, or a fair division of caring labor – that is, actions we do to bring about the well-being of others. If one person is always deferential, then the other always gets their way; from the point of view of concern theories, though, the first person is simply acting lovingly.

Furthermore, as it's articulated, this concern theory seems to require unlimited concern: the person who loves has to do everything they can do bring about the well-being of the other. Again, because one person's self-interest becomes satisfying the other person's needs and interests, it is impossible to distinguish between other-regarding and self-interested actions. And even if there were self-interested actions, we would seemingly have to put them aside. The basic idea is that love gives you reasons to act to bring about the other's well-being. But how can these reasons come to an end? If love has to do with acting for the other's benefit, it's unclear how we can ever have reason to act selfishly.

These points about equality and fairness are especially significant because social norms deeply affect what we consider to be our interests and desires, and these norms are often gendered. In our society, women are often taught to care about others' well-being and to sacrifice their own desires and interests for those of others, especially those of family members. If the example in which Sydney is deferential to Taylor concerns a heterosexual partnership in which Sydney is a woman and Taylor is a man, then Sydney's deference may lead her to believe that it is her special job to make sure everyone in the family has their needs met. Her interests, then, are to bring about the well-being of others. Taylor may think that caring for others is part of how women should be. In a case like this, the woman might have the interests that she prepare food, take the kids to the doctor, etc., and her partner will also have the interest that she prepare food, take the kids to the doctor, etc. The union view and caring-concern view would result in Sydney's doing all the caring labor around the home. In the union view, the shared interests would include an interest that she perform the caring labor. In the concern view, her love would support her idea that she should do caring labor – and interestingly, even if her partner loves her back, her idea that women "should" take care of others will mean that satisfying her interests to care for others could be a way of fostering her well-being.

The same applies for Morgan and Nico. If Morgan is a woman who is deferential because of gender norms, she may decide that Nico's happiness is most important for her to consider, and therefore may weaken her own commitment to staying put, to embrace a desire for Nico to take the job. In that case, the merging of interests would simply result in a move, with no sense of necessary reciprocity on Nico's part. And in the concern view, she would be right to go along with Morgan, since in the concern view we can't distinguish deferential from non-deferential actions. If love requires Morgan to take on the promotion of Nico's well-being, there is no sense in which Morgan has done something for Nico, and so there is no sense in which Nico is obligated by equality and fairness to reciprocate.

The problem is especially interesting for couples who have divergent sexual desires. Women are often socialized to think that their sexual pleasure isn't as directly important as that of men, and that it is their job to please. Suppose a woman wanted to please her boyfriend because she'd been brought up to think that's what a good woman does, and the boyfriend wanted her to please him, because he'd been brought up to think that's what a good woman does. In the union view, not only would it be best overall for the woman to just please the man, since this best satisfies their shared ends and desires, it's difficult to even articulate what might be nonideal about this solution. In the concern theory as well, the woman's love would give her reason to do what pleases him, and thus in pleasing him she would be acting "self-interestedly" and thus asserting her selfhood. Again, it becomes difficult to even frame the issue of equality and reciprocity.

Essentially, when interests are merged, it is impossible to say that a pattern of decision-making is unequal or unfair, because there is no sense of self-interest weighed against other-interest. And when concern requires unlimited care for the other's well-being, it is difficult to say that an outcome is unequal or unfair. Earlier in this chapter, I argued that rendering these theories in terms of balancing and shared egalitarian deliberation is a move in the right direction but that doing so in the right way leads to approaches that are not really theories of love at all since they do not show what is distinctive about love as compared to other relationships. So, in the next section, we revisit the question of why love may be thought to be a distinctive thing for which we need a special theory.

Why a theory of love, revisited

I've been arguing that there are challenges with certain union and concern theories of love: when they're interpreted literally, they encounter a range of difficulties, and when they're modified to be more plausible, they show how love is much like other relationships. The fact that shared egalitarian deliberation and appropriate balancing of concerns are characteristic not only of love but also of other relationships like friendship suggests that the difficulty lies in the idea that we need a distinct theory of love in the first place. The need for such a theory rests on the idea that the relations we have with people we love are radically different from the relations we have with others: not just different in degree, but different in kind. To think we can have a theory of love is to think that love is somehow importantly different from other relationships. But, as we've seen through these chapters, a plausible view of love is one in which love relationships are a lot like other caring relationships. They are different in degree, perhaps, or in emotional texture, but they are not deeply different in kind.

As we've touched on before, one reason to want a theory of love may be because of the potential conflict between the caring and selflessness of love and the individualist model of people in public life. In modern, liberal, capitalist societies, we're encouraged to see ourselves as self-interested people looking out for our own needs and desires, who then interact with others primarily through the model of negotiation and contract. In public life, liberal society frames us each as individuals whose freedom to act on our own rational autonomous interest is paramount; capitalism means that in our relations with others public values encourage a spirit of contract and negotiation: if we need something from another person, we assume that getting it will be a matter of finding an appropriate exchange. We pay others to do things for us and they pay us to do things for them; negotiation means looking out for yourself. In this individualist perspective, rationality means "self-interested" rationality: you do what is good for you with regard to your own well-being. And "autonomy" means self-regarding autonomy: you are "self-governed," making your own decisions without influence from others.

But love and family life challenge the social individualism we encounter in our culture more broadly. Love is generous and caring, not self-interested. We want to feel giving toward the people we love, not that we're always looking for some return on our investment. If rationality is understood as self-interested maximizing of our own well-being, then the generosity of love might seem irrational. If autonomy means "self-governed" in the sense of not being influenced by others, then how could love, which involves constant mutual influence, ever be compatible with autonomy? The felt need for a theory of love might have to do with finding a way that interactions with those we love can be completely different from interactions with everyone else.

Among other things, if the same spirit of negotiation and contractual exchange that characterizes our public lives also dominated our private lives, it might be intolerable and exhausting. Don't we need a place where we can rest and feel a spirit of caring and nurturing, instead of a spirit of competition and calculation? With the traditional system of gender roles and marriage, men could be self-interested and competing in public, with home as a sanctuary for a different atmosphere: kind and loving. In the intimate sphere, instead of looking out for your own interests and trying to get what you need and want through exchange, a man could feel that someone else was looking out for their interests, taking their wants and needs as a priority (see Lasch 1979).

As we've seen, though, in this set-up, the sanctuary of home is attained at the cost of women's individuality and autonomy. Historically, the sanctuary of home was sometimes attained because marriage formally subsumed the will of the woman into that of the man. When one group of people is subordinate and the other is dominant, it is easy to have union and caring concern in love: interests are merged because one person takes over; the nurturer provides caring concern because that's what nurturers do. The specialness of the love relationship functioned partly through sexist inequality.

One reason to want a modern theory of love might be to try to find a solution to this same problem that doesn't require one person to be subordinate and another to be dominant. Union theories and caring-concern theories both emphasize the difference between the way we interact with those we love and the way we interact with others. Both try to create a mode of interaction between people that is diametrically opposed to the self-interested negotiation and competition that is taken to be characteristic of other kinds of interactions in democratic capitalist societies.

As we saw toward the end of Chapter 5, the idea of love as union constructs our relationships of love as radically different from other relationships like friendship or the fondness and caring we may feel for relative strangers, so the selflessness of love is restricted to a specific context; the "we" also emerges as an individual with needs and interests of its own. As we saw in Chapter 6, in Frankfurt's concern theory, love has to do with our volitions and thus with what we have reason to do; it affects who we are at a deep level. From this it follows that the person who acts lovingly toward another is, in a sense, acting autonomously and rationally for themselves. Generally speaking, if addressing the conflicts between social individualism and love is one motivation for wanting a theory of love, this would explain why the theories and analysis have had so much to say about topics like rationality and autonomy.

But I've argued that union and caring concern don't address the conflicts in a satisfactory way. Once you eliminate the idea that one person will be subordinate and the other dominant, the idea of union and caring concern don't function well: they elide the important distinctions between individuals and the couple, and they get in the way of understanding equality and fairness. And in reality, competing interests don't magically dissolve when people love one another. As anyone who has argued over housework or childcare or time in the bathroom or any of the million things that couples argue about every day knows, you can love someone completely and passionately and still have different interests from them. Deciding what to do in cases of divergent and competing interests in ways that respect gender equality and fairness requires balancing our own interests and those of the other person and the couple in appropriate ways, and taking up a deliberative egalitarian perspective. But so do many human relationships. That it is so difficult to articulate a sense of the specialness of love that both mitigates the individualism of public life and also makes sense of fairness and equality suggests that carving out protected domains of love in family life is more difficult than it may appear.

Conclusion

This chapter has explored the idea that trying to show how love is special may be a misguided enterprise. One reason to think love has to be special is that it seems to create a context that is fundamentally different from those of public life, one in which caring for someone else, for their own sake, is a paradigmatic attitude. In liberal societies, the assumption is that each person should be free to pursue what is good for them individually; in capitalist societies, the assumption is that we will generally get the things we want and need through negotiation and exchange. These assumptions seem inappropriate for contexts of love. It might seem a theory of love can help us explain these divergences.

I've argued, however, that some theories of love face challenges related to fairness and equality, especially when it comes to competing interests. Altering the theories, through the use of balancing and shared egalitarian deliberation, creates a plausible view of love, but one in which love is not all that special. While union and concern may function to create a special context of caring context against a background of asymmetrical gender roles, they are ill suited for gender equality, since they elide the distinctions that are necessary for making judgments about fairness and reciprocity.

One of the more striking things about these theories of love is that they seem designed for understanding love as a thing that happens at home among small groups of people. You could never have union or caring concern for a large group – or for everyone in the world. There is no way this sense of "love" could be at play with respect to the idea that you should "love thy neighbor." But why not see the kind of caring we have toward intimates and the kind of caring we have toward strangers as existing along a continuum, instead of as completely different kinds of things?

8 Orientations of sex and love

Introduction

"Orientation" has become one of our society's principal terms for discussing how people experience attraction and love. We commonly describe individuals in terms of their orientations, as "gay," "lesbian," "straight," and "bisexual," though, as we will see, these hardly scratch the surface of the many ways people experience attraction and orientation. Though orientations are often discussed as matters pertaining specifically to sex, orientations obviously relate also to love, romance, and family life. That's why this chapter is called "Orientations of Sex *and* Love."

The term "LGBTQ" stands for "lesbian, gay, bisexual, trans, and queer and/or questioning"; other initials are sometimes added – for example, A for asexuality or I for intersex. For simplicity, I'll use the abbreviation LGBTQ+. This chapter begins with an explication of this terminology. When we discuss why LGBTQ+ people should be afforded equal rights and respect, we often hear about the idea of "born that way" and "not a choice": that because we are born with certain orientations, and thus cannot change them, orientations cannot be a justification for discrimination. Relatedly, there has been a lot of recent scientific research into orientations, with the implication that the science will be relevant to politics: if orientations are genetic and biological, the thinking goes, they are fixed and stable aspects of a person, aspects that must be treated with respect. But, as we'll see in this chapter, the "born that way" and "not a choice" arguments have various conceptual and ethical complexities, and they are insufficient for grounding the relevant equal rights and freedoms. Furthermore, taking a scientific view of orientations can have surprising negative effects. What is needed, I'll argue, is positive affirmation and valuing of the ways of life of LGBTQ+ people.

As we've seen in the Introduction, I write from the widely shared philosophical perspective that queer and same-sex partnerships are as ethical as any other relationships and don't require any special defense. But some people believe that LGBTQ+ relationships are wrong, for religious or other reasons, and not that long ago in North America being gay or lesbian was illegal. As we'll see in the first section, the history and context of political and social discrimination against gays and lesbians is essential for understanding how orientations and public identities have been conceptualized and how they are studied and understood.

Concepts, terminology, and history

A rich and complex vocabulary for discussing these issues has emerged in recent decades. The characterizations offered here are rough and introductory because the best ways of defining these concepts are contested and evolving. Sexual orientations and identities have to do with the question of whom a person has sex with or wants to have sex with; these are distinct from sex and gender identities, which concern which sex or gender a person is. Typically, sex identities like "male" and "female" are understood to refer to biological categories, while gender has to do with the characteristics and roles that a society or culture delineates as masculine or feminine.

Roughly, "gay" refers to people who only, or primarily, want to have sex and romantic relationships with people of the same sex. Sometimes it is used particularly for men, sometimes for people in general. "Lesbian" refers to women who only, or primarily, want to have sex and romantic relationships with other women. "Bisexual" refers to people who want to have sex and romantic relationships with both men and women. "Transgender" people experience their gender identity as different from the sex they were assigned at birth; "transexuality" refers to a person transitioning physically from one sex to another, for instance through the use of hormones. "Cis" is the opposite of "trans", so a "ciswoman" is a woman who was assigned "female" at birth and a "cisman" is a man who was assigned male at birth. Some people identify as "genderqueer" or "nonbinary," meaning that they do not subscribe to the idea of sorting everyone separately into the categories of "men" and "women," or want to be identified with neither, or both. Finally, "intersex": this is the term that was "adopted by science in the early 20th century and applied to human beings whose biological sex cannot be classified as clearly male or female" (OII 2017). "Intersex" people might identify primarily as male or female, might identify as simply "intersex," or might identify in some other way.

We're not going to be talking a lot about gender and sex identity here because we're focusing more on the sex that you want to have than the sex that you are, but it is crucial to understand that gender presentation, gender identity, sex identity, and sexual orientation are all distinct and don't align in any necessary way. A person assigned female at birth might identify as a man, and may want to have sex with men. A person might identify as a man, enjoy dressing in a feminine style, and want to have sex with women. Some people who transition to female are lesbians, and some who transition to male are gay. It's sometimes thought that gayness for men is associated with femininity and lesbianism with masculinity for women, but it's important to realize that there are no necessary connections here. People vary a lot.

Any analysis of sexual orientations has to start by observing that people whose sexuality is seen as different from the socially dominant norms have been subjected to extraordinary persecution and violence. Around much of the world, and through much of history, there has been hatred and fear of sexuality outside the cis-hetero norm, manifesting itself through official criminalization and unofficial – but often socially sanctioned – personal violence, from bullying to murder. In the 1950s it was especially difficult to be gay or lesbian in North America, with the FBI and Canadian RCMP both tracking suspected gay and lesbian activity, aiming to stamp out homosexuality altogether. In the 1960s, gays and lesbians began increasingly to agitate for change – and in the case of the Stonewall riots, using violence to make their point.

Currently, countries vary enormously with respect to the rights and protections they accord. Canadian laws are among the most progressive in the world and allow most formal kinds of equality – such as marriage, adoption, and employment equality. In the United States, a Supreme Court ruling legalized same-sex marriage nationwide in 2015, though there is still debate over some forms of discrimination – such as whether to allow retail providers to refuse service to same-sex wedding couples. However, across North America there is still violence, hate crime, and bullying against people whose sexuality differs from social norms. Trans people especially face great hostility, violence, and threats of various kinds. Intersex people are often surgically altered as infants, before they can consent, and in ways that harm their sexual identity and their capacity to experience sexual pleasure. In some places, things are improving, but not everywhere, and in some places, things are getting worse.

It is against the backdrop of the twentieth-century oppression of LGBTQ+ people that the idea emerged of a distinction between a sexual "orientation," which is thought to be a stable, underlying quality about a person, and a sexual "identity," which refers to a way of being in the world that one can choose to adopt. Orientations are understood as features of a person's constitution that determine whom they are attracted to. Identities, by contrast, are associated with living publicly and identifying in a certain way. In the mid twentieth century, organizations formed to promote respect and equality for LGBTQ+ people; having an "identity" was – and is – meant partly to assist in this: if you declare that you have a certain identity, you take on a certain social position: you declare who you are, and whom you stand with. This traditional distinction makes sense of the idea that someone might identify as gay only later in life, despite being gay from very early on. When people talk about "coming out of the closet," or just "coming out," they are referring to the process of coming to identify publicly with a certain felt orientation.

The concept of "identity" has acquired such significance partly because of the political context surrounding LGBTQ+ issues. In other domains of life, we don't generally use this concept: you needn't adopt a special identity to do what you want to do openly and freely. If you like to watch documentaries, and none of your family and friends do, you don't have to adopt a special identity as a "documentary watcher" when you decide to do it and talk about it. You might enjoy meeting up with other people who also like to watch documentaries, but you don't "come out" as a documentary film watcher, and, if you don't want to, you don't have to associate yourself with other documentary film watchers. You can just watch documentaries. What makes sexual identities different is that they evolved in response to the cultural and political attitudes against sexual activity that falls outside the heterosexual norm. The concept of a sexual identity developed originally, in part, as a tool that would help in the political struggle for liberation and equality.

Some people identify as "asexual": this term refers to people who experience little or no sexual attraction to anyone. This is plausibly another orientation and identity a person might have. It is distinct from the condition of choosing celibacy, that is, choosing not to have sex, as encouraged for instance by some religious traditions; celibacy is entirely compatible with intense sexual desire, whereas the essence of asexuality is the absence of attraction or desire. Theoretical work on the idea of asexuality is relatively new, and so the term is sometimes not included in existing discussions of orientations.

The term "queer" used to be an insult associated with anti-gay and lesbian persecution, but, beginning in the late 1980s, activists and others "reappropriated" it and started using it with a positive self-referential meaning. Many people now use "queer" as a broad concept referring to all those who experience their sexuality outside the cis/straight norm; it is thus associated with an idea of challenging norms and breaking rules. Among other things, those who feel that sex, gender, orientation, and identity categories can themselves be restrictive or oppressive might adopt the label "queer" instead. "Queer" in this usage can include people who mostly have sex with the opposite sex – if, for example, they are into domination or role-playing or other practices seen as outside the norm.

As with the idea of "identity," the concept "queer" has political overtones, and these have generated debate. Both theorists and activists have asked whether the term is more or less effective in the political struggle for recognition and equal rights (Jagose 1996). On the one hand, it is an appealingly broad term, applying to all people whose sexuality is in any way diverges from the standard cis-heterosexual narrative. It can, for example, include people who are into ethical nonmonogamy – that is, who want to form love and sex relationships with multiple people at one time (a topic we'll discuss in depth in Chapter 14) – and also people into different kinds of sex like BDSM. On the other hand, its breadth might undercut its power. How far does the concept extend? In particular, if straight people can identify as "queer," then the concept may lose its power to reflect the particular marginalization experienced by gay men and lesbians.

The "born that way" and "not a choice" arguments: conceptual complexities

Central to the North American fight for equality and respect are the "born that way" and "not a choice" arguments, centering on the idea that our sexual desires and attractions are not simply lifestyle choices to be taken up or discarded on a whim but are embedded deep in who we are and so demand respect. While an "identity" may be chosen, an orientation is not. In this way of thinking, being gay is not like choosing to smoke, or choosing to play the guitar, or choosing to live in one kind of place rather than another. Instead, the desire to have loving and sexual relationships with some people rather than others reflects a deep, innate, and unchangeable fact about a person. If orientations are inborn and unchangeable, rather than a matter of choice, the thinking goes, it would be wrong to make laws and other policies that discriminate against people who are born this way.

These ideas have become deeply embedded in our culture. In 2012, the actress Cynthia Nixon caused a huge controversy when she said that for her, gayness was a choice: she had had relationships with men and with women, and was now choosing to have one with a woman. This remark angered some people because it seemed to undermine the fight for respect and equality. After a storm of controversy, Nixon clarified her remarks. What she meant, she said, was that she had an innate and unchangeable identity of being bisexual, and that within that she had "chosen" to have a relationship with a woman rather than a man (Grindley 2012). Likewise, after the Orlando Pulse gay nightclub shooting in 2016, a storm of complaints resulted when the French prime minister, François Hollande, said, "It is America that has been hit but it is also freedom, the freedom to choose one's sexual orientation and to determine one's style of life." People objected to Hollande's implication that orientation was a choice (France 24 2016). And Lady Gaga calls her youth organization the "Born This Way" Foundation, again suggesting the idea that qualities you're born with have a special claim on other's respect; that's simply who you are.

It is partly because the "born that way" and "not a choice" arguments are entwined with the LGBTQ+ political movement that the *science* of orientations has come to seem so important. There is sometimes an expectation that studying the biological aspects of orientations will help bring moral clarity to our social world. Some contemporary scientific research into orientations is devoted to finding out whether they are natural and biological, with the implication that this will bear on ethical and political debates: if they are, this would mean people are "born that way"; it's "not a choice" and therefore sexual orientation cannot be grounds for discrimination.

But this way of seeing things is complicated by various factors, and science is unlikely to yield impartial solutions to ethical and social questions. For one thing, orientation concepts are complex and can be understood in various ways. Is an orientation toward a certain sex, a certain gender, or both? How do nonbinary sex and gender categories fit in? Do orientations concern a person's behavior and activities, or their attractions and fantasies? What about the distinction between emotional attraction and physical attraction?

In the 1970s and 1980s, Michel Foucault's groundbreaking work on the history of sexuality argued that we conceptualize orientations in contingent and culturally specific ways. These concepts are products of culture, not nature, and thus vary from one society to another. For example, Foucault argued that in Ancient Greece there was no such thing as "gay" or "straight." Instead, there were simply acts of sexuality between same-sex or opposite-sex couples. A person might have sex one way more often than another, but this pattern of choices did not say anything about who the person was: the choice to have sex in certain ways was just that – a choice to have sex in certain ways – and did not indicate that the person themselves had any particular underlying quality.

Concepts that are contingently connected to culture are sometimes called "socially constructed." In our society, an example of a concept that is socially constructed is "married." Unlike concepts such as "having blood type A" or "being a member of the species *Homo sapiens,*" there's nothing in nature that distinguishes married people from unmarried ones, and the kinds of relationships or social institutions we might be inclined to count as being like "marriage" vary around the world. Being married doesn't mean that you have some deep natural quality, it just means you're married. It's a social category. Same thing with money. Money is a social construct: something counts as money only because we decide that it does, and different things count as money in different societies. There's no part of nature that "being a dollar" refers to; it's not a biological or physical or chemical concept. Foucault believed that our orientation concepts function similarly, emerging in a certain way out of a specific social context.

From a scientific point of view, while research into the nature of orientations began in the 1860s, the first major tools developed to assess orientation for purposes of research were the Kinsey Scale, introduced in 1948, and the subsequent Klein Sexual Orientation Grid, developed in the 1970s (Galupo et al. 2014). Interestingly, Kinsey's scale was developed in part to illustrate that sexuality does not fall neatly into separate categories of heterosexual or exclusively homosexual but rather forms a continuum. In assessing orientations, Kinsey asked people about both experiences and fantasies, and he did not use his scale to imply that these would correlate with being a specific kind of person. He specifically avoided using orientation labels like "gay" and "bisexual" as nouns (Galupo et al. 2014: 406), showing his reluctance to think of people as falling squarely into one category or another.

In keeping with an emphasis on sexual diversity and fluidity, Klein's later classification system considers various dimensions, distinguishing among factors like sexual attraction, emotional preference, self-identification, and community. People are asked questions not only about past experience but also about an idealized future – what they hope or wish to do. Kinsey and Klein's focus on sexuality as continuous, fluid, and difficult to label is at odds with how orientation labels are used today, both in ordinary life and in scientific research, where it has become common to simply lump people together into categories like "gay," "straight," and "bisexual."

In a recent philosophical analysis, Robin Dembroff (2016) calls attention to the fact that typical ways of categorizing orientation concepts not only assume binary sex and gender categories, they also collapse the distinction between sex and gender. Terminology like "gay" or "same sex" implies people have a single sex/gender in the binary and also elides the possibility that we might be attracted to someone because of their gender characteristics or because of their sex characteristics. Orientation, Dembroff concludes, must be "bidimensional" to allow for either or both of these possibilities.

The legal theorist Ed Stein (2011) argues that partly because of these kind of complexities, when we talk about the questions raised by the "born that way" and "not a choice" arguments and the relationship between science and politics, we're interested in distinct matters that it's easy to run together. We might be interested in whether orientations are biological or socially constructed. We might be interested in whether orientations are genetic or environmental in origin. We might be interested in whether orientations are fixed qualities that a person cannot change, or whether they are more like choices, aspects of the self that can be changed.

It's easy to confuse these questions, but in fact they are importantly different. For example, to ask whether something is biological or socially constructed is different from asking whether it is genetic or environmental. Consider the effects of lead poisoning. A person who gets lead poisoning gets it from their environment. But it's not a cultural construct. A person who has it has a real biological condition with particular risk factors – it's not at all a question of how we think about it, and it's not something that would vary from one culture to another. Another example concerns the way the environment of the uterus affects development before birth: this is an environmental and not genetic matter, but it is also a biological one. Orientations do not have to be genetic or inborn to be real biological qualities. It's doubtful that orientations function like lead poisoning, but the examples show that a quality that is environmental can also be biological. There is no neat divide between "nature" and "nurture."

Being genetic or biological is also different from being unchangeable: "born that way" and "not a choice" are two different things. A condition can come from any number of sources and still be impossible to change. Stein (2011) points out that there is some evidence that sexual orientations are very difficult, if not impossible, to change. But to know this does not require biological or scientific research on "genes" or causes – all it requires us to know is that orientations are the kind of quality that people experience in a certain kind of way. If unchangeability – "not a choice" – is what we're interested in, then research into biological or genetic causes of orientation is really beside the point. It doesn't tell us what we need to know.

Given all of these distinctions, it's interesting to consider whether orientations can be both socially constructed and also unchangeable. This might seem counterintuitive. If a concept is shown to be socially constructed, then you might think it is not really "real" or objective – thus undercutting the idea that a person could really have this or that orientation. Foucault's idea that orientations might be socially constructed is sometimes interpreted in this way. If orientations aren't biological, the thinking goes, then it can't be true of anyone that they are "gay" or "straight." How can an orientation be unchangeable if orientations do not exist?

Against this, it's important to realize that concepts that are socially constructed are still real in a sense. Whether a person is married has big legal and social implications for their life, even if marriage is a socially constructed concept. Money is a socially constructed concept, but whether you have money has huge consequences for your life and for how you live. And the same goes for other socially constructed concepts. As we'll discuss in Chapter 10, even though "races" are not biological concepts, people are socially racialized: they are treated as members of certain races, and this has powerful and real effects on their lives.

Sexual orientations may seem different – unlike race and money, they're not quite things society dictates for you. But there could still be ways that our social world constrains what orientations people can be. For example, your preferences might be stable and directed in a certain way even though the concept of orientation is a social one. One way this might be true is if people cannot change whom they are attracted to, but if, living in a society with different categories, they would interpret their own desires and attractions differently. In our society there is huge pressure to decide: are you gay or straight or lesbian or bi or what? And despite the complexity of orientations discussed above, it's common to lump people together into the basic and broad categories of "gay," "straight," and "bisexual." Remember how Foucault said that in Ancient Greece people didn't really think in terms of orientations – there were just people who did certain things, but those actions weren't thought to reflect something deep or important about who they were. In a society without orientation concepts, you might still have the same pattern of desire, but you wouldn't come to see yourself in a certain way. But in our society, this is very difficult – people are always asking you to categorize yourself.

Issues like these mean it is probably impossible to separate the scientific investigation of orientations from our moral and social beliefs about them. Our understanding of orientation is complex, and so also are the questions we might be interested in when we study orientations scientifically. There is no simple way to go from a biological basis for orientations to simple conclusions about how desire and attraction function in our lives.

The "born that way" and "not a choice" arguments: ethical and political complexities

From an ethical and political point of view, things are even more complicated. As Stein (2011) points out, most basically, many of the things LGBTQ+ people want to do to live their lives – like marry or date certain people – really are a matter of choice, even if orientation itself is not. Engaging in queer sex, identifying publicly as a person with a certain orientation, living in a family with a specific partner, raising children as an open LGBTQ+ person – all of these are things people choose to do. Regardless of your orientation, it is a choice to set up house with someone, it's a choice to come out as LGBTQ+, it's a choice to have a family that falls outside the cis-heterosexual norm. At a basic level, it's even a choice to have sex at all. Indeed, many religious people counsel that if one experiences attraction outside the heterosexual norm, the thing to do is simply to not act on it. As Stein says, it is possible live a "celibate, closeted, single, and childless" life (2011: 639). Forming family relationships, having children, and living publicly as LGBTQ+ people are all choices. But protecting and validating these choices are central to LGBTQ+ politics in the contemporary world.

So the ethical and political issues go beyond innateness and unchangeability. What's at stake is not just having the orientation but also living a certain way. And living a certain way is, in fact, a choice. The "born that way" and "not a choice" arguments don't have anything to say about these choices – since they are, in fact, choices. The ethical claim, Stein (2011) suggests, is that these are the kinds of choices that should be respected; politically, we should have equal rights to make choices based on whatever orientation we have. The arguments about orientations being inborn and immutable have no bearing on this central ethical issue and in fact may distract from it.

Furthermore, some important aspects of orientation itself have elements of choice. As Kinsey and Klein emphasized, some people experience patterns of attraction and desire that are more fluid and open to change than others. As Cynthia Nixon's remarks show, bisexual people also make a choice to have sex with the same sex. Bisexual people are attracted to both men and women. So any time they have sex with same-sex partners, this is, in some sense, making a choice. Finally, some women make a political choice to have sex only with other women. We've talked in previous chapters about the relentless pressure women feel to objectify themselves. In some relationships, men are able to exert control over women in the household – using physical abuse or emotional pressure to enforce a role as primary decision-maker. For these and a wide range of other reasons, some women decide that they cannot live as full human beings if they live in intimate contact with men, and so they decide to have sex with women. This is a choice. Seeing orientations less as fixed categories and more on a continuum may be important to our cultural and political self-conception. For example, the poet and activist Adrienne Rich (1980) proposes that all women exist along a kind of lesbian continuum that they move in and out of, depending on how their relationships with other women evolve, and that women need to understand themselves primarily in relation to other women is necessary before they can engage in heterosexual relationships and still be themselves. This suggests an interplay between desire and self-understanding in which we may make choices about how to understand ourselves.

Some scholars have taken this line of thought further still and have argued that there is generally an element of choice to sexual orientation itself. William Wilkerson (2009) focuses on the idea of interpretation, pointing out that people must interpret their own feelings and desires to come to conclusions about their own sexuality, in the process making many choices. When we interpret, we decide what has significance and what doesn't, we make choices about how we think some things are related to other things, and we assign meaning to experiences and emotions, to understand what we think they signify.

As a really simple example, suppose you find yourself feeling sexually aroused when in a certain circumstance – perhaps when you're with a certain friend doing a certain activity. It is not obvious what significance to attach to this arousal. It might mean you are sexually attracted to your friend. Or it might mean that the activity is one that excites you in a way you don't quite understand. Maybe being with your friend makes you feel sexually attractive to others, and this turns you on. Maybe your friend is attractive to others, which makes people pay attention to you in a new way, and this is arousing. There are many possibilities. It's not until you've had other experiences, assigned those experiences a certain kind of significance, and reflected – thus interpreting – that you can come to even tentative conclusions about what it means for your sexuality.

Wilkerson points out that if our orientations were obvious and clear, then it would be impossible to be in denial or mistaken about them, and yet people often are. Because of our society's taking "straight" as a default, this is most common for people who come out as gay or lesbian or bisexual. Before coming to grips with their orientation, gays and lesbians may experience feelings and desires for people of the same sex that they try to "explain away" – imagining, for example, that the arousal and desire are really prompted by something else, or by thoughts of something else, rather being directed at same-sex partners. But if orientations didn't require interpretation, they would be obvious to us – it would be impossible to be deceived or in denial about them.

Crucially, self-interpretation happens in a social context. As we saw in the previous section, when we interpret ourselves, the orientations we choose from are the ones our society makes available to us, the ones it sees as making sense. We live in a world where there are certain orientations to choose from, and where people are often asked to pigeonhole their sexual experience into a specific pattern or box. Those boxes might not always fit our feelings and experiences.

An old episode of the sitcom *30 Rock* offers a useful example. The show is about a team of writers and performers who make a TV comedy show, and in one episode, Frank, a writer who is kind of a guy's guy – the kind of guy who wears trucker hats with slogans on them and doesn't shave – meets a young cute coffee-delivery guy, Jamie. Frank thinks of himself as straight, but he says, "That guy is adorable. Maybe I am gay – for that little peach. I wanna kiss him on the mouth. I wanna hold him. I want Jamie." He's so taken with Jamie that he keeps vying for his attention, even though Jamie is not interested. Later, his friend Liz tells him to stop it, and Frank says, "I can't. I'm gay for Jamie," and Liz responds, "No, that's not a thing. You can't be gay for just one person." Frank replies, "I got some real thinking to do. It's scary, but also exciting."

Liz's comment reflects something true about our culture that we don't often talk about: we don't accept that you can be gay for just one person. But why not? Why couldn't a person be attracted almost always to the opposite sex, then develop a passionate crush on one member of the same sex? Why don't we have a concept for that? Someone like Frank either has to buck the trends and be a true individualist or has to figure out more clearly how his attraction to Jamie fits in with everything else.

In response to Wilkerson's argument, it might be pointed out that just because there are various ways of seeing similarities and differences among desires doesn't mean that orientations themselves are radically unfixed. For example, Esa Díaz-León (2017) says that there is a difference between saying that desires can be interpreted in a number of ways and saying that there is no underlying reality about them. Among other things, even a person who can find various plausible ways to interpret their desires might also know that some interpretations are definitely false. Imagine a man who finds themselves uncertain about their pattern of arousal but never feels desire to have sex with a woman. Many people go through stages of uncertainty before coming to understand their own sexuality, and in our society, there is a huge amount of pressure to be straight. Young men who think they might be gay sometimes date women and have girlfriends, bowing to social pressure or hoping they might not be gay after all. If a man dated a lot of women but never felt any desire to have sex with them, describing that person as "straight" might seem to be more like a mistake or a mislabeling than an "alternative interpretation." This opens up the possibility that while there is an element of choice to interpretation, those choices are also constrained. Some interpretations just are not on the table.

With respect to the ways that some orientation concepts become socially available while others do not, scientific research can reinforce the ways that concepts become cemented in our culture. In his work on human natural kinds, Ian Hacking (1999) has called people "interactive kinds" – he says that, unlike frogs or plants or planets, people change when you study them, as a result of being studied. It's interesting to think about the effects scientific research on orientations has had in making us think of them as real. Imagine you grew up thinking in other terms than "gay" "straight" etc., and you were volunteering to be in a study about the biology of orientations. The first thing they might ask you is your orientation. You might decide, on reflection, to interpret your desires and patterns of attraction in certain way – and boom! All of a sudden, a person who didn't have an orientation has one. This shows how the social categories available to us can have a profound effect on how we see ourselves.

Orientations and values of sex and love

A further problem with the "born that way" and "not a choice arguments" is that some qualities that are innate and unchangeable do not engender respect or even tolerance. Suppose a person is born with a propensity toward violent behavior, and this propensity is very difficult to get rid of. Or maybe someone has a pattern of sexual desire in which they are excited by seeing other people being hurt or forced to have sex they do not want. No one would say that because these people are "born that way" and it's "not a choice," they should be encouraged to act on these patterns and desires in order to be "who they really are." Instead, they would be expected to stop acting in ways that hurt other people.

This further illustrates how the question of what deserves respect versus condemnation cannot be based on biology or unchangeability alone but must involve some value judgments. What matters is seeing LGBTQ+ ways of life as valuable and good. In fact, in a social context of negative attitudes toward LGBTQ+ people, the linking of an orientation with innateness and biology could have dramatic negative implications, encouraging people to see the quality as a defect to be eliminated not a quality to be respected. Stein (2011) tells the story of the gay-rights activist Magnus Hirschfeld who tried to use the "born that way" argument in early twentieth-century Germany to further the cause of equality for LGBTQ+ people. Late in life, Hirschfeld said his project had failed dramatically – that his use of the "born that way" argument had contributed to the persecution of gay people by lending credence to the idea of them as biologically defective. Seeing gayness as innate made it seem more like a birth defect or inborn disorder – the opposite of what was intended.

It is instructive in this context to consider the example of Alan Turing, the brilliant logician who invented many of the concepts of modern computing and proved some deep mathematical theorems. He worked for the British government during the war at the famous Bletchley Park, where he was central to the successful effort to break German codes and defeat the Nazis. Turing was gay, and since sex between men was criminal in 1952, he was prosecuted for the crime of homosexuality. He was given a choice between prison and chemical castration – which entailed the injection of estrogen, reducing his sex drive and potential for sexual arousal – and chose the castration. Turing killed himself two years later – at least, he died from eating an apple laced with cyanide, and an inquest determined it had been a suicide.

In 2009, Britain officially apologized for "the appalling way" that Turing had been treated, and he was granted a posthumous pardon in 2013. The choice to grant Turing a pardon was controversial because it seemed to suggest that Turing was specifically deserving of pardon. After all, what about all the other people who were convicted of homosexuality in Britain at that time? The pardon just for Turing seemed to convey the idea that the law was appropriate but that he was not guilty, as opposed to saying that the law itself was unjust and an ethical violation. In response, in 2017, Britain passed the "Turing Law," which posthumously pardoned all men who died before gay sex was decriminalized and makes it possible for living convicted gay men to seek pardons for actions that are no longer illegal. To some, though, the idea of a "pardon" wrongly implies there is something to be forgiven: what they want is not a pardon but rather an apology (Dewan 2017). The Turing example fits with Stein's (2011) idea that seeing orientations as biological can lead to more persecution rather than protection of rights. In this case, the hormonal and thus biological aspect of his desire led authorities to try to eliminate that desire rather than respect it. Innateness and unchangeability can lead to the opposite of equality and respect.

Today, research on the genetic origins of sexual orientations opens the door to the possibility that people will try to find interventions to prevent their offspring from being lesbian or gay. Currently, people have prenatal tests for various disabilities like Down Syndrome, and if those tests are positive, they often choose abortion. These practices have been criticized by disability-rights activists, who point out that they amount to an attempt to eliminate a whole class of people and also reinforce the stigma and negative stereotypes associated with disability. What if you had a prenatal test for orientation? Would that be seen as a socially acceptable cause for choosing abortion? What if, instead of abortion, there was a simple method for altering the fetus so that the person would have some specific orientation? Would it be ethical to do so?

In a recent discussion of this issue, the psychologist J. Michael Bailey and his co-author Aaron Greenberg argued that if a prenatal intervention would determine the infant's future orientation, that parents should be allowed to choose, since choosing does no direct harm to anyone (Greenberg and Bailey 2001). The possibility of prenatal tests and interventions shows some limits of thinking of sex and love in terms of freedom and autonomy and the need for value judgments. If an argument for respect and equality is based simply on freedom of choice and consent, then it seems that selecting for some orientations rather than others would be permitted; it is, after all, itself an exercise of freedom of choice. Given the prevalence of homophobia, many people choosing would probably choose to select for straightness. To protect gay and lesbian identity, to really promote equality and respect, we need a positive value, and not just "acceptance," for all sexual orientations. An ethical framework that seeks to protect LGBTQ+ orientations should move beyond the rights of people to do as they please and should say something substantive about LGBTQ+ orientations as valuable. For this project, the "born that way" and "not a choice" arguments do not help and might do harm.

Conclusion

In our society, questions about sexual orientations and identities inevitably have political overtones because of the long history of persecution to which sexual minorities have been subjected. That history has encouraged many theorists and activists to look to science for answers; if orientations are matters of birth rather than choice, that would seem to provide solid arguments against discrimination. But this chapter has explored the problems with the "born that way" and "not a choice" arguments. Much of what is most important in LGBTQ+ sex and love is a matter of choice; we need positive values to showcase why these choices are worthy not only of rights against discrimination but also of respect and validation. The person who chooses LGBTQ+ sex and love is just as deserving of, and just as much in need of, political recognition and protection as the person with an inborn or unchangeable pattern of desire. This need for positive values illustrates how frameworks of personal autonomy and free choice can be insufficient for addressing the ethical and political questions of LGBTQ+ rights and respect.

9 Love and marriage

Introduction

Especially in contemporary contexts, marriage is a multilayered, complex set of practices. Marriage is a social and cultural institution, a way a community chooses to conceptualize partnership and family life. Marriage is also a legal entity, embedded in a system that accords specific legal rights and obligations to the married. Marriage is also highly personal, involving an intimate commitment to care for and love the other person. These different meanings of marriage fit awkwardly with one another, and there are also questions arising within each conceptualization.

For example, if marriage is a promise or contract, then how do we deal with the fact that love and commitment are sometimes things that are beyond our control? What happens when love fades? If we see marriage as an institution, how do we deal with its roots in patriarchal societies, where marriage often created gendered and unequal distributions? Can marriage be changed to fit with equality? If marriage creates obligations, as many people think it does, how do we deal with the fact that obligations are often antithetical to the feeling of love, especially over time?

In addressing these, it can be tempting to make marriage more flexible and personalizable, so that each person can find their own way. But, as I see it, there is an interesting tension between the idea of marriage as a shared social concept that means the same thing to everyone and the idea of marriage as something flexible and personalizable. On the one hand, embracing a fixed sense of marriage means that marriage might not work as well for some people as others; it also means we risk carrying along outdated social norms. On the other hand, there are risks associated with flexibility: people may disagree about the right interpretation, leading to mismatched expectations or disappointment. Also, with too much flexibility, we may lose the special bindingness often associated with helping married people get through difficult times. This tension is an example of how new problems and questions arise when we take marriage out of a traditional context – in which marriage is patriarchal, heterosexual, and typically lifelong – into a more modern individualistic and equal one.

The nature of marriage

As we saw in our discussion of love, historians say that it's only relatively recently in Western history that romantic love became an important component of marriage. Before then, marriage was primarily focused on building appropriate practical and political bonds – it was most important that the marriage partner be a suitable person, someone you could trust, a person who would keep up their ends of various family-related obligations. It was around the seventeenth century that people began seeing romantic love as important to marriage (Coontz 2006). Marriage also used to involve more of a permanent commitment, with divorce only possible in cases of serious problems like cruelty or abandonment. Divorce is still expensive and complicated, but it has become much easier and more commonplace than it used to be. Starting in the late twentieth century, people started discussing the nature and point of marriage a lot, because of the widespread shift in many places from thinking of marriage as only appropriate for heterosexual partnerships to seeing it as appropriate for all partnerships.

One of the many contested questions about marriage is whether it is primarily an institutional matter, related to laws and policies, or whether it is primarily a private matter, something two people make an agreement or contract about. Marriage might seem like a contract: a promise or agreement between people to do certain things. But the image of marriage as a contractual promise raises several puzzles. For one thing, we usually think of promises as things that must be kept. But if marriage is a promise, this would mean that unilateral divorce – divorce in which one person decides to leave another – would always be unethical. While the decision to divorce is often regarded with sorrow, and might be prohibited within certain religions, it is generally not seen as an immoral action. In addition, the society and the state often intervene in family matters, for legitimate reasons. Some of the burdens and benefits of marriage concern society at large. Spouses, for example, have extra visitation rights in hospitals and do not have to testify against one another in court; they may be required to provide health care or other services to the partner. How would a private promise make sense of these facts? Finally, if marriage is a contract, it is a strange one, because it is completely open-ended. Rather than an agreement to do this or that particular thing, it's an agreement to love and stay committed to the other person – no matter what happens.

On the other hand, it can also seem strange to think of marriage as an institutional affair. Some of the burdens associated with marriage may be ones we want to opt out of. For example, marriage laws say that marriage requires sexual exclusivity: to have sex with someone outside of marriage is seen as a violation. As we discuss further in Chapter 14, in some jurisdictions in North America adultery is against the law. But what if individual people do not want to arrange things this way? If marriage is a personal promise, this is easy to accommodate, but from the institutional view of marriage it is more difficult. Does this mean we cannot have marriage on our own terms?

Is marriage a promise?

When you think of marriage as a promise, one of the first questions that you might ask is what, exactly, you are promising. In many Western marriage ceremonies, the vows exchanged include a promise to love and stay committed to the other person forever, "till death do us part," as they say. But is this possible? How can you promise to love someone for ever, if love is beyond our conscious control? How can we promise to stay committed, when we know that our commitments and priorities might change as time goes on?

Some people think there's something absurd about promising to love, on grounds that love can fade, and there's nothing you can really do about it. In our discussion of theories of love, we saw how even though the union theory and the concern theory had a lot to say about how, once you were in love or bonded together, you would have reason to do this or that thing, they didn't have much to say about the falling in love, or, notably, about falling out of love. If romantic love is wanting to form a union, what happens when you no longer feel that feeling, no longer want to be part of that union? If love is volitional, what happens when those volitions are no longer part of who you are because you just don't feel that way about the other person anymore? How can you promise to do something that is outside your control? It would be like promising not to be bitten by mosquitoes.

Commitment might seem simpler, on grounds that it's more a thing you "do" than a thing you "feel." You might promise to stay married, to honor your partner's various wishes, and so on. Unlike the amorphous "feeling of love," these are choices you can make and carry through on intentionally. Even with commitment, though, matters are complex. Honoring previous commitments requires staying committed to the goals that they encapsulate, and sometimes those goals change. Then how can you honor the commitment? If you form a commitment to stay together forever, for certain reasons that are important to you at the time, and then later you cease to care about those reasons, you may find yourself unable to keep your commitment.

From one point of view, these kinds of considerations suggest that you can't, or shouldn't, promise unending love or commitment, because they are things you can't make happen in the first place. Normally, people shouldn't promise things they know they can't make happen, and especially things they know are going to be difficult. And unending love and commitment are very difficult!

In fact, they've begun to seem implausible as well as difficult, because there are very good reasons to think you'll be unable to carry them out. Now that divorce is easier to obtain and less stigmatized, the divorce rate in North America is between 40 and 50 percent. That means almost half of all people who make promises of unending love and commitment fail to keep those promises. Assuming you are typical, your odds of failing are pretty good. Anyone knowing this would have to contemplate the possibility that they, too, will get divorced. So how can they make a lifelong commitment, knowing that divorce is so common? All of those other people also promised to stay together for ever, and yet they failed.

Elizabeth Brake (2011) says that promising to love is sufficiently odd that you can't even do it. Even if you say the right-sounding words, and pronounce "I promise ...", you haven't really succeeding in making a promise, because you can't make a promise when the outcome is beyond your control. Imagine: could you promise not to shoot yourself when playing Russian roulette? Could you promise not to die if you do a bungee jump with a frayed cord? What about promising to succeed in a surgical operation, or baking a soufflé? Suppose someone you care about is bungee jumping with a frayed cord, in a place where there have been known deaths in the past few months. You beg them not to do it. "Don't jump! You might hurt yourself! Please!" and in response the person says "Oh, don't worry. You're being silly! I promise I won't get hurt." I think this response would feel cynical and manipulative, and certainly wouldn't feel like a promise. It would feel more like they're just looking for a way to shut you up. I agree with Brake that if you know you have a 50 percent chance of failing, you can't really promise to succeed. All you can promise is to do your best.

In response to this it might be said that marriage promises are different from bungee jumping because the variables are internal rather than external. A frayed bungee cord is something completely beyond your control. But your feelings of love are part of you. So maybe despite that 50-percent failure rate, you have reason to believe that in love, you will be special. "I'll be in the 50 percent of successes. I promise!"

But I think that even with these internal variables, there are reasons to think you can't promise when the odds of failure are high. Think of other cases where people promise to do difficult things and the challenge is due to internal, personal factors. For example, suppose your friend oversleeps all the time and finds it really hard to get up early. They're used to sleeping in every day, and when they have to get up early they succeed only about half the time. You know they are constantly missing early meetings and getting in trouble for lateness at work or school. Now imagine that you need an early ride to the airport, and your friend feels they owe you a favor, and so they begin insisting that they'll pick you up at 6:00 a.m. You might think, "No – this is ridiculous. You always oversleep!" You might argue with your friend, saying "You can't make a promise like that. You're always oversleeping!" Now imagine that your friend says, "Yeah, I know I never get up on time. But tomorrow I'll be there, I promise. Even though I've never got up before 9:00 in my whole life, and even though I've slept through my alarm about half of all mornings this year, I'll be there. I promise!" I don't know how you'd feel, but I'd be inclined to regard this as an annoying and hypocritical failure of self-knowledge rather than a genuine promise to do something helpful.

Against this perspective on promises, Susan Mendus (1984) says that a promise isn't a prediction of success: of course, people can always fail. If guaranteed success were required, we would never promise anything. A promise, she says, is more like a statement of intention. Especially with long-term promises, you're not predicting that something will absolutely happen, you're signaling what your current state of mind is. Your current state of mind is that you intend to carry out the action. More dramatically, Mendus says that a commitment to "try" or "do your best" isn't enough and signals a lack of seriousness about what is going to happen. You can, she says, be unconditionally committed to your spouse, even while acknowledging that you might give up that commitment in the future. Your state of mind is: "I promise to love and to honour and in so doing I cannot now envisage anything happening such as would make me give up that commitment" (1984: 247). After all, even though a lot of people divorce, a lot of people do stay married.

From this perspective, promising to love and honor someone just means expressing that you find yourself surely and squarely expecting to find yourself among the people who succeed. With promising interpreted this way, it seems like only a cold-hearted or unprincipled person would refuse. What kind of love is it where the person is already imagining and foreseeing the end of the relationship? What unprincipled person is unwilling to even state an intention over something so important? Imagine you are in love and talking about marriage and commitment, and you say, "I will love and honor you – I know life is complicated but I can't imagine anything that would make me give that up" and the other person says something like "Well … I can't say the same. Who knows what will happen? Who knows what kind of person I will be in the future"? In this case refusing to even state an intention might be like declaring they can already see the beginning of the end. It's either very cold or very flippant. What kind of lover is already thinking about when love will end – and not just thinking about it but also planning for it?

Brake (2011) disagrees with Mendus's idea that a promise is more like a statement of intention. For one thing, she says, we generally expect one another to actually keep our promises. An intention isn't really sufficient. I think this point of view is supported by our earlier example of the oversleeper. What if that person said to you, "Yes, I know I always oversleep. But I have every intention of being there for you bright and early, and I cannot now foresee anything that will cause me to be late. Of course, I can't predict the future! But right now I have every intention of being there." I would probably roll my eyes at this. Sure, the person may have good intentions. But if they're not going to be able to follow through, they shouldn't promise.

Furthermore, Brake says that it is not cold-hearted or unloving to rationally contemplate the possibility that love may end. You can hope that it will not, while recognizing that it might. In fact, she says, if a marriage promise forces a denial of the mere possibility that love will end, then it is intrinsically delusional. And delusional people are in no situation to be making big decisions – like the decision to get married!

For her part, Brake says that marriage vows aren't really promises at all. They can't be, since you can only promise what you can control. It's interesting to consider the question: if Brake is right that wedding vows don't succeed in making promises to love, does that mean we shouldn't state those vows as promises? In that case, should we state other promises instead? Or say something else entirely?

These practical questions are where things get complicated. Our first reaction might be, "Well, so what if vows are not really promises?" Wedding vows are traditional statements, intended to convey love and caring. Brake and Mendus agree that those getting married intend to stay together and love one another forever, whether or not they can really promise to. Sometimes people who get married don't give any thought at all to what they'll be saying during the ceremony, trusting instead that the person running things will just tell them what to say. The fact that these people aren't particularly concerned with the details might suggest that what seem like "vows" aren't really intended as vows or promises at all. They're more like a bit of nice-sounding boilerplate, or more like poetry than a promise. Maybe, even though the statements have the form of statements of promise, the true, underlying meaning is more like Mendus's "I love you, and I can't now imagine anything that will happen to that love, and I intend to love you forever and do the things that will foster that love. I will do my best."

But, as I see it, there is one big problem with that analysis, and that is that it opens the door to huge misunderstandings on the part of the people getting married – which is, of course, a highly significant undertaking. What if you have two people stating vows, and one of them is thinking "Oh, it's just nice-sounding words meaning I'll stick around and do my best," but the other one is thinking "We are truly promising to stay toge-ther no matter what! After all, that's what the vows say, and vows are serious business." This seems like a potential disaster, with two people having different ideas about what exactly they were conveying to one another about the future. If your intended spouse said, "Sure, of course, I'll stay faithful to you," and they really meant, "Well, I'll do my best," you might regard them as a bad and manipulative person. This example highlights one way that flexibility – in this case, in how the formal vows are interpreted – is in tension with the idea of marriage as a shared social concept. Sure, people are free to interpret their own vows as they think best. But if the people getting married aren't on the same page about that interpretation, that's a problem.

For these reasons, it might be better to insist on honesty and modesty in wedding vows: "I can't promise to love you forever, but I will do my best." I do wonder whether these kinds of honest vows would seem awkward, especially in the context of an elaborate ceremony. Imagine you're getting married, and it's a fancy wedding, and you're up there in front of all those people, all dressed up in your wedding clothes, and you say to one another: "I love you and nothing I can see now will ever change that; I'll try to stay with you and love you. Even though I can't promise success, I will try to do my best." That's honest. But does it sound a bit peculiar? Of course, you can always avoid this dilemma by choosing not to marry at all.

At the end of her paper, Brake describes some advice from *Brides* magazine on wedding vows (2011: 38):

> "Write your vows separately and keep them secret from each other until your wedding day, which will up the emotional factor ...
> Set a 30-second time limit – this will force you to really think about what you're saying and make each word count."

As she says, "This secrecy and brevity seem like bad policy." I agree!

Gender and the institution of marriage

We've seen how the view of marriage as a promise opens the door to varying interpretations of what, exactly, is being promised. Seeing marriage as an institution might seem to better support the shared social concept. To examine whether this is so, let's first take a step back and look at the kind of institution marriage is thought to be and whether it is functioning in our lives the way we want it to. In 1996, Claudia Card wrote an article provocatively titled "Against Marriage and Motherhood." At that time, the United States was starting on progress toward marriage equality and same-sex marriage rights; against this backdrop, Card chose her title to showcase the possibility that because of the kind of institution marriage is in our society, the fight for marriage rights could obliterate or obscure a radical feminist critique of existing marriage and family life relationships.

Understanding that critique requires first examining "radical feminism" itself. There are many strands of feminism, and several can be understood as "radical," but basically radical feminism sees the set-up of society as oppressive to women. Thus, that set-up must change radically. "Liberal" feminism, to which radical feminism is often contrasted, emphasizes the importance of individual choices and sees the protections of individual freedoms as crucially important. As in our discussion of the "liberal" perspective on sex work, the word "liberal" here has its traditional core philosophical meaning of being in favor of individual freedom of choice and not the meaning its come to have in "liberal" versus "conservative."

Rather than shifting away from existing social structures, liberal feminism often aims to increase choices and promote equality within those structures, for example through laws protecting reproductive choices and banning gender discrimination.

Radical feminism's critique sees patriarchal gender relations and resulting injustice as essentially harmful to women and points to the necessity of changing not only legal structures or the distribution of money and goods but also social relations – and especially gendered social relations – at a fundamental level. While liberal feminists promote individual rights, radical feminists are more likely to think that "individualism" might be part of the problem. From the radical feminist point of view, the kinds of change that can happen through legal change and equality of rights is somewhat limited: if part of the problem is in people's deeply held attitudes and their associated practices, social progress of all kinds will require deeper forms of change. Though each form of feminism is multifaceted, liberal feminists are more likely to seek equality in the sense of equal rights, protections, and status to men's rights, protections, and status, while radical feminists are more likely to think that women, being different from men, might require different rights, protections, and status – and even a radically different organization of society – to lead flourishing lives.

It's important to realize that the specialness of such rights and protections does not mean "special" in the sense of "greater" – feminism is not about saying women are better or more deserving than men. And many radical feminists would say that their idea of "social progress" would include changes that are good not only for women but also for men. Everyone in our society finds themselves affected by deep and pervasive attitudes about gender roles. Men are expected to be tough, to be successful breadwinners, to be strong; women are expected to be nurturing, passive, caring. The more these roles and expectations are entrenched, radical feminists sometimes point out, the worse things are for everyone. No one can really be themselves, everyone must act as something they're not. For people to live good lives, in this view, a deep reordering of how people relate to one another is required.

To see the difference between radical and liberal feminisms, let's look at the example of the "gender wage gap," which refers to the fact that women earn less, on average, than men. In the United States, the gap is about 22 percent, which means that for every $1.00 earned by a male worker, a female worker earns 78 cents (O'Brien 2015). This is an "unadjusted" wage gap, which means it does not control for factors like women having different kinds of jobs: some of the gap is due to the fact that more women are in lower-paying jobs like being a nurse and more men are in higher-paying jobs like being a surgeon. When adjusted for factors such as job position, total hours worked, number of children, and the frequency at which unpaid leave is taken, the wage gap in the US is between 4 and 7 percent; this is the part due to factors like discrimination. The total, or unadjusted, wage gap is thought to be caused by various factors beyond discrimination, including women choosing or needing to leave and re-enter the workforce in order to meet family caregiving responsibilities, occupational segregation in historically undervalued and low-paying jobs, such as childcare and clerical work, traditionally lower levels of education, and less unionization among female workers. For our discussion, the difference in family caregiving responsibilities is the most salient of these.

In an innovative analysis of choices, family life, and oppression, Ann Cudd (1994) points out that one reason women do more caring work is pretty straightforward: in heterosexual couples, because of the wage gap itself, it often makes more financial sense for the woman to do more childcare and the man to work harder at his job. A heterosexual couple who share equal career aspirations but also want one parent to stay at home while their kids are small will generally be better off financially if the man goes to work – because of the wage gap, he'll be likely to make more money. This factor then perpetuates the wage gap, because leaving and re-entering the workforce is just the kind of thing that leads to lower earnings over time. While the choice is rational overall, the woman's income is adversely affected.

A liberal feminist might have the goal of equal wages, brought about by fighting discrimination, and perhaps also through initiatives like improved day care or mandated paternity leave for new fathers. But a radical feminist might focus attention differently, on the ways the problems go beyond basic wage inequality and thus beyond financial and legal matters. They might point out the deeply ingrained and gendered social expectation that women will stay home with children, and they may think it's important to challenge that social expectation. They might add that our society values work outside the home more than it values caring for others: work outside the home often brings prestige and status along with money and transferrable skills, while taking care of others is seen as low-status "women's work." If caring work were properly valued, perhaps we'd come to see "wages" as an unacceptably narrow indicator of well-being.

Some radical feminists have imagined a utopia in which childcare is shared by everyone equally: instead of parents taking care of their biological children, everyone would care for all the children. Shulamith Firestone argued in the 1970s that women would not be truly equal and free until technology freed them from their biological roles in pregnancy and childbirth: only when gestation could happen outside the body would women be generally free from what she considered the "barbaric" experiences of pregnancy and birth.

In her analysis of marriage, Card notes that the word "family" comes from the Latin word *familia* meaning "household," which itself came from the word *famulus*, which itself once meant "servant." Historically, women were people, like servants, over whom other people just had control – to order around, to abuse if they felt like it. From the point of view of radical feminism, traditional family roles, in which women stay home with children and are thus dependent on men and men's earnings, can't help but recreate this same problematic connection to control and abuse. And monogamy, which is socially enforced more for women than for men, can be seen as another societal tool for controlling women, by controlling their sexuality and tying them to sex with one man for ever, as if she belonged to him.

As we've seen in earlier chapters, some radical feminists become lesbians to avoid recreating the pattern of heterosexual domination in traditional relationships. Gay men, too, have challenged the status quo, with some directing their energies less toward conventional parity with straight people – in the form of marriage, adoption rights, and so on – and more toward a radical reconfiguring of society (Warner 2000). Sexuality, in this reconfiguration, might be more open and free, so that anyone could have sex freely with whomever they pleased, promiscuity would be as worthy of respect as monogamy, and sex would be freed from the secrecy and oppressive social rules of our current way of life. It's easy to see how these "radical" perspectives might resist pushing toward marriage equality, which is really aimed at joining and supporting an existing conventional social institution. If marriage is a flawed institution that perpetuates social injustice, destroys love, and functions coercively, why should we expand it? It would be better to get rid of it altogether.

Furthermore, an institution of marriage that confers benefits on married people might be coercive to those who need those benefits. Marriage is associated with a wide range of benefits impossible to get in any other way. Workplace benefits are extended to spouses of employees, and even in countries where there is universal health care, there are many employment-related benefits such as long-term care insurance, medical benefits for mental health, physiotherapy, and so on. As we've seen, legal family members have "visitation rights": if someone you love is in the hospital, you might not be allowed in to visit them unless you are officially a member of the family. Before same-sex marriage, gay and lesbian people were being turned away from hospitals where they were hoping to visit their life partners, on grounds that they were not formally married. For some people, especially women, the economic benefits of marriage are such that they could not afford not to marry. If you have to marry to get these, Card suggests, this is a kind of coercion: you are, in a sense, pressured into marriage through other factors, and thus you cannot make a free choice. Your motives will always be mixed.

More pointedly, if divorce is difficult, you're trapped. As we've discussed, many women in heterosexual couples take time off from work when their children are small. It is often impossible to return to work making anything like what you would have earned if you had stayed working, and often a person in that situation makes far less. If a couple has children, a woman may feel she must stay married to keep the economic benefits of marriage, especially for her children. It is part of the current institution of marriage to make divorce difficult: expensive, risky, and time-consuming. Even spouses who, in Card's words, "have grown to hate each other" sometimes stay married because divorce is so painful, emotionally draining, and costly. If these costs and benefits are why people get or stay married, this doesn't square very well with the feelings of love and care that are usually taken to be necessary for a good marriage in the contemporary world.

With respect to divorce, though, it's interesting to consider whether there are any positive aspects to the pressure to get or stay married. The practical and legal difficulty of divorce is sometimes considered one of the positive aspects of marriage. That is because, as we've seen in our discussion of promising to love, when people spend many years together, they often go through periods when the relationship feels difficult, or their affection fades, or they begin fantasizing about being with other people. Maybe it's harder to see the romance in a relationship when there are small children, or there is a lot of hard work to do, or times are tough financially. Maybe people panic when they reach middle age, thinking they should have tried to have a wider range of experiences. If these conditions are temporary, people might be grateful for the difficulty of divorce, because they would be glad, when things improved, to have stayed with the person they made a commitment to. You'll be put off divorcing because divorce is difficult, and then having failed to divorce, you'll find yourselves staying together and perhaps finding a renewal of love and affection.

We might see this through the lens of the story of the ancient Greek king Odysseus, who was said to have told his men to tie him to the mast of their ship as they went past the "sirens." Hearing the song of the sirens was said to make people incapable of rational thought, and Odysseus wanted to prevent himself from acting irrationally and possibly throwing himself into the sea to try to join them – which would have meant death for him. So they tied him up. Indeed, as they passed by, he was said to have gone insane and struggled to break free. But his bonds held, and when they were safely out of reach, he was untied, unharmed and grateful.

The Odysseus story is often used to illustrate the idea that people who want to tie themselves to some commitment might create external conditions that will ensure they keep their commitment even if they feel like changing their minds. The difficulty of divorce might be seen in this light. People marrying know they will be tempted to break up, and so marrying is like tying yourself to the mast of a ship, making it so that you can't break up – or, at least, making it time-consuming, expensive, and stressful.

As a social institution, marriage used to be embedded in a certain set of social ideas: that sex was only appropriate within marriage, that marriage was between a man and a woman, that marriage would last until one partner died. I think this discussion highlights how many new questions and possibilities arise when we confront marriage from within a set of values based on equality, gender-neutrality, and individual autonomy. In this new context, long-standing assumptions about the nature of marriage – like the idea that marriage should come with specific legal burdens, protections, and constraints – no longer seem obvious. We pursue this theme in the next section, where we consider further the way the commitment of marriage requires certain things of us.

Is marriage bad for love?

Earlier, I suggested that the metaphor of Odysseus might help us see the good in the external constraints associated with marriage. Against this idea, though, Eric Cave (2003) says that the obligations of marriage, however you interpret them, can damage love. Even without the kind of formal institutions mentioned in the previous section, Cave says that these problems result from what he calls the "marriage bond," which is the "set of extra legal obligations" that marriage imposes on the participants. For example, we might have obligations to constrain our sexual experience with others, an obligation to share the burdens of domestic life, and an obligation to be there for the other person in times of need. Whether it's a promise or an institution, formal or informal, most of us think that getting married to another person involves some such obligations. Cave says that the way marriage generates these obligations can damage love because you have to act lovingly even when you don't feel like it. And that feeling of "have to" might make you less inclined to want to. The generosity of love gets undermined, and so love itself suffers.

If you've ever heard someone refer jokingly to their spouse as "the old ball and chain," this is a good example of what Cave is talking about. If out of love you nurture and care for your partner or constrain the kinds of romantic and sexual attention·you pay to others, you do so because of your love. But if you do those actions because you are obligated to do them by a marriage contract, then they are suddenly not your free choice. You are being forced. And if you feel forced, you may come to resent the marriage bond – and your spouse – for imposing all of these burdens on you, precisely at the moment you would like to be doing something else. Then you will love them less fully and deeply.

We might recall here our old examples from Chapters 5–7. Remember Morgan and Nico, where Nico got the job offer far away? Suppose Nico gives up the job so Morgan can continue to enjoy life in their home city. If Nico does that out of love, it will be Nico's choice, and Nico will feel good that they were able to choose an act that expresses love and caring in this way. But if Nico chooses this because they feel forced to by the marriage bond, because fostering Morgan's happiness is required, then Nico will not feel they freely chose a loving act. Instead, they'll feel that a sacrifice was demanded of them – a sacrifice Nico may well resent. This may make

Nico reassert their own independence from Morgan, damaging the love between them.

Things might be even worse for Quinn and Robin who enjoy different sexual activities. If Quinn loves to receive oral sex and Robin doesn't love to perform it but does like to make Quinn happy, imagine what would happen if they started to think of Robin's satisfying Quinn as an obligation. If performing oral sex is something Robin must do, then the loving feeling – the feeling of wanting to do it to bring Quinn pleasure and make them happy – may well would fade away. Especially for such an intimate kind of interaction, the obligation could foster a feeling of resentment rather than generosity.

Worse, marriage may leave you in doubt about whether your lover reciprocates your love. Suppose you undertake the actions required by the marriage bond out of love: you make dinner, and take care of the kids, and go see your in-laws, and help your spouse with whatever they're doing. Then suppose your spouse does things for you, too. Now you might wonder: is your spouse is doing those things out of love or out of obligation? Nico thinks, *Is Morgan being nice to me out of duty rather than love? Does Morgan resent me?* Quinn thinks, *Does Robin only perform oral sex out of obligation? Is the feeling of love gone?*

To avoid these problems, Cave proposes that instead of thinking of specific "contracts" or "promises," we should explicitly think in terms of commitments that can change over time. Use your love to inform which commitments seem right to you when. For example, you might plan to act lovingly far into the future, and form a commitment to do so, but whether you keep this commitment will depend on how you feel when the time comes. Morgan would only move for Nico if doing so reflected what they felt was the best thing to do at the time, given their love for Nico. And Robin would only perform oral sex if that reflected a loving desire to do so, to make Quinn happy.

It's interesting to notice here an echo of Frankfurt's theory of love. When Frankfurt calls love "volitional," he means that love concerns your will and intentions, and that love gives you reasons to do one thing rather than another. If one loves another, then they have reason to intentionally do things for them. It seems that if you put Cave's idea about marriage commitment together with Frankfurt's theory of love, you might get the result that if you love someone, it makes sense to reaffirm your commitment to them – where, again, this commitment then comes from inside you and what you care about, as opposed to being an external constraint imposed upon you by a promise or contract agreement. This leads to the appealing conclusion that reasons and love go together: when you act lovingly toward your spouse, you do so out of a feeling of love that gives you reason to act that way. The ball-and-chain image disappears.

It's a lovely idea. And yet, I think it's worth noticing that the "flexible commitment" interpretation of marriage doesn't say much about why you might try to stay together, or even to foster love, when times are tough and you feel love fading. In fact, it seems like when your love wobbles, there's no reason to do anything except what you already feel like doing. If you're not feeling loving at some moment, you wouldn't be obligated to try to see things from the other person's point of view, or to act lovingly even if you're not quite feeling it. Maybe a marriage bond should include the obligation to act lovingly – even when it's the last thing you want to do.

This gets into interesting questions about why people get married in the first place and what role they hope that commitment will play in their lives. As we saw with our discussion of Odysseus, for some people marriage is a way of binding themselves. Especially if you see yourself as fickle, changeable, and bad at forming lasting relationships, you might see marriage as a way of making yourself into someone who is able to form these. This is an idea we often encounter in novels and movies. A person who is ambivalent about marriage goes ahead with it not because they're confident about keeping the marriage commitment but precisely because they feel they will have trouble doing so. They hope the institution of marriage, with its attendant social meanings and obligations, will turn them into the kind of people they want to be. It's a leap of faith. These people would not be well served by flexible commitments.

Given the possibility that different people seek different things in marriage, Cave proposes that we might be best off in a society with multiple forms. Some people, who find their love is not weakened by external commitments and who want to be bound, Odysseus-style, when things get tough, might want a promise-based contractual marriage. Others, who want to feel their actions are motivated by love, might want an open-ended commitment-based marriage.

While it would be wonderful for everyone to have the kind of marriage they want, I think there might also be challenges to the idea of allowing multiple forms of marriage to coexist. What if two people who want to get married prefer different kinds of marriage? Suppose one person wants the traditional promise-based marriage and the other doesn't. I can imagine the first regarding the second as kind of a weak-minded or unloving person – someone who is just unwilling to really commit and instead wants to have their cake and eat it too. If you're the kind of person for whom the obligations seem appropriate, you might think that the whole point of marriage is to create a lasting and dependable bond, with shared expectations that you can trust the other person to carry out. If marriage includes shared obligations regarding caring actions, then isn't it a little precious to be overly concerned with whether they are done out of "love" or out of obligation? After all, many people have mixed motives even in the best of circumstances.

I can also imagine the second regarding the first as an unrealistic idealist or puritan, someone trying to shackle them for ever to some preexisting set of agreements. If you're the person whose love is destroyed by the feeling of obligation, as Cave so vividly describes, you might think the other person is asking too much and putting you in an impossible position: you do not want to create a contract or promise with obligations, but you know you are letting them down if you do not. You might regard your potential spouse as an imposer of impossible burdens. Allowing multiple forms of marriage could exacerbate these differences because it would require each relationship to confront all the possibilities head-on. Sometimes having a new option available creates a burden rather than removing one because you have to confront all of the potentially uncomfortable reasons you are choosing or not choosing it. Trying to convince your partner to adopt a less restrictive version of marriage than you would like yourself – that could feel like a sad and awkward position to be in. But trying to convince your partner to adopt a more restrictive version of marriage than you would like yourself – that could *also* be a sad and awkward position to be in!

Conclusion

Marriage is complex: if it's a promise, it's unclear what kind of promise it can be; as an institution it is embedded in gendered social norms; as a set of fixed commitments it may undermine our loving generosity toward one another. Marriage is rooted in a patriarchal past, and its meaning used to be linked to inflexible, gendered social assumptions. In exploring the issues, we've seen multiple ways that marriage and loving commitment might mean different things to different people. I've suggested, though, that embracing variability may have complex consequences, especially when people come to the marriage question with different background assumptions, desires, and life plans. It's not always easy to have social concepts work the way each person would like best.

10 Sex, love, and race

Introduction

Choices, preferences, and decisions in sex and love perpetuate racial injustice in a range of ways. As an entry point for examining some of them, we'll be focusing in this chapter on racialized preferences in sex, dating, love, and marriage. "Racialized" preferences are those that are caused by, or based on, considerations of race, and can include both aversions and attractions. Sometimes preferences that track race have to do with complex issues involving culture, ethnicity, and religion, as when people choose to marry or procreate with people like themselves for reasons having to do with the preservation of culture, the importance of a family with shared values, or the desire to raise children in a certain tradition. They're not specifically about race. In the kind of cases we'll be discussing, though, race is central to people's sexual and romantic preferences and decisions. Maybe you've heard of "yellow fever," a slang term referring to white men having a preference for dating and having sex with Asian women, or maybe you've heard people say they just don't find people of a certain race attractive. Some people specify on their online dating profiles they will not date people of a certain race.

One question we'll consider is whether racialized preferences can be innocuous expressions of taste, or whether they are generally racist or bad in some other way. An intuitive way of framing this question focuses on the causes and nature of our preferences: if preferences are based on stereotypes, or if they exoticize and objectify people, then they are wrong. As we'll see, however, these connections are contested. Sexual desires are often based on superficial characteristics and projected qualities – what makes race special? And we've seen how the ethics of objectification is contextual and complex. A different perspective on this question is oriented not toward causes but rather toward effects: as we'll see, not only are the discriminatory consequences of racialized sexual aversions a form of sexual racism, racialized sexual attraction can harm people by forcing them to wonder whether their partners see them as individuals or just as representatives of a certain race. This leads us to consider the delicate

interplay between potentially objectifying sexual desire and the non-fung-
ibility associated with love. A second set of issues has to do with whether
we have ethical obligations to make certain choices in sex and love because
of sexual injustice or to promote racial solidarity.

I'll suggest here that racialized sex and love preferences are controversial
partly because they lie at the intersection of two social norms. On the one
hand, because they are such intimate and personal domains, we tend to
think we have rights to make decisions in sex and love for our own reasons, whatever those reasons are. On the other hand, our sexual decisions
reflect and reinforce the social racial attitudes of our society, and from this
point of view can lead to social injustice and racism, which would make
them appropriately subject to ethical evaluation and criticism. Reflection
on race, sex, and love shows how dramatically these two norms can
conflict.

Race in cultural context

To discuss sex, love, and race, a basic understanding of race and racialization and the idea of a dominant race is necessary. There is widespread
agreement among scholars that race concepts are "socially constructed":
as we saw in Chapter 8, this means race concepts emerge from a social
environment and there is no biological underpinning on the basis of which
we could classify people into races. Different societies use different racial
classifications so that a person classified one way in the United States
might be classified differently in South Africa or Brazil. And there is no
set of biological factors that correlate with race. Genetic variability
between the populations of Africa or Europe or Asia is not much greater
than that within those populations (Appiah 1985: 21). For these and other
reasons, racial distinctions are typically understood to be socially rather
than biologically based.

As we also saw in Chapter 8, the fact that races are socially constructed
does not mean that races aren't "real." How the people in your society
classify you racially, and how you identify racially yourself, can have huge
implications for your life, in ways that go beyond your control, and these
effects are a matter of objective fact. Social scientists use the term "racialization" to refer to the process through which people come to be treated
as being part of one racial group rather than another. How people are
racialized varies from place to place and time to time, but within a particular society it can be inflexible and utterly out of any individual person's
control how they are racialized. In the United States and Canada, people
who have one white parent and one Black parent are typically racialized
as "Black" because of social and historical factors, whether they want to
identify that way or not. The concept of "ethnicity," which refers to cultural identification, is interconnected with that of race but the two ideas
are distinct. For example, a Korean child adopted by an Italian family,

who grows up in Italy, will likely experience herself as having Italian ethnicity, growing up speaking Italian and eating Italian food, but if she moves to Canada as an adult, she will likely be racialized as Asian.

Our modern race concepts have to be understood in connection with the social and political history in which they emerged. Broadly speaking, the concepts of race we use in North America emerged in connection with European imperialism, colonialism, and slavery. The details are complex, but basically Europeans invading and colonizing other societies used race concepts to justify to their actions: since they saw the white race as inherently superior, they felt entitled to enslave, dominate, and control people they racialized as not-white. Previously, other distinctions, such as religious ones, had been seen as more central. European imperialists then used race concepts to categorize the people they encountered in other places, introducing hierarchical judgments based on how close physiognomy and appearance was to their white ideal. In this historical sociopolitical context, the racial categories that emerged were hierarchical, with the white race understood to be superior to others, thus justifying imperialist attitudes and colonialist actions (Taylor 2013). The idea of the supremacy of the white race persists today, as do many effects of historical oppression. Because of implicit and explicit racism, in North America white people are generally better employed and wealthier than people of other races, and whiteness is seen as normal, a "default" from which other races are seen as deviations. In this sense, white is a dominant race in our society: as we'll see below, this dominance plays a role in how we understand racialized preferences in sex and love.

Racism has to be understood against this backdrop of how race concepts emerged, what races are, how people are racialized, and the idea of a dominant race. There is a lot of debate over how to define racism, but for our context it is useful to consider Tommie Shelby's (2002) idea that racism is fundamentally about what beliefs a person has. Beliefs are racist when they buy into or perpetuate the beliefs associated with the ideology embedded in European imperialism and the slave trade: for example, that white people are naturally superior to people of other races, or that "darker" races have inherent or biological characteristics that render them inferior, or that this justifies the exploitation and domination of other races by the white race. This helps explain why racial stereotypes are racist: the stereotype of Black people as lazy or of Asian people as deferential wrongs people by inappropriately generalizing, but it also wrongs them by propping up an ideology that white people are superior. Whether Shelby is right that racism is fundamentally about beliefs is contested (see, e.g., Garcia 1996). For our purposes, it is the contextualization in social and historical factors that is useful; so let's allow here for the possibility that racism has to do with beliefs and other attitudes that perpetuate the ideology of white supremacy. The phrase "people of color" refers to people who are racialized in ways other than white; it allows for a positive rather than negative description of races that are not the dominant race, and avoids the problematic associations with "minorities" – especially given that people of color are not always in the minority.

Some problems with racialized preferences

There are various ways in which racialized sexual and romantic preferences have been thought to be a problem, a manifestation of what Nathaniel Adam Tobias Coleman calls "sexual racism" rather than mere preferences. First, some people express an aversion to people of a certain race, an aversion that might seem particularly problematic if the subject of the aversion is not the dominant race, raising the question of whether they are racist against the group in question. For example, in a 2010 *Playboy* interview, John Mayer, a white pop star, said in response to a question about Black women that while he had a "Benetton heart" – Benetton being famous for racially diverse advertisements – his penis was a "like a white supremacist" (quoted in Chideya 2010; Mayer later apologized). That is, he just didn't find Black women sexually attractive.

There are several ways an aversion might be a problem. When the aversion is in favor of the dominant race, this can be because of racist beauty ideals. We live in a society that showcases some kinds of appearances as "beautiful" and not others. In North America, beauty is often associated with whiteness: fashion models are overwhelmingly white, and blondness is seen as particularly attractive. Whiteness is shown associated with beauty, sexual attractiveness, health, and success, and it is difficult for anyone not to absorb and internalize these messages. They may then form beliefs such as "White features are more beautiful than others." If white people or people of color absorb and internalize these messages and this is part of why they seek out white partners or avoid partners who are people of color, this would seem a regrettable manifestation of a racist society rather than an unproblematic simple preference or desire.

Aversions can also be caused by stereotypes and other racist associations; these can be consciously held, that is, known to the person who has them, or they can be "implicit." Implicit associations are held in our subconscious that cause us to have feelings and attitudes about other people based on factors like race (and others like age, appearance, and so on). These implicit associations can inform our conscious beliefs and attitudes without our realizing that they are there. For example, Black people are often stereotyped as lazy or aggressive; if belief in such a stereotype causes an aversion, then the aversion would be racist. As to "other racist associations," think about how popular culture presents people of different races romantically and how that might affect how we all think of people. Some people, like Black and Latino women and Asian men, are seldom depicted as romantic leads. In Chapter 1, we talked about the Bechdel test: typically, women are not shown in movies talking to one another unless it's to discuss a man. These depictions both reflect our sexist social reality, in which women are often seen as valuable only for their attractiveness or romantic suitability, and reinforce that social reality, by conforming to it. In an analogous way, people of color are represented in popular culture in ways that are marginalizing, one-dimensional, and stereotyping. Black women are often depicted as maids and servants or as working low-status jobs; Black men are often depicted as aggressive criminals; Latinas are often depicted as domestic servants; Middle Easterners are often depicted as terrorists; frequently the story line is one in which the plot is centered around white characters. In his 2013 memoir *Fresh Off the Boat*, Eddie Huang describes his indignation at the way Hollywood movies depict Asian men, as sidekicks or shopkeepers but never as romantic leads. In 2016, *New York Times* film critic Manohla Dargis proposed the "DuVernay Test" (in honor of director Ava DuVernay), picking out movies in which people of color have "fully realized lives rather than serve as scenery in white stories" (Dargis 2016). In so far as an aversion is caused by our experience of these cultural depictions, it is connected to racism in our social reality.

But positive attraction can also be a problem. In her 1992 essay "Eating the Other," bell hooks describes young white men who go out of their way to seek out sex with members of other racial groups. They don't think of themselves as racist. But they seek out these sexual experiences – with "the Other" – as a route to self-transformation, a way of becoming more worldly. They assume that people of color are more experienced, more sensual, and by exoticizing them they reduce them to symbols for something they want for themselves. Just because the attention is "positive," and not aversive, in the sense of pursuing a sexual encounter and finding people more attractive rather than less, doesn't make it acceptable. Treating people as "exotic" and as tools to your purpose of living a certain kind of life is a way of mistreating them.

Attraction to people of a certain race can also be bad in virtue of stereotyping. Writing about "rice queens" – white men who are exclusively or primarily attracted to Asian men – Daniel Tsang (1992) points out that not only does the practice inappropriately lump "Asians" together as a racial class, ignoring differences between men who are Chinese, Japanese, Vietnamese, etc., it also seems to rest on stereotypes. The white men, he says, are attracted to Asians because of their perceived youthfulness, submissiveness, and dependence. As Robin Zheng (2016) explains, this is similar to stereotyping thought to be in play in "yellow fever": white men are attracted to Asian women because they associating them with the same kinds of qualities of delicacy and submission.

Racial stereotyping is wrong because it perpetuates false and damaging ideas that people of a certain race share certain qualities rather than acknowledging that individuals are different. Racial stereotyping can also be racist because often the stereotypes in question are linked in some way to the "ideology" mentioned above. For example, the idea that white people are assertive and self-directed while Asian people are self-effacing and deferential is part of, and helps perpetuate, an ideology in which whiteness is better and other races form a different and lesser "Other." In Shelby's definition, when beliefs support and perpetuate this ideology, they are racist. In this way, racialized sexual preferences can be seen as linked to racist beliefs.

In a 2007 paper, Niels Teunis describes a gay male community in San Francisco in which white men want to hook up with Black men but consistently look for, and even insist on, the same kind of thing from them: that the Black men be in control, dominant, and on top in sex. If the Black men aren't interested in this mode of interaction, the white partners aren't interested. Teunis argues that this trend rests on stereotypes about Black men and their sexuality: that they are dangerous, powerful, and hypersexual. Teunis argues that because white men in this community consistently refuse to have sex with Black men who do not want to play this role, Black men are forced "to play specific roles in sexual encounters that are not necessarily of their own choosing" (2007: 263). Teunis says that because of this, the practice objectifies Black men and is wrong. Again, in so far as these stereotypes reflect and perpetuate beliefs enmeshed historically in the set of beliefs that Europeans perpetuated to promote the idea of white supremacy, they are racist beliefs.

In an analysis of sexual racism, Coleman (2011) discusses a range of evidence for the conclusion that Black people are subject to sexual racism both in online dating and in offline encounters; Coleman argues that the result is less bargaining power for Blacks and thus Black people get less of what they want out of sexual interactions. In one study, researchers placed identical personal profiles for men on dating sites, varying only the race; in all cases, Black men received the fewest number of responses (Brown, 2003, cited in Coleman 2011). Black men also suffer from the kind of stereotyping patterns that Teunis found in his study: if white men want Black men only when they are willing to play a certain role, Black men are at a disadvantage when it comes to having the kind of sex they want to have; to get what they want, they may have to do more of what the other person wants. Especially in the context of men having sex with men, Coleman argues for a causal relationship between this kind of sexual racism and negative health outcomes for Black men: because Black men have less bargaining power, they have to do more of what the other man wants to have sexual interactions and pleasure; if this includes having unprotected sex, this could be a causal factor for increased rates of HIV for Black men over white. In that case, Coleman says, agencies like the Center for Disease Control should not focus attention on early detection but rather on eliminating the sexual racism that creates the problems in the first place (2011: 14).

We see in these examples how understanding racialized preferences is complicated by the way races relate to one another in society and the fact that white is a dominant race. The context in which the white race is dominant and others are subordinated or oppressed creates evident asymmetries when it comes to racialized preferences in sex and love. We also see in this discussion some ways that stereotyping, exoticization, and objectification can function to make racialized preferences unlike other, innocuous preferences. While preferences of sex and love are intimate and personal, they are also shaped by, and contribute to, the culture we live in. When preferences track racial attitudes – correlating, for instance, with favorable attitudes toward a dominant race and aversive ones toward an oppressed one, they may reflect and reinforce the existing ethical and social problems with the racial landscape. In the next section, we go more deeply into the question of how to evaluate racialized preferences.

Further evaluation: causes and consequences of racialized preferences

In evaluating racialized preferences, we can distinguish between the problem of why a person has the racialized preferences that they do and the consequences that follow from certain patterns of racialization. We saw in the previous section how the reason a person has a racialized preference can indicate that their preference is a problem: it might be stereotyping or exoticizing and therefore racist.

However, Raja Halwani (2017) says that looking at the reasons for racialized preferences shows that these preferences do not have to be a problem. Evaluating racialized preferences, he points out, requires us to look not only at the pattern of desire but also at the reasons for those desires. These reasons may or may not be stereotyping, and they may or may not reflect racism. After all, he says, in general people are sexually attracted to some and not others because of physical and nonphysical attributes. And these attributes often correlate with race. A white person may find themselves frequently dating Latino/Latina partners not because they are exoticizing them but simply because of their appearance, taste in music, clothing style, or whatever. Or they might date Korean people because they like dark hair and K-pop. In some cases, a pattern of racialized preferences need not really be about race at all. For example, imagine a person thinks to themselves, "I really find Latino/Latina partners attractive," and goes out of their way to date them, then one day finds themselves falling for a person and then finding out they're actually Middle Eastern. If this person thinks "Oh, I guess I am attracted to Middle Eastern people as well," then in that case, Halwani says, the racial pattern of desires may not have had specifically racial reasons and thus need not have anything to do with stereotyping, exoticization, or treating the person as merely useful to your purposes.

More contentiously, Halwani argues that even when racialized sexual preferences do have to do with stereotyping, they may not indicate that the person who has them is racist. This is partly because a person who has sexual desires based on stereotypes may not carry the relevant beliefs over to other contexts. For example, a white person who finds Asian people attractive may be sexually excited by qualities of submissiveness and deference associated with the stereotype but may not carry the belief that "Asian people are submissive and deferential" outside of the sexual context – knowing, intellectually, that the stereotype is generalizing and false. Furthermore, a person can take a range of attitudes toward their own desires. A person who has racialized preferences based on stereotypes may experience those desires but also rationally disavow the beliefs and stereotypes associated with them. For example, a white person who has a sexual aversion to Black people may feel the aversion but regard it as regrettable and something they hope to change. They disavow, rather than endorsing, the desire; this, Halwani suggests, may block the conclusion that the person themselves is racist.

It is interesting to consider this last point with respect to our discussion of reflection and selfhood in Chapter 6. There, we discussed the idea that some desires and impulses can be seen as outside the self because what we rationally endorse is a better reflection of who we really are.

If it were correct, that framework would help make sense of Halwani's idea, since the person who experiences desires based on racial stereotypes but does not rationally endorse or stand behind them would be identified not with their stereotyping desire but rather with their non-stereotyping thoughts. Their true self would thus be clear of racism. In Chapter 6, we also discussed a few challenges to this way of seeing the self, including the example of an LGBTQ+ person raised in a homophobic family or society. If this person desires queer sex but has internalized the idea that such sex is morally wrong and thus disavows these desires, then it might seem their desires are more a reflection of their true self than their homophobic reflective endorsements. Such examples challenge the theory that reflective endorsements are a better reflection of a person's self. Whether the racism example seems to support that theory because the thoughts are the true self, or challenge it, because the desires are, depends on how we conceptualize what racism is: is the person who experiences racist attitudes and beliefs but regards them as wrong and actively tries to distance themselves from them racist?

A different perspective on the issue emerges when we shift from thinking about the reasons for the racialized sexual preferences to thinking about the effects of racialized sexual preferences. Discussing the example of white men who desire Asian women, Zheng (2016) argues that whether or not we see the reasons for those desires as a problem, the phenomenon harms Asian women. For one thing, in being targeted by white men, Asian woman confront constant doubt over the reasons their partners are interested in them. Is it because of who they are as individuals or are they just here to fulfill a generic desire for a certain type of person? If they are approached or asked out, is the man interested in them for who they are or simply as an "Asian" woman? Asian women dating white men thus feel lumped into a category and treated as interchangeable within that category, as if their individuality' doesn't matter. Asian women are also "otherized" – their difference from whiteness becoming seen as central to their identity – and "hypersexualized" – perceived in ways that place their sexuality at the center of their identity, even when they prefer not to be regarded this way. Regardless of whether a man desires an Asian woman because of stereotypes, the effect of the pattern of racialized preferences creates harms and for that reason is bad.

It's interesting to consider these ideas in light of our discussions of objectification and love in previous chapters. On the face of it, when they arise because of stereotypes or exoticization, racialized preferences objectify: among other things, the targets are treated as instrumental – as a means to an end – and as fungible – interchangeable with others of the same race. As Nussbaum says, however, in evaluating objectification a lot depends on context and tone and on the way people are treated in the relationship outside of sexuality. This may relate to what Halwani was saying about the person who is sexually excited by a stereotype but doesn't have that stereotype outside of sex. If love means caring for the other person for who they are as an individual, then maybe it is possible to be sexually attracted to a person in part because they are a certain race but also to care about them as a whole person, in a non-stereotyping way, the rest of the time. In this direction, Halwani also says that there's a difference between the reason we are initially attracted to someone and the reason we come to love them: we might be attracted to a person for a range of features they share with other people – appearance, wit, and maybe race; at the same time, we might come to love them as an individual, for who they are.

Zheng points out that among the effects of racialized desires is the way they reinforce and prop up existing, pernicious, forms of racialization. Maybe part of their power to do so is linked to the particular way they form patterns. As Zheng points out, the phenomenon of white men being attracted to Asian women is common and widespread – enough so that the slang definition UrbanDictionary.com has twenty-seven different definitions of the term. And as we saw in hooks's (1992) piece, people of color are generally often exoticized and hypersexualized – regarded as sex objects, evaluated in terms of their physical characteristics and sexiness, and seen first through the lens of a sexual stereotype. As we discussed in Chapter 1, women are often disproportionately valued for their appearance and sexual attractiveness. The critical race theorist Kimberlé Williams Crenshaw coined the term "intersectionality" to refer to the way people have overlapping social identities through which they experience oppression or discrimination (see Crenshaw 1989); from this point of view it may be significant that the Asian women Zheng describes experience objectification as women and as racialized targets of hypersexualization. The concept of social autonomy we saw in Chapter 2 might help us understand the potential harmful effects of racialized preferences, particularly when they involve patterns. When racialized dating preferences reinforce the way that Asian women are seen through a sexualizing lens, this plausibly undercuts their social autonomy – their ability to be who they want to be in the world and be seen as they want to be seen. As we saw in Chapter 2, if you can't opt out of something, you can't choose it freely; this may be another context where people can't opt out of being sexualized and objectified. Zheng cites an Asian woman in a study who says, "I hate seeing Asian women with a white man. I hate it, I just hate it … I guess it feels especially weird, because every time I see that, I know that's what I'm looked as. That's how people see me, as somebody who should be with a white man" (Lee 1996: 119, cited in Zheng 2016: 411).

Focusing on the effects of racialized preferences also fits with what Teunis says about Black and white gay men. He ties the negative aspects of white men wanting only certain things from Black partners to considerations about the nature of the act: that it is objectifying in and of itself to want only specific things from people of a certain race, to want to interact with them in only a certain kind of way. But we might also, as Zheng does, look at the effects. The Black gay men in this community may suffer harms whether or not the desires have a problematic source. Again, among other things, the social autonomy of the Black men may be hindered: as Coleman says, relative to others, they are less able to engage in the kind of interactions they want to engage in.

In response to some of these thoughts, it might be asked, well what are we supposed to do? Sexual attraction is often seen as mysterious and beyond our control. You can't just decide to find someone, or not find someone, sexually attractive. Attraction is often not subject to our immediate control, and just telling people they should or should not find certain people attractive might not get you very far.

But recall the distinction Halwani draws between the desires a person has and the attitude that person takes toward their desire: it's possible to have racialized sexual desires that one does not approve of. In that case, we might note that desires are shaped by many things, and are not simply given. Popular culture informs many of our racist stereotypes and therefore plausibly contributes to racialized sexual preferences. If we recognize stereotypes in our thinking, we might go out of our way to find experiences that challenge those stereotypes – avoiding, say, big-budget Hollywood films that constantly depict Middle Easterners as terrorists, Black and Latina women as domestic help, Black men as violent criminals, and so on, and seeking out popular culture and art that centers the full-fledged experiences of people of color. Changing how we see people may change our pattern of attraction. Furthermore, as Zheng points out, desires are often partly a matter of choice: as in William Wilkerson's (2009) approach to orientations, that we talked about in Chapter 8, if understanding our own desires requires interpretation, this is a way that conscious choice comes into play. If you find yourself attracted to certain people, you might try to interpret your choice for yourself in terms of qualities you like rather than races you like, thus undercutting your own racialized preferences and pushing yourself to see people more as individuals and less as symbols.

Speaking of orientations, we might consider: if racialized sexual preferences are harmful in the sense that they dehumanize the target and subject them to doubt as in Zheng's analysis, can the same be said for gender-oriented preferences? If it's wrong to seek out Asian partners because they are Asian, is it also wrong to seek out and prefer female partners because they are female, or genderqueer partners because they are genderqueer, or whatever?

This is a very interesting and difficult question. One possibility is that the answer is no, because race and gender are culturally different. As Zheng points out, people do not seem to feel depersonalized knowing that their partners chose them partly on the basis of their gender, and knowing their partner has a specific gender orientation does not lead us to feel interchangeable with other people of that gender. So that problem of "doubt" – having to wonder whether you are being treated as an individual rather than a fungible member of a category – while salient to the race context, might not be relevant to the gender context. It's interesting to consider why this might be so. Zheng suggests maybe it's because we see gender as already part of the dating and relationship system so that no one feels "singled out" on the basis of gender, the way people feel singled out on the basis of race. Maybe this has to do with our history of sanctioning only heterosexual relationships.

A different and more radical possibility is that the answer is "yes," and that preferences that "discriminate" on the basis of sex and gender are also a problem. We might ask ourselves what, exactly, it is that we find we want in a partner, and whether or not those qualities might be found in people of various sexes and genders. In our society, there is increasing recognition of intersexuality, where bodies have physical traits of male and female and some intersex people do not identify with either. Some trans people choose to identify as male or female but choose only selective physical changes – for example, they may take hormones but not have surgery. Genderqueer people reject the whole male/female distinction. If sex and gender stop being so black and white, maybe insisting on dating people of a certain sex or gender will come to seem regressive, discriminatory, or objectifying.

In thinking of the various ways that our desires and affections are open to interpretation and choice, it's worth remembering that in relationships desires can be shaped by emotions. Often people in long committed relationships say they were initially not attracted to the other person, and started off as friends, but with time they came to fall in love with them and then became sexually attracted. In many cultural communities and other parts of the world, it is common for romantic relationships to be based first in marriage, with marriage choices typically guided by parents and other family members. Often the people don't know one another very well at the start. The matter is complex because people's experience of this varies widely, but certainly love and desire can flourish in these relationships just as they do when we choose for ourselves. Desire, attraction, and love are not simply given: they are shaped by circumstance, and just choosing someone can sometimes bring about, rather than being based on, initial attraction.

One reason we may be reluctant to submit our sex and love preferences to ethical evaluation is that because we cannot simply choose or control those preferences easily we feel should not be held responsible for them. But this discussion shows that taking responsibility for preferences is a subtle and matter. Maybe you can't wake up one morning and desire a completely different set of people. But you can take responsibility for your preferences. You can decide what stance to take toward them, you can interpret them, and you can choose how you engage with your social world to shape them.

Marriage and racial solidarity

In a 1994 article, Charles Mills poses the question "Do Black Men Have a Moral Duty to Marry Black Women?" He surveys and evaluates a wide range of possible responses for why the answer might be "yes." Some of these relate to ideas we've already discussed, about motivations, but the article also brings up new issues related specifically to the Black–white divide in the modern United States.

For example, given that whiteness reflects a beauty ideal and a status ideal, one question would be whether Black men dating white women are motivated, perhaps unbeknownst to themselves, by these factors instead of by more genuine attraction, caring, and love. If these motivations are in play, then whether or not the white woman is OK with it, the marriage would be endorsing the same racist set of values that motivates it in the first place and would therefore imply "a lack of respect for oneself and one's own race" (Mills 1994: 148). Of course, motivations are always complex and difficult to sort out, but, as Mills points out, a Black man's choice to marry a white woman may nonetheless be interpreted as expressing the same kind of thinking and thus constituting a "slap in the face" to Black women by implying "you're not good enough" (1994: 149).

Another idea that Mills considers has to do with demographics. Because of the disproportionate number of Black men who are in jail, dead at an early age, and unemployed, there are more Black women who want to marry than there are "marriageable" Black men. (Even setting aside the possibly classist concept of "marriageable," and its relation to employment, the first two factors create a significant imbalance). Because Black women are seen as less attractive marriage partners, of lower status than white women, if Black men do not marry Black women, many Black women will be unable to find marriage partners.

Mills discusses various aspects of this proposal. For one thing, he wonders how strong the obligation is and whether it would be strong enough to override male preferences. If a man fell in love with a white woman and wanted to marry her, does his general obligation to help out Black women override his right to marry as he pleases? Mills doesn't come down one way or the other, but he does suggest a possible line of argument. I mentioned above the way that preferences for white people as sex and romance partners might be generally a product of living in a society that promotes whiteness as beauty and status norms. Perhaps Black men who want to marry white women are potentially subject to these pressures in ways they do not recognize. In this case, their desire to marry a Black woman could be the result of a kind of brainwashing; the obligation to marry a Black woman would not be such a burden, really, because it would be an obligation to do what is ultimately in their best interest, reflecting preferences they would have had in the absence of discriminatory attitudes formed from living in a racist society. This would lessen the burden, supporting the idea that the obligation would be in force.

One of the most interesting aspects Mills brings up about this proposal has to do with whether the motivations in question would be insulting or unwelcome to the woman in question. Likening the motivation to "charity," he wonders how it would feel to know that you'd been sought out by a marriage partner as a charity case. If someone marries you out of "duty" and likens their motivation to similar motives of helping homeless people, doesn't this seem insulting? It's interesting to consider how this idea fits in with cultural expectations of what kinds of attraction, attitudes, and love are currently thought to be the norm, against which this motivation would be anomalous and damaging. If marrying something in order to do something nice for them, something that would address a societal injustice, is not the right reason, this implies that the modern "right" reasons for selecting a marriage partner might have something important to do with selfishness. As we talked about in Chapters 5–7, I think this is true: our conception of romantic love often includes the idea that for X to really love Y means X should regard Y's presence in their life as something good for X themselves! So we want our marriage partners to be self-interested in a sense. Marrying out of charity undercuts that idea. The proposal also raises issues related to Zheng's analysis. Even though a Black person marrying another Black person may not be "othering" or "exoticizing," there still might be the unnerving sense of having been selected for one's race rather than for one's individual qualities. Do these problems derail the idea of marrying in one's own race for reasons related to demographics? Or would marrying in one's own race express a different kind of meaning? I wonder if there is a way to endorse the demographic argument in a way that wouldn't invoke a mood of "charity" so much as "solidarity," an attitude with a different aspect to it.

This discussion shows the importance of context in thinking about sex, love, and race: the question, and the answers, in Mills' discussion are tied to specific cultural factors about race and racism in the United States. Furthermore, if there are reasons Black men should marry Black women, this is another sense in which preferences of sex and love are appropriately subject to evaluation and responsibility.

Conclusion

While racialized sex and love preferences might seem, on the surface, similar to other innocuous preferences, we've seen in this chapter many ways in which they are not, and several reasons to be wary of both racial aversions and racial attractions. Sometimes these preferences are exoticizing and objectifying. Sometimes they are caused by or perpetuate racist stereotypes. Sometimes they are informed by beauty and status norms that favor whiteness. Sometimes, even when they are positive, they can cause doubt and harm to the people who are their target.

While preferences of sex and love are personal and intimate, they are also shaped by and contribute to the racialized attitudes and facts of injustice in our society. They are therefore connected to the broadest social structures. And, as we've seen, even though they may seem beyond our control, there are also senses in which we can take responsibility for them, and there are occasions where we are ethically obligated to do so. There are therefore limits to the sense in which we can say we are free to have and express whatever sex and romance preferences we want: sexual liberty must be interpreted if it is not to conflict with anti-racist social obligations.

11 Sex, love, and disability

Introduction

Discussion of sex, love, and disability is complicated by various factors. Often, people with disabilities are desexualized, that is, seen not as sexual persons at all. Sometimes they are seen as having a malignant form of sexuality that is dangerous or sexually out of control. In various times and places, people with disabilities have been sterilized, often against their will, sometimes as part of a program of eugenics that sought their elimination. People with disabilities face various kinds of discrimination, are disproportionately the targets of sexual misconduct and violence, and are often not seen as romantic partners.

Recent anthologies like Robert McRuer and Anna Mollow's (2012) *Sex and Disability* show the vast range of topics to be considered in this area. I focus here on just two specific areas that illustrate a basic idea: that understanding the issues requires investigating context and social values, and thus goes beyond individual desires and decision-making. First, I discuss the role of sexual surrogates for people with physical disabilities, with particular attention to questions of love and intimacy, and then I turn to the question of sexual consent for people with intellectual disabilities. Of course, there are overlapping issues in these topics, since some people have various kinds of disabilities; in addition, it is important to remember that people with disabilities are a heterogeneous group along multiple dimensions. "Intellectual disability" is the preferred term for "conditions creating significant limitations in both intellectual functioning and in adaptive behavior" (American Association on Intellectual and Developmental Disabilities 2017). I also follow Janine Benedet and Isabel Grant in using the term "mental disability" as an umbrella term for people whose disabilities "affect cognition, perception, intellectual ability or decision-making" who may be an otherwise heterogeneous group (Benedet and Grant 2014: 133); this can include some forms of mental illness as well.

Much of our discussion focuses on ensuring that people with disabilities are able to exercise their rights to freedom of sexual and romantic expression. Especially when we talk about rights in the domain of sex and love, how we should interpret those rights and their associated obligations is complex and contested. I'll argue that properly understanding these issues, we should adopt a broad social and political perspective organized around equality and antidiscrimination rather than appealing to specific judgments about romance and relationships.

Disability in context

In Chapter 4, we mentioned briefly the story of Mark O'Brien, the writer who had polio and saw a sex surrogate, Cheryl Cohen-Greene. Like many people with disabilities, O'Brien says that through the course of his life he was never encouraged to see himself as a sexual being, and that, on the contrary, he was raised to have a fear and anxiety around sex. He describes how, in his thirties, he was still "embarrassed" by his sexuality: mortified when he became physically aroused while being bathed by attendants, too ashamed to talk to anyone about the orgasms he had sometimes had as a result, and always imagining that they hated him for becoming excited. He talks about how he always dreamed of having a romantic and sexual relationship, but how he waited passively, hoping to be approached or asked out, something that never happened. He laments that education for people with disabilities includes things like "how to cook from a wheelchair" but not how to deal with a damaged self-image or how to love and be loved through sex.

In their 1996 edited collection, *The Sexual Politics of Disability*, Tom Shakespeare, Kath Gillespie-Sells and Dominic Davies point to a wide range of scholarship showing how people with disabilities have long been seen as either asexual or "malignantly" sexual. They examine sexual politics from a "disability-rights" perspective, and it is striking that even so relatively recently they describe having to "start from scratch" with their research because there had been so little work from this perspective previously (Shakespeare et al. 1996: 11). In their 2016 book *Sexuality, Disability, and the Law*, authors Perlin and Lynch describe widespread resistance to discussion of disability and sexuality, especially for people with mental disabilities, and especially for people who are living in institutional settings. A widespread "sanism" means that people with mental illness are treated as "deviant, morally weak, sexually uncontrollable [and] emotionally unstable" (Perlin 1992: 393, quoted in Perlin and Lynch 2016: 8), but also as "asexual" (Perlin and Lynch 2016).

People with disabilities, and especially women, are disproportionately the target of sexual abuse, sometimes by caregivers and sometimes by intimates. Revisiting the experience of working on *The Sexual Politics of Disability* some years later, Tom Shakespeare describes how, when he and his co-authors began interviewing people with disabilities, interviewees raised a wide range of issues like body image and identifying "differently" as men and women, because of the intersection of "gender, sexuality, and disability," but they also talked about their experiences of abuse and pain (Shakespeare 2006: 168). As Benedet and Grant explain, women with mental disabilities are particularly vulnerable; they may feel powerless to reject demands of caregivers; they may comply with demands without understanding what is being asked of them; and they may be induced to comply by offers of "compensation, companionship or simply social acceptance" (2014: 131–132).

An important part of the disability-rights perspective has to do with the possibility of seeing disability through a social lens rather than a medical one (Shakespeare et al. 1996). The "social model" of disability challenges the idea of disability as a medical condition that makes a person inherently worse off and replaces it with an understanding of disability as seen through the lens of social oppression. For example, if a person who uses a wheelchair cannot get into a building when stairs are the only option for getting inside, the social model teaches us that the problem is not the person's condition but rather the environment, which hasn't been set up to work for people in wheelchairs. The way our environment is set up for people with some specific abilities and not others is the result of social factors and choices, and what counts as a "disability" is the result of social beliefs about what is normal, not objective medical facts. Hence the idea of a "social" model.

There is debate over the status of the "social model" and how it should be interpreted, but there is widespread consensus on two matters: that living with a disability is an experience profoundly affected by one's social environment and surroundings, and that seeing sexuality from the "disability-rights" perspective means including the voices of people with disabilities themselves rather than deferring to the opinions of just physicians, psychologists, sexologists, and the like (Shakespeare et al. 1996: 3; for discussion of an "interactional" model, see Shakespeare 2006).

Physical disabilities and sexual surrogacy

In 2012, Mark O'Brien's experience was made into a film called *The Sessions*. While partner surrogacy for people with disabilities was not new, the film prompted fresh debate and discussion over the issue. In practical terms, sexual surrogacy usually entails clients meeting with a surrogate for between six and ten weekly sessions in consultation with a referring psychologist; all collaborate to ensure the treatment is going well for the client (Mintz 2014). The International Professional Surrogates Association (IPSA) is a nonprofit organization dedicated to advancing the science, art and availability of surrogate partner therapy; they have a code of ethics, provide certification, and offer clients assistance with a range of problems, including anxiety, medical conditions, emotional abuse and/or trauma, and lack of desire (IPSA 2017).

Global attitudes toward surrogacy vary greatly. In France, surrogacy has been condemned as a form of prostitution (de la Baume 2013). In

Denmark, it can be a care worker's duty to facilitate sexuality for people they care for, whether this means assistance in facilitating partner sex, masturbation, or a visit with a sex worker. In some countries, "limited touching" services exist, organized by nonprofit organizations. (Perlin and Lynch 2016: 109).

One source of controversy concerns the conceptual understanding of surrogacy in relation to sexual objectification and gender inequality. In her 2008 article "Disability and the Male Sex Right," Sheila Jeffreys says that the idea of surrogacy is conceptually linked to seeing men's sexuality in terms of an entitlement to sexual pleasure; this, she says, reinforces the same social factors that lead to people – especially women – with disabilities being the target of sexual abuse. There are two connections here. First, the idea of surrogacy as satisfying a "right" to sex supports the idea of sexual pleasure as a male entitlement; for straight men, this suggests women are mere providers of that pleasure rather than sexual beings on their own terms. Second, the practice of sexual surrogacy teaches disabled men a depersonalized, objectifying form of sexuality. Because this form of sexuality constructs women as sexual objects, it "requires that a woman suffers emotional and/or physical abuse" (Jeffreys 2008: 334). As in Nussbaum's discussion of objectification in Chapter 1 and Estes' discussion of sex work in Chapter 4, Jeffreys' perspective conceptualizes mutuality and respect for partners as full human beings as important aspects of healthy sexuality. Because surrogacy lacks mutuality and a caring respectful relationship, the sex is objectifying.

In response to Jeffreys, Tracy de Boer (2015) challenges the idea that surrogacy involves an "inferior" form of sexuality and emphasizes the importance of sexual inclusion for people with disabilities. In discussing what healthy sexuality should be, de Boer draws on Jacqueline Fortunata's (1980: 394) distinction between an "artistic" lover – who responds to their partner as a unique person and values the sexual act "not for its outcome but for its structure in the present" – and a "scientific" lover – who "focuses on what all partners have in common (for example, mouth, genitals, and so on)" (de Boer 2015: 72). Appealing to various first-person accounts, including Cohen-Greene's (2012) memoir *An Intimate Life: Sex, Love, and My Journey as a Surrogate Partner*, de Boer suggests that surrogacy can function to enable "artistic" sexuality. As Cohen-Greene says, while a client might experience typical sex work as being like a visit to a restaurant, "seeing a surrogate is like going to culinary school" (2012: 161); because the aim is to model healthy relationships and not just provide sexual pleasure, surrogacy aligns with the best kind of sexuality and is not "inferior."

I agree with de Boer that surrogacy need not involve any kind of inferior sexuality. I would go further and say that even without an "artistic" and individualized approach, the sex involved in surrogacy would not necessarily be an inferior form of sexuality. As we discussed in Chapters 1 and 2, in my view the context of the relationship is not the crucial issue distinguishing ethical from unethical forms of objectification. From this point of view, the kind of depersonalization described by Jeffreys may not be unethical. It depends on the background context; as long as the activity is autonomously chosen and consensual, the fact that it involves fungibility is not, itself, a problem. In fact, as we discussed in Chapter 1, some theorizing about gay male sexual culture has linked a "fungibility" of sex partners with a kind of democratic equality: seeing everyone as interchangeable, one also sees them as equal. That sex is depersonalized does not necessarily make it wrong.

Furthermore, in keeping with my theory that objectification should be understood not in terms of the interaction or relationship of the participants but rather in terms of its social and political context, I would emphasize the gendered component of analysis. As we saw in Chapter 2, among gay men, fungibility takes on a certain aspect since men are typically regarded socially as individuals and not as mere bodies, whereas seeing women as fungible supports an existing problematic status quo. In Chapter 4, we talked about Laurie Shrage's (1989) idea that the social meaning of a practice is contextual. Given that we already live in a society where men are more often assumed to be sexual actors and women are more often regarded as sexual objects, surrogacy may take on a different social aspect depending on whether it is mostly male clients and female surrogates or whether the sex and gender breakdowns are all over the map. As Mintz (2014) says, it is relevant to understanding surrogacy that 30 percent of clients are women, often treated by male surrogates (Fox 2013), and that surrogates are highly trained professionals who can change careers if they choose (Mintz 2014: 11).

With respect to the question of gender equality, Perlin and Lynch point out that stereotypes do sometimes play out in current surrogate situations, especially the stereotype that men "somehow need sex, or need to orgasm," while women "may enjoy it but have no analogous physiological need" (2016: 109). Japan's White Hands, for example, "provides a service that allows only men to be masturbated" (Perlin and Lynch 2016: 109–110); Perlin and Lynch say that, when asked, staff responded that they "haven't received any requests from women" (2016: 110). As we know from our previous discussion, there could be many reasons for this, having to do with factors like social perception, gendered norms, and the possibility that a woman would be unable to protect herself from a man who didn't respect her boundaries and specific desires. From this point of view, whether the sex is depersonalized or objectifying would depend on factors related to the gender equality within the practice and also in the society more broadly. As in Shrage's analysis of sex work, if the practice props up social ideas that male pleasure should be prioritized, that would make it a problem.

One way to conceptualize the issue is in terms of a fundamental right to sexual pleasure. Embracing this idea, Jacob Appel says that where sex work is generally illegal there should be exceptions for "people whose physical or mental disabilities make sexual relationships with non-compensated adults either impossible or highly unlikely" (Appel 2010: 153). As Alida Liberman (2018) points out, however, the question of sexual rights can be complex. We do not interpret sexual liberty as meaning anyone can do as they please: public masturbation and sex with unconscious people are prohibited, and they are so whether or not this prohibition leads some people to have unsatisfying sex lives. Furthermore, it's important not to make disability a proxy for sexual exclusion. Some people find it difficult or impossible to find uncompensated sex partners and so are "sexually excluded," but there are disabled people who are not sexually excluded and also sexual excluded people who are not disabled. Sexual exclusion can happen for many reasons: a person may have an unusual fetish, or may be perceived as unattractive, or may be a misogynist man who repulses those around him with his sexist remarks (Liberman 2018: 3). If the central issue is sexual exclusion, why not address that directly? To frame the issue in terms of disability implies that disability is always a cause of sexual exclusion; this, Liberman says, is socially harmful to people with disabilities.

In accordance with the idea of analyzing surrogacy from a social and political perspective, but framing the issue more in terms of anti-discrimination rather than a general sex right, Kevin Mintz proposes a conceptually original approach in which the issue of surrogate partner therapy for people with disabilities is an issue of "fair equality of opportunity in health" (2014: 4). Mintz draws on the idea that justice in health care means that people should have equal access to the elements of human functioning that society recognizes as affecting social opportunity. Arbitrary factors like disabilities should not affect equality of access to these elements; otherwise, the social situation is unjust. In this framework, "health needs" are "conditions constituting a relevant loss of normal species functioning" (see, e.g., Daniels 1985). People with disabilities, then, are owed whatever is available that would bring them to normal functioning. In the case of sexuality, Mintz argues that sexual health is among the elements of well-being that should be included so that surrogate partner therapy would be evaluated as a potential health-related intervention, potentially supported through considerations of equal rights and justice.

To make this case, Mintz says that sex is a component of normal species functioning partly because it is central to the intimacy that most people consider crucial to romantic relationships (2014: 6). Such relationships are an important part of the formation and ongoing maintenance of "families" – which here means any long-lasting partnerships. So equal access to sexual functioning is important for being able to participate in one of the practices widely agreed on to be crucial to a good life. This doesn't mean people are required to share these goals and access treatment; it just means that, in fairness, they should have the opportunity to access relevant treatment. Given the complex nature of "dysfunction" (which we'll discuss further in Chapter 12), and given that there may be different kinds of sexual practices that are best for various people with various conditions, enabling people with sexual function need not require specific goals like penetrative intercourse. Instead, people can collaborate with their partners to engage in whatever sexual behaviors are "satisfying and safe for all participants" (Mintz 2014: 7). The proposal is focused on antidiscrimination and equality in making options open to able-bodied people also open to disabled people, rather than starting from a general right to sexual interaction or pleasure. This frames the issue in terms of equality of opportunity rather than a general right to sexual pleasure.

Surrogacy, intimacy, and love

Sometimes an emphasis on sexuality or surrogacy is seen as conflicting with, or at least edging out, an emphasis on intimacy and love. In the Introduction to their 2012 collection *Sex and Disability*, editors McRuer and Mollow point out that after co-authoring the *Sexual Politics of Disability* (mentioned above) in 1996, Tom Shakespeare went on to suggest in his 2006 book that this emphasis might have been somewhat misplaced: "by making sexuality our primary concern," he writes, "we failed to understand that intimacy is perhaps a greater priority for disabled people" (Shakespeare 2006: 168; quoted in McRuer and Mollow 2012: 29).

Relatedly, surrogacy, especially if used in certain ways, can be seen as medicalizing. As we saw above, the medical model sees a condition as something to be treated or cured in a context of provider care; if the surrogate is seen as a part of the healthcare team, then the effect may be to reinforce the idea of impaired sexuality as part of the condition that needs "treatment" rather than a normal part of a person's life. In a defense of the French decision against allowing surrogate partner therapy, Anne-Cécile Mailfert, a member of Osez le Féminisme (Dare to be Feminist) said, "It's like telling disabled people that since they will never have a sex or love life, we'll prescribe them sexual assistance as a palliative" (de la Baume 2013); she says sexual assistance can create a "dangerous emotional dependency" between surrogates and clients. Related to this, we might interpret Jeffreys' charge of "depersonalizing" sex as improperly interpreting sexuality in the disability context as sex divorced from intimacy and partnership.

Against this, proponents emphasize the importance of the autonomy of a people with disabilities to make their own decisions about sex and love. With respect to the decision in France, a Dutch surrogate says, "In Holland, we have integrity over our body" (de la Baume, 2013). And we've seen the emphasis on surrogacy as a practice that aims toward the client developing their own sexual health and well-being rather than acting as a pleasure provider or a substitute for other relationships.

This emphasis on the client's development fits with Mintz's proposal, that sex be conceptualized as connected to intimacy and partnership, and with Cohen-Greene's and de Boer's conceptualization of surrogacy as a practice that teaches sexuality rather than providing it. Mintz (2017b) also emphasizes, however, that while surrogacy can be appropriate, it must not be seen as a panacea, as solving all problems. When a clinician is too quick to say, "Oh, they're disabled and a virgin. Send them to a surrogate or a sex worker," this can be medicalizing and commodifying. Mintz describes his own experience and perspective:

> I began seeing a sexologist at 22 because I had not yet been in a relationship. We explored my seeing a male surrogate, but decided against it because of logistics and money. However, I will tell you that every time, until I actually started dating my current partner, I would talk about my sexual concerns with other sexologists, the reaction would be, "why don't you see a surrogate or hire a sex worker?" I am a sex worker advocate, and I have no moral objections to either option, but I deeply resented the idea that my sexuality would be yet another thing I'd have to pay a professional for me to experience. Disabled people like myself have to pay for so many extra supports just to go about their daily lives and I find it problematic, personally and professionally, that the assumption in my interactions with sexologists is that seeing a surrogate or sex worker would be the default option.
>
> (Mintz 2017b)

In describing his own experience with surrogacy, Mark O'Brien mentions an experience relevant to the relationship between sex and love. He sees Cohen-Greene a few times, and after a few frustrating experiences they finally do have intercourse. He decides to stop seeing her after that, partly because of the money – it's pretty expensive – and partly because there doesn't seem to be anything else left to conquer. He ends his essay on a sad note, however:

> I began this essay in 1986, then set it aside until last year. In re-reading what I originally wrote, and my old journal entries from the time, I've been struck by how optimistic I was, imagining that my experience with Cheryl had changed my life. But my life hasn't changed. I continue to be isolated, partly because of my polio, which forces me to spend five or six days a week in an iron lung, and partly because of my personality. I am low-key, withdrawn, and cerebral ... I wonder whether seeing Cheryl was worth it, not in terms of the money but in hopes raised and never fulfilled.
>
> (O'Brien 1990)

O'Brien realizes that just having sex doesn't change his life much. He notes that most women he finds attractive would never want to date him, a man with such serious physical problems, and that his desires were, in a sense, for something beyond merely having sex.

On the one hand, this sentiment might seem to complicate the pro-surrogacy argument, tinged, as it is, with disappointment. But I think that this would be a misinterpretation. Many people, maybe even most, have had this same reaction to a sexual experience: it was not as life-changing as they might have thought it would be, and was disappointing in retrospect. What could be a more human emotion? If experience with surrogate partnership doesn't always provide life-changing magic, and if it sometimes leaves a person wistful or sad, that makes it a lot like sex generally, for anyone. If surrogacy enables some people to have a set of conflicting and unpredictable emotions about a sexual experience, that's an argument for it, not against it.

With respect to sex, love, and intimacy, it's worth noting that some of the obstacles that people with disabilities face in accessing sexual pleasure and fulfillment are the same ones they face in accessing love and intimacy. Some of these have to do straightforwardly with discrimination and the social tendency to see only able-bodiedness as sexually attractive (McRuer and Mollow 2012). But there are subtler reasons as well, and Elizabeth Emens points out that it would be a mistake to see personal or individual factors as distinct from social and legal ones. In discussing the complex ways that social factors create "intimate discrimination," Emens (2009) points out that background legal and societal structures have substantive impact on whom we meet, whom we form relationships with, and whom we choose to partner with or marry. These structures include the way some spaces are inaccessible for people with disabilities, the way a public transit system enables or prevents people from visiting various areas of a town or city, or the way subsidies for caring attendants may or may not be discontinued in the event a person marries.

Emens asks us to imagine two towns, A-city (relatively accessible) and I-city (relatively inaccessible) and a lawyer, Janet, who is a triple amputee who uses a wheelchair (Emens 2009: 1370–1372). In A-city, Janet meets someone, and they form a romantic relationship: it's easy for Janet to get around on the accessible transit; bars and restaurants are generally accessible; and the city is in a state with a welfare system that provides for daily self-care tasks (as needed), and ensures that state assistance would continue as before were she to marry. Her romantic relationship goes really well. Then Janet moves to I-city for a new job. There she meets someone new, but I-city creates problem after problem. Difficulties with the inaccessible transit system make Janet late for work unless she leaves early in the morning, annoying her new partner who is not a morning person. Most restaurants and homes are either inaccessible or difficult for a wheelchair-user; because people feel awkward about this, the couple stops getting invited out to dinner. Janet becomes frustrated and unhappy, and then annoyed when her partner tells her to take a more "positive" attitude, failing to share her perspective. In I-city, assistance for personal care would cease in case of marriage, so the new partner would have to take on many personal care tasks. The new partner's family start to exert pressure against the relationship, asking, "Are you sure you want to face a lifetime of these constraints?"

As Emens says, Janet's prospects as a dating partner look starkly different in the two towns, based on decisions by the state about infrastructure, policy, and enforcement (2009: 1371). What this shows is that issues of access to sex, love, and intimacy cannot be framed purely on the individual level – that is, as a question of how individual people relate to one another, as lovers, or as surrogate and client, or as friends with benefits, or whatever. While these are all important, the broader social structures are as well; creating a society in which people's choices for sex, love, romance, and marriage challenge entrenched inequalities rather than increasing them requires change on a broad social and legal scale (see also Teunis and Herdt 2007).

Our discussion in this section highlights the ways that understanding nondiscrimination in contexts of disability goes beyond ending the stigmatization of people with disabilities and involves reflection on how social and cultural structures make the goods of sex and love available or unavailable. With respect to surrogate partner therapy, I've argued that the question of objectification or depersonalization is less important than the broader question of gender equality; with respect to sexual rights, Mintz's framing of the problem in terms of fair opportunity usefully centers the issue of equality and nondiscrimination for people with disabilities; with respect to forming romantic relationships, Emens' thought experiment shows how fairness in sex and love is related to a vast range of other matters like infrastructure and transportation.

Intellectual disabilities and complexities of consent

Of course, people with intellectual disabilities face many of the same problems discussed above, of finding partners, overcoming practical problems, and dealing with a generally hostile social world. And, as we've seen above, there are forms of abuse and mistreatment that especially affect those with intellectual disabilities, including high rates of sexual abuse and violence. Some people with mental disabilities live in institutional settings, where caregivers not only can exert control over their behavior but also may fear legal liability for failing to protect people under their care from rape and sexual assault. So framing issues of sexuality for people with intellectual disabilities is particularly complex.

Central among these challenges is the problem of consent. Legally and morally, consent is usually thought to provide the criterion we expect to use in distinguishing appropriate, ethical sexual interaction from sexual assault. As we discussed in Chapter 3, setting out the expected workings of consent can be difficult, but it's generally thought that people must be "competent" and capable in order to genuinely consent. But, as Perlin and Lynch point out, what it means to be able to consent to sexual activity is unclear, and to assume that people with certain conditions are generally incapable of consent would be a mistake. "Competency" is a legal assessment, but what it means to be "competent" varies with context: as Judge Harry Blackmun said, "A person who is 'competent' to play basketball is not therefore 'competent' to play the violin" (Perlin and Lynch 2016: 58). As Alexander Boni-Saenz explains, in the United States, most states have incapacity tests that focus narrowly on assessing a person's cognitive abilities, and while these tests work well for some situations, as when a person is "incapacitated" by drugs or alcohol, when applied generally they improperly bar many people with persistent forms of incapacity from having any sexual activity (2015: 1204). Perlin and Lynch emphasize the importance of a "functional" rather than "diagnostic" approach: the important question is what the person can do, which must in turn be understood contextually.

Some existing thinking about consent and capacity is informed by underlying assumptions about the nature and role of personal autonomy in decision-making. As we've discussed in previous chapters, "autonomous" generally means self-directed, authentic, or uncoerced. Traditional theories of autonomy often interpret autonomous behavior as requiring a reflective decision-making ability using sophisticated cognitive resources. These perspectives often emphasize a distinction between a choice – which may reflect a mere desire or impulse – and an "autonomous" choice – one that reflects the person's self-directedness, ability to weigh and reflect on various considerations, or deeper underlying values. For example, as we saw in Chapter 6, Harry Frankfurt's view of autonomy distinguishes between mere desires and those higher-order desires that the person identifies with, which better reflect who the person really is.

Such theories have been generally criticized both for an implicit masculinism that conceptualizes personhood in an excessively individualistic kind of way (Stoljar 2015) and for their exclusion of people who do not fit an ideal of independent, cognitively typical, people (Boni-Saenz 2015: 1223; see Kittay 2011). The first critique starts from the observation that traditional views of autonomy set up an ideal of self-sufficiency, rationality, and disconnection from other people. As feminist theorists point out, however, people are socially embedded beings. Women, in particular, may prioritize relationships and care, and to hold up self-sufficiency as an ideal would be a mistake. This thinking has led to the development of a family of theories called "relational autonomy," which emphasize instead the idea that "agents are socially and historically embedded, not metaphysically isolated, and are, moreover, shaped by factors such as race and class" (Stoljar 2015).

The second critique is that centering rational independence improperly and unjustly excludes some people with disabilities because they would then be seen as unable to make autonomous choices. The concept of autonomy can therefore raise problems when used to demarcate genuine, self-directed choices from mere desires or actions. When traditional thinking about autonomy informs ethical judgments, policy judgments, and the law, as it often does in discussions of sexual consent, this can lead to exclusion and to the rights of people with disabilities being ignored or erased. As Boni-Saenz says, this exclusion creates a need for a new way of thinking about decision-making that is inclusive for people with a range of cognitive impairments (2015: 1224).

Boni-Saenz suggests using a "capability" approach that starts from the idea that sexual activity is an "opportunity" to pursue functionings associated with sex. People see and evaluate sexual options differently, and they may pursue options that ultimately make them unhappy; the point is in prioritizing a person's right to pursue their own path. Not all opportunities are on the table, of course, and everyone must respect the sexual capabilities of others. From this conceptualization, Boni-Saenz says that a minimal requirement for sexual agency is the ability to form and express positive willingness to engage in sexual activity. This, he says, is necessary to establish sexual consent, and also important because it is the only way to know "what a person's internal mental states regarding sexual desires might be" (2015: 1226). Using the idea of a "functional" instead of "diagnostic" approach, Murphy and O'Callaghan (2004) propose a range of relevant criteria such as "basic sexual knowledge," "knowledge of the consequences of sexual relations," "an understanding that sexual contact should always be a matter of choice," "the ability to recognize potentially abusive situations," and "the ability to show skills of assertion in social and personal situations and to thereby reject any unwanted advances at the given time" (2004: 1349; for discussion see Perlin and Lynch 2016: 59).

As Boni-Saenz (2015) and Andria Bianchi (2016) point out, there are particular challenges to using supported decision-making in contexts of sexuality. For one thing, people in a support network may have the kind of societal biases we've seen above: that people with disabilities should not be sexual, or that their sexuality is a danger. The background opinions of the people we talk to about a decision affect our decision process, and, as David DeVidi says, there is always a risk of people in support networks shifting from "helping someone to think something through" and "doing someone's thinking for him" (2012: 197). In part, this is because often the people in someone's support network are family members and close friends who are especially concerned to protect the person from harm, and the urge to preempt perceived mistakes can be "overwhelming" (DeVidi 2012: 197). In the sexual context, this may lead members of a support network to pressure a person, consciously or not, away from sexual decisions they perceive to be physically or emotionally risky. In addition, able-bodied people in support networks may be prone to projecting their own ideas and opinions onto a person with a disability rather than actively listening to what the person is trying to say.

Furthermore, given that sexuality is a heavily moralized topic about which people have a wide range of values and opinions, family and close friends may bring to the table a very different set of background assumptions about what is, and is not, healthy and appropriate (Bianchi 2016: 115). For example, what if the people in the support network have more traditional or risk-averse sexual values and disapprove of the person's sexual choices? This is obviously a particularly strong danger for LGBTQ+ people whose support networks may not share their sexual values. In a study of attitudes of support workers and their clients, Jami Petner-Arrey and Susan R. Copeland (2015) found that support workers often prioritized the protection and safety of clients, in ways that interfered with individual autonomy and decision-making. In addition, people often have certain emotions when it comes to the sexuality of family members: parents may not want to see their children as sexual; children may not want to see aging parents as sexual, and so on. Mintz points out that romantic relationships between disability-related professionals and their clients develop with "relative frequency," and that families "sometimes have trouble accepting those relationships" (2017a: 3–4). Bianchi suggests that perhaps for decisions related to sex, it might be better to have a special committee, formed with people who are not in the person's family, which would explain sex and answer questions and thus facilitate decision-making that better reflects what the person themselves wants (2016: 116).

From a theoretical perspective, the idea of "balancing" rights and potential harms is crucial to evaluating these proposals. No policy will prevent all cases of abuse: as Boni-Saenz points out, for any criteria we introduce, a person intent on committing sexual assault will be able to find a way around the relevant restrictions. The question, in his view, is not about preventing all assault, since this is impossible, but rather about finding the best way to reduce sexual violence while limiting the restriction on sexual opportunities for people with disabilities (Boni-Saenz 2015: 1244–1245). Since people with disabilities are disproportionately the targets of sexual abuse, appropriate frameworks must rest on finding a "balance" between "empowering people to claim their sexual rights and protecting them from abuse" (Murphy and O'Callaghan 2004: 1347; see also Perlin and Lynch 2016: 79). Experiencing risk itself is an important human right: as Petner-Arrey and Copeland point out, not only is denying this right to people with intellectual disabilities inherently wrong, but excessive risk management can also put people with disabilities at increased risk – "because they have not been educated on how to interpret and respond to risk themselves" (2015: 45).

To investigate how well people with intellectual disabilities were able to understand concepts of consent and abuse, Murphy and O'Callaghan (2004) showed participants pictorial vignettes and asked questions about what was going on and how the people felt. Not surprisingly, there was a lot of variation. In discussing the implications of their research, they point out the difficulty of finding a set of criteria: the lower the criteria are set, the higher the number of people who would be construed as having the capacity to consent to sex. There is a careful balance, they conclude, "to be struck between requiring people to know enough without requiring them to know everything" (Murphy and O'Callaghan 2004: 1355). As Michael Gill says, any process of determining capacity to consent must be individualized, situational, and flexible, changing along with increased sexual knowledge and "ability to act with intention," with the understanding that there is always a risk that the moral standards or religious doctrines of a particular supervisor can influence how a policy is carried out, blocking a person's ability to exercise sexual freedom of expression (2015: 39).

This discussion of sexual consent as involving a balance among complex factors shows the importance of a broad social perspective: instead of finding a morally bright line applicable to all cases regardless of context, we must consider which rights and harms are at stake more generally and find a way to weigh them appropriately. As we saw in Chapter 3, sexual consent always involves a complex balancing; the principles of fairness and equality should function as a guide to how that balancing should be carried out.

Conclusion

Our discussion has centered on the rights and abilities of people with disabilities to live lives with freedom of expression, sexual fulfillment, and love. I've argued that interpreting these rights and abilities raises complex questions: about whether depersonalized sex is unethically objectifying, about whether gender inequality affects our understanding of surrogate partner therapy, about how our social fabric creates inequalities of sex and love, about how to balance the rights and potential harms in sexual consent. For these complex questions, I've suggested that we should go beyond individualized perspectives about the nature of sex and love to base our judgments on equality and antidiscrimination. In contexts of structural discrimination and stigma, to say that everyone has a right to personal sexual freedom and autonomy is surely true, but it raises more questions than it answers.

12 The medicalization of sex and love

Introduction

Because they're so closely bound up with the body and its needs, love and sex have long attracted the attention of physicians and other medical practitioners. That long-standing interest has intensified in recent years with the success of Viagra and its sibling drugs and with the recent search for the elusive "Viagra for women." This engagement is commonly described as "medicalization," meaning the process by which some physiological or behavioral aspect of the human experience comes to be treated as something we study and improve through science and medical intervention. This chapter examines some of the issues surrounding this tendency toward the medicalization of sex and love. Especially when new treatments like pharmaceuticals are involved, medicalization is often accompanied by a shift in our understanding of what is a problem or dysfunction. As we will see below, when it comes to sex and love, judging what is a problem or dysfunction is a complex evaluative matter with a deeply social dimension. To a large extent, values and commitments, rather than biology, shape what we see as healthy.

Some recent research into women's sexuality illuminates those social dimensions of medicalization and its relation to norms of sexuality and appropriate sexual function and behavior. Reframing traditional models of sexual function shows that what may seem dysfunctional from one point of view may seem entirely normal from another. For example, some research suggests that, for women more than men, physical arousal and subjective feelings of sexual pleasure don't always go together and that desire may emerge more in response to sexual activity rather than spontaneously. These patterns could seem like "dysfunctions," or they could be understood as part of normal sexual function and thus not problems at all. Similarly, people in long-term monogamous relationships often find their sexual desire for their partner diminishes with time. Is this a problem to be solved with treatment? Or is the social norm of monogamy the problem? As we'll see, either way there are questions about the relationship of desire to the self, the relative importance of lust, and what is or isn't the kind of sex we hope to want. While it might seem surprising to think that "love" could be medicalized, recent philosophical research has investigated whether we should have the right – or even the obligation – to take love drugs if they existed. In the case where they could save a marriage, some philosophers think the answer might be "yes."

In this chapter, I will focus on a few specific issues to show how our judgments about what is disordered rest on our social and ethical evaluations. This is not meant to suggest that the development of new treatments for dysfunctions and enhancements should cease: many people have health conditions that get in the way of satisfying and pleasurable sex, and the more options they have to address this the better. The point is rather that when medicalization brings about new options – such as the option to take a pill – this has complicated effects. For one thing, it highlights the distance between the way we are and the way we want to be. Medicalization thus focuses attention on the question: when it comes to sex and love, what is the way we want to be?

Medicalization and the "Viagra narrative"

As we've seen, medicalization is a social process having to do with a shift toward using scientific methods and frameworks to study and change aspects of human life. For example, nutrition used to mean food: what people ate had to do with resources, culture, and social patterns more than anything else. Food wasn't something people studied and measured scientifically or tried to improve through science and double-blind studies. Over the past couple of centuries this has changed dramatically, with food being broken down into the study of calories, vitamins, minerals, and so on. Now, people talk about food as if it is, in a sense, a kind of medicine. Nutrition has been medicalized.

In Chapter 8, we saw an example of how sex and love can be medicalized, with the question of how orientations are understood and studied. Michel Foucault's work argues that sex and other human activities are increasingly medicalized, especially when it comes to orientations: what used to be more a matter of individual people choosing to do different things on different occasions for a mix of reasons has come to be studied in terms of people having fixed orientations that can be studied through biological and physiological sciences. Because humans are "interactive kinds," studying them through the lens of particular orientation concepts can reinforce the sense that those concepts are natural and inevitable.

While the question of what is healthy or dysfunctional might seem to be a straightforward matter of medicine and biology, the distinction has a profoundly social dimension. The story of Viagra is an interesting case study in how social factors affect what is or is not seen as a dysfunction or problem to be solved. Before the introduction of Viagra in 1983, "impotence" was the word generally used for a man who didn't get an erection during sexual activity. In an erection, blood flows quickly into the penis, increasing its length, width, and firmness; impotence occurs when this physiological change fails to happen in tandem with sexual activity or subjective feelings of sexual excitement. Before the 1980s, the study of impotence and the discussion around it focused on a range of factors: a man might have problems with his relationship with his partner, generating a mental and emotional difficulty; there might be other psychological factors like anxiety or stress; impotence might be a side effect of some other health treatment; it might be a physiological issue related to hormones or the arteries or something like that.

Crucially, impotence is mostly normal, in the sense that every man will experience it at some time or other and that it can be a healthy and appropriate response. If a man is angry, or stressed, or frightened, or exhausted, maybe it's not the best time to be having sex; the lack of an erection is the body's way of responding to this appropriately. As men get older, they often get fewer erections and their erections take longer to develop; this, too, is normal and part of aging for a healthy man.

When Viagra was introduced, the cultural discussion around impotence changed. Originally designed to treat the pain caused by heart disease, Viagra works by dilating blood vessels, thus improving blood flow. Scholars of gender and sexuality say that the introduction of Viagra changed our collective understanding of impotence. Jay Baglia says that the rhetoric associated with Viagra replaced "impotence" – a "psychologically and relationally flaccid term" – with the term "erectile dysfunction" – a term that is not only "masculinized and structurally based" but also focuses our attention on physiological issues alone, pushing aside relational and psychological considerations (2005: 3).

Baglia and Leonora Tiefer (2006a, 2006b) point out that pharmaceutical corporations have an interest in creating and supporting a certain understanding of what happens when an expected erection does not occur: the more impotence is seen as a failure or dysfunction, the higher the demand for the treatment, and the higher the sales and profit. Tiefer says that making Viagra a successful drug required that "what the penis should do needed to become more and more important and demanding," so that "most penises would fail or falter at some point" and the incidence of erectile dysfunction would escalate (2006b: 279). This, she says, was accomplished partly through ad campaigns reinforcing the idea that successful hetero sex requires penetration. Rather than being a completely normal part of life, what used to be called "impotence" was now a dysfunction, a failure, needing treatment. Tiefer calls this cultural understanding the "Viagra narrative": in it, impotence – and what counts as "normal sex" – is medicalized.

Framing impotence as a dysfunction rather than a normal part of life has several implications. As Baglia points out, taking a pill discourages men from thinking about the effects of stress, poor diet, and alcohol or drug abuse and how these are affecting their lives more generally (2005: 3).

The "Viagra narrative" reinforces the idea that "sex" for men requires an erection, obscuring the idea of other possibilities like giving oral sex or gaining pleasure from being stimulated in other ways. And there are effects on our cultural understanding of masculinity as well. As Tom Digby (2014) explains, masculinity in our society is profoundly impacted by themes of toughness and invulnerability; Digby argues that the suppression of empathy and caring emotions required by norms of modern masculinity is damaging not only to men but also to women, for the way it creates pressures on men to act badly to women. Baglia (2005: 4) points out that the construction of masculinity as requiring erections may block progress on finding alternative conceptualizations of masculinity, opening up space for men to be who they are instead of conforming to existing problematic masculinity norms.

The social control of women's sexuality

Once Viagra existed, it was inevitable that there would be increased interest in creating a similar drug for women: as Tiefer says, from the successful branding of Viagra, we are now so accustomed to thinking of sex through the lens of something that can be enhanced and corrected through drugs that it seems only fair that such a drug would be available for women (2006b: 287). But sex researchers say that when it comes to women's sexuality we should be especially cautious about the ways that research and new treatments can shape our understanding of what is and isn't a problem.

As with Viagra itself, the introduction of these drugs risks casting as dysfunctional what is normal; psychological, emotional, and relational factors are set aside in favor of a focus on physiology. As with men, there is a risk that lack of sexual desire or arousal because of relationship problems will be interpreted as medical dysfunctions to be solved by popping a pill, and the waning of desire associated with aging, which can be seen as completely normal, will be recast as a problem.

But it's also said that the potential problems with medicalizing women's sexuality are particularly acute. Partly, as we'll see below, this is because of new understandings of the workings and variability of women's sexuality. There are also risks associated with the way social control can be, and historically has been, especially asserted over women's sexuality. John Bancroft, a physician who served as director of the Kinsey Institute, attributes this potential for social control of women's sexuality partly to the disjunction women experience between orgasm and reproductive behavior: for women, unlike for men, the activities that cause orgasm are not generally the same as the activities that cause conception (Bancroft 2002: 453).

For men, having an orgasm generally involves semen coming out of the penis, and this is how people get pregnant. But there's no such connection for women. As we saw in Chapter 2, the act that brings about conception, penetration of the vagina with the penis, does not typically bring about orgasm for women; the activities that bring about orgasm, like stimulation of the clitoris, do not themselves bring about conception. This disconnect means that social norms that impede and obscure women's pleasure and orgasm can flourish without adverse effects on reproduction, and so it is easier for these norms to take hold and persist.

As we've seen, some social norms function to channel women's sexuality into structures like monogamous marriage and encourage a double standard, endorsing male promiscuity as normal or even good, and classing promiscuous women as "sluts" and "bad." As in the case of impotence, the creation of pharmaceutical options for women's sexuality is likely to go hand in hand with a certain conceptualization of what is and isn't dysfunctional. If women's sexuality is more susceptible to influence from social norms, this could have a particularly dramatic impact. As we'll see in the next section, the complexity of women's sexual response shows multiple ways in which what seems like a "problem" is shaped by social and cultural factors and cannot be seen simply in terms of biological function or health.

Recent scientific study of women's sexuality

Formulating a drug like Viagra for women has turned out to be challenging, partly because women's sexuality is not well understood; since it's not obvious what an analogue to impotence is, it's not obvious what "like Viagra" means in this context. Is the problem a lack of desire to have sex? Is it subjective desire that doesn't produce physiological changes associated with arousal? Is it having sex without having an orgasm? Is it a combination of these or something else? As Emily Nagoski says in her fascinating book *Come as You Are* (2015), recent scientific research about women's sexuality not only shows why developing drugs is difficult but also helps us understand women's sexuality in new and fruitful ways. Nagoski and others emphasize that interpreting women through the lens of a traditional model of sexuality, one perhaps more suited to men, can cause us to incorrectly see something as a problem or dysfunction. Very roughly, a traditional model of sexuality is that desire (wanting to have sex) leads to arousal (physiological, bodily changes in the body such as lubrication or erection), which leads to sexual activity and pleasure, which lead to orgasm and thus resolution. But some researchers suggest this model isn't always apt, especially for women, and that there are features of women's sexuality we should try to understand on their own terms.

One such feature is nonconcordance. This refers to the fact that the things that create physiological responses and the things that create subjective feelings of arousal often don't go together; while this is true for both men and women, the disconnect is greater for women. Physiological effects of arousal for women include lubrication, the stiffening and enlargement of the clitoris, and a raised heart rate, and these don't always go together with a woman feeling turned on. The reporter Daniel Bergner describes one researcher showing male and female participants movie clips: bonobos having sex, men and women having heterosexual sex, men and women having same-sex sex, a man masturbating, a woman masturbating, a chiseled man walking naked on a beach, and a naked, well-toned woman doing calisthenics. Men responded in mostly "category-specific" ways: men who self-identified as gay showed physiological arousal in response to men and reported feeling turned on by men; straight men for women likewise; none were aroused by the bonobos.

But the women's responses were all over the map. Physically, straight women and lesbians responded to the bonobos while reporting no subjective response, and they responded physiologically more to the exercising woman than the strolling man. Viewing the lesbian and gay scenes, women who identified as straight reported less subjective excitement while their bodies were more responsive, and conversely for the clips of straight sex. In a 2013 review of Bergner's book, Amanda Hess summarizes this way: "Straight women claimed to respond to straight sex more than they really did; lesbian women claimed to respond to straight sex far less than they really did; nobody admitted a response to the bonobo sex." Some studies have suggested that women experience more nonconcordance than men do: with men, the degree of concordance is about 50 percent – about 50 percent of the time, physical and subjective arousal go together – but for women it's only about 10 percent. That would mean about 90 percent of the time a woman is either experiencing bodily changes without subjective changes or subjective changes without bodily changes.

Another interesting feature is responsive desire. Recent research suggests that women's desire may often occur in response to sexual activity. In the traditional model, desire leads to arousal; in people with healthy sexuality, desire itself occurs spontaneously. But women may often engage in some sexual activity that causes them to feel desire for more sexual activity. In a paper that prompted a great deal of attention from sex researchers, Rosemary Basson notes that women may "move from a sexual neutrality to seeking stimuli necessary to ignite sexual desire. This sexual desire would be experienced as a craving for sexual sensations for their own sake, it also might involve a desire to experience physical and subjective arousal and perhaps release of sexual tension" (2010: 53). That is, a woman might seek out the experiences and interactions that will lead to her having sexual desire rather than having sexual desire and being motivated by that to seek out certain experiences and interactions.

Related to desire and pleasure, Nagoski emphasizes a distinction between "eagerness" and "enjoying": "eagerness" refers to that lustful craving we might have for sex we anticipate while "enjoying" is experiencing a good feeling in the moment. As responsive desire illustrates, these don't have to go together, and you don't necessarily need eagerness to get to enjoying. A lot of sexual pleasure has to do with knowing yourself and knowing your partner, knowing the kinds of things that each of you likes to do, and caring enough to make it work well. We don't need the feeling of eagerness to get started on sex that turns out to be incredibly good.

In general, women vary with respect to what turns them on and why and how what seems like a low or high sex drive can be produced by different mechanisms. Nagoski uses the metaphor of "accelerator" and "brake" for the various internal processes that affect how women experience sexual desire, with the accelerator pushing us toward feeling desire for sex and the brake dampening it. Not surprisingly, stress, fatigue, anxiety, and fear can often cause the brake to kick in. In what may be a result of evolution, it's been suggested women have strong psychophysiological mechanisms of inhibition: if there is something wrong – wrong partner, wrong moment, bad feelings, whatever – women's desire and arousal are more likely than men's to shut down (Bancroft 2002). A woman who experiences herself as having a high sex drive may have a strong accelerator – or they might just find it easy to switch off the brake; conversely, a woman whose desire feels low may have a weak accelerator or may just have a very responsive brake system. Women who have different underlying systems may respond differently to different contexts when it comes to feeling lust and desire. This shows that "lack of sexual desire" is not a simple phenomenon and that it has multiple potential causes.

As we've seen, many women do not orgasm just from penetrative heterosexual intercourse, and physiologically a woman's orgasm is often caused by direct or indirect stimulation of her clitoris. For a mix of reasons, women generally have substantially fewer orgasms than men in heterosexual sexual encounters overall, a fact that's been referred to as the "orgasm gap." Women having sex with women and women masturbating both have orgasms more often than women having sex with men, and while the gap between men and women is more dramatic in short-term hooking up, it persists even in longer-term couples (Mintz 2018).

Because of all of these factors, if we interpret women's sexuality along the lines of the traditional model – desire leads to arousal which leads to sex which leads to orgasm – we might be led to conclude that women's sexual response doesn't work as well as that of men. Relatively speaking, desire occurs less spontaneously, subjective desire and physiological arousal do not go together, sexual activity does not lead to orgasm. This could lead one to conclude that there is a lot of seeming dysfunction in women's sexuality to be addressed. But this conclusion could be mistaken. The orgasm gap has to do with context and the specific activities, not a woman's malfunctioning physiology. And, as we'll see, nonconcordance and responsive desire can be understood as a normal part of women's healthy sexuality, not as problems to be solved. We can change the model, not ourselves. Changing the model leads to some philosophically interesting questions, as we'll discuss below.

Nonconcordance and the interpretation of desire

First, let's look more at nonconcordance, when subjective enjoyment and physiological arousal do not always go together. Sometimes this means physical changes do not accompany subjective ones so that the body is not responding in ways we might have expected. For example, a woman may be making out with a partner and feeling a high degree of subjective arousal – she is really into it and enjoying it – but her body isn't producing vaginal lubrication.

Other times, nonconcordance means that physiological arousal effects happen in ways that do not track subjective experience. For example, Nagoski tells an interesting story of a woman experimenting with dominance and submission, whose partner rigged up a device where she was perched with a bar horizontally between her legs, pressing against her vulva. The partner tied up her hands and left her for a while. She said it was totally boring and she wasn't into it at all, but when the partner came back, her body had produced a lot of genital lubrication. Her partner thought she must have been into it: wasn't this lubrication proof of what she "really" liked? "And I was so confused," she said, "because I definitely wasn't into it but my body was definitely responding" (Nagoski 2015: 192).

Sometimes women experience physiological arousal in response to things they are not only not interested in but emphatically do not want, for example in the case of rape. It's hypothesized that lubrication may be an evolutionary adaptive mechanism, protecting the vagina and vulva from harm. That is, if the body's response to unwanted sex did not involve lubrication, and the sex happened anyway, the woman could be hurt. But if the body's response does include lubrication, harm is less likely (Suschinsky and Lalumière 2011).

Understanding this disconnect as normal and common, we need not think of it as an episode of "dysfunction." For example, if desire is present but the physiological changes associated with arousal are not, saliva or other kinds of lubrication could be used to make interacting with the vulva and vagina feel good. If lubrication is present but the person isn't into it, why not just do something else? Nagoski cautions that we tend to see the body's responses as somehow "real" or as clues to what a person really wants, to think that the body tells the "truth" while the mind, complicated as it is by social and cultural layers, is somehow confused or obfuscating; thus the phrasing in terms of what women "claimed" or "admitted" to wanting. But Nagoski rejects this framing. To think that "genital response is enjoying" or that the genitals somehow tell the truth about a person and what they want, so that if their subjective state or mind doesn't line up then the person is confused, or worse, lying, is a mistake. Nagoski call this a "lubrication error."

The woman whose boyfriend said she must be really into it because her body responded was making this error, treating the body as a source of truth for no reason. It's doubtful that the women in the bonobo study had an underlying desire to have sex with bonobos. In *Fifty Shades of Grey*, the hero dominates Anastasia, and, noticing the wetness of her vulva, says "Feel this. See how much your body likes this, Anastasia." In Nagoski's terms, this is another lubrication error: the body is responding to a sexually relevant stimulus, not showing us what we really want and like.

Nagoski's book has heartbreaking stories of women who experienced lubrication and bodily responses during rape and how this caused them to feel intense shame and to second-guess themselves. Understanding their response through nonconcordance allowed them to let go of the idea that their bodily responses reflected something about themselves, and this allowed them to thus to let go of the shame. This applies to men as well. Even if they have a greater degree of concurrence, men also have a lot of nonconcurrence, and it's just as important not to take the body as a source of truth. Nagoski describes a man who sees a violent sexual assault and experiences an erection, to his great shame. The shame is unwarranted: the body's physiological response does not reflect who we are.

As in the Viagra narrative, if we think of nonconcordance as a normal part of life rather than a dysfunction, we start to think of all the things that affect our brakes and accelerators, something a pharmaceutical treatment might encourage us to ignore or push aside. Again, it's only if you think the higher degree of concordance is "normal" that you would think of desire nonconcordance as a problem.

But while there is a clear sense in which the body is not a source of truth about a person, there are still philosophical complexities associated with nonconcordance, because norms and context profoundly affect what we give ourselves permission to want and thus how we interpret our body's responses. As we saw in our discussion of the Viagra narrative, social expectations about sexuality can affect and change what we see as normal. It is certainly possible that women have been taught to see certain things – like hetero sex for women who identify as "straight" – as the things they "should" want. In that case, their subjective experience may be affected in ways that guide them away from what the might otherwise have enjoyed.

In this direction, it is intuitive to say that if you live in a sexually repressive society, and because of this you lack subjective interest in sex, then the experience of physiological arousal could be seen as a sign of your true sexual interests. The same applies to LGBTQ+ people raised in homophobic cultures or families, or anyone who lives in a society where there are pressures to conform to a certain model of sexuality. If a gay man is in denial because of internalized homophobia and tries to date only women but never experiences physical arousal with them, we might want to say that the problem is the homophobia, and that the body is telling him something. Couldn't accepting and acknowledging our physical responses be liberating and good? In this sense, we might want to say that genital response could be a window into another version of a person's self, the person they might have been had they not been socialized in a certain way. Even if it is a mistake to assume that the body is generally a source of truth, maybe sometimes it is a source of relevant information.

With respect to the greater degree of nonconcordance in women, Bergner cites Meredith Chivers as pointing out that there may be reasons that men learn over time, more than women, to connect the physical with the subjective (2013b: 15). Because the penis is visible and unsubtle in its growing and shrinking, boys grow up with a continuous source of vivid information about their bodily responses, and because they are aware of these responses, a positive "sexual loop" might develop over time, allowing a developing boy to integrate physiological and subjective responses. So the higher degree of concordance might have a cause. It's often pointed out that adolescent girls are taught about sex in ways that make them gatekeepers rather than sexual beings: they're supposed to tell other people when "no" is appropriate, and conventional sex education has little discussion about how girls and women experience pleasure in sex. The gatekeeper function and social norms may interrupt the possibility of a positive sexual loop. If women don't make those connections partly because double standards and social norms about "good girls," this is regrettable.

William Wilkerson's idea of interpretation from Chapter 8 might be useful here. When you notice a physiological response, you always have a choice of how to interpret it, as showing something about yourself or as really having nothing to do with who you are. While the body is not a source of "truth" about a person, it can be one component in the raw data that we subject to interpretation. Social repression of sexuality suggests that sometimes the body could be a source of information worth listening to.

Worth listening to – but when? If regarding the body as a source of insight into our sexuality is sometimes a lubrication error and other times a liberatory act, is there any way to distinguish our appropriate response? I don't think there is general answer to this question. Sometimes your physiology might be worth listening to, and sometimes it's not; the difference has to do with complex value-laden social factors. A woman who experiences arousal in response to oral sex but not subjective pleasure might ask whether her "brake" is kicking in – perhaps she feels awkward or embarrassed – and, if it seems so, she might be best off relaxing and trying to connect the experience with subjective pleasure. But the man who experiences an erection in response to rape should certainly not try to connect the experience with subjective pleasure or see it as what he "really wants": this response is usefully seen as a bodily response having nothing to do with the man's subjective identity. The difference between these two cases is that rape is morally wrong and oral sex is not. There is no way to divorce the question of how to interpret our desires from the evaluative question of what we think it is good to want and do, and from the social and ethical meanings of certain acts.

This discussion of nonconcordance shows the deeply social dimension of sexual well-being. From the point of view of the traditional model, nonconcordance looks like a dysfunction; acknowledging nonconcordance as normal, it is not. But when we experience nonconcordance, trusting the body can be a liberatory act in a context of social repression, or it can be a lubrication error and a terrible mistake. The difference has to do with values and social norms, illustrating how social factors affect what we think is normal and what we think is a problem.

Lack of desire and eagerness versus enjoying

Similar considerations apply in the case of responsive desire and the distinction between eagerness and enjoying. One of the main aims for "Viagra for women" is to create a drug that will cause women to feel more desire and thus have increased interest in having sex. In his reporting on this topic, Bergner (2013a) describes one notable target population: women in long-term monogamous relationships who have stopped feeling sexual desire for their partners. In many cases, he says, these women still experience a great deal of sexual pleasure with their spouses: once they start having sex, they get into it, and they have pleasure and orgasm. But they no longer feel that intense lustful drive for sex. In fact, sometimes they feel reluctance; they start adopting strategies like going to bed earlier to deflect their spouses from initiating sex. Some statistical studies suggest that in monogamous couples (gay and straight), while men and women both experience a decline in spontaneous desire for sex with their partner, for women the decline is substantially more dramatic.

Is this kind of waning desire a suitable target for intervention? In one sense, it could easily be seen as a dysfunction: if lack of desire causes women not to engage in sex, and they are unhappy about that, wishing the desire to come back, it's natural to think of "lack of desire" as a problem. But there are two perspectives from which this could be a mistake. First, if the waning of desire happens in contexts of monogamy, why not challenge monogamy itself? Second, why should we prioritize eagerness over enjoying?

Especially for women, monogamy is not only socially expected but also seen as a natural state of desire. That is, the way we talk about women's desire often supposes that monogamy and the emotional closeness that comes with it are what they want and need most – so that failing to experience desire in those contexts would be especially aptly seen as dysfunctional. But what if that is an artifact of our social understanding of sex?

You may have encountered the idea that men are "naturally" more promiscuous and women "naturally" more suited to monogamy. The idea that these patterns are found in nature is sometimes supported by appeal to an evolutionary argument that goes something like this: men are promiscuous because being promiscuous is "adaptive" for men; male promiscuity makes it more likely that a man's genes will be passed on to the

next generation; evolutionary pressures in the past meant that more promiscuous men passed on more of their genes and others did not; so the
men who exist today inherited that trait. Women, on the other hand, are
thought to be monogamous because, biologically, they have to devote a
huge amount of time to their offspring; trying to stay with one man max-
imizes the chances the man will help her take care of them. Sometimes this
goes along with an idea you find in a lot of advice columns: that women
crave safety and emotional closeness in sex, most naturally found in a
long-term committed and loving relationship.

But the evolutionary gendered perspective on monogamy has been criticized from scientific and philosophical perspectives. For one thing, evolutionary arguments are difficult to assess in social areas like sexuality,
where culture has so much impact on our practices. The strategy of evolutionary arguments is always difficult because you are observing a phenomenon and then crafting an explanation of how it got to be that way in
terms of evolution. But the phenomenon being observed often has complex social dimensions. When it comes to understanding monogamy and
marriage-like relationships, anthropologists describe a wide range of social
arrangements including monogamy, polygyny (one man with more than
one woman), polyandry (one woman with more than one man), same-sex
relationships, and relationships that don't involve sex at all. As Carla Fehr
(2011) says, the variation of social institutions makes it difficult to see
what is the cross-cultural phenomenon to be explained and also makes it
easy to make false assumptions that what we happen to observe in our
own culture is somehow universal.

It's also common to hear that safety and emotional closeness are central
to women's sexuality. You may also have encountered the idea that for
women, emotions and relationships are what matter and that feeling in a
relaxed and trustful state of mind facilitates sexual pleasure. But it's also
been said that safety and closeness might get in the way of sexual desire
and thus get in the way of the eager lustfulness that some people want to
be part of their sexual experience. Esther Perel, the author of *Mating in
Captivity* (2006), argues that desire requires distance and that domestic
closeness and love can sometimes get in the way of that. Citing the
research of psychologists like Martha Meana, Bergner says that often for
women what ignites passion is not safety and emotional closeness but
rather unpredictability, novelty, and a sense of urgency and passion from
their partners. Relatedly, for women feeling the waning of desire, one fairly
reliable way of bringing back lustful feelings is a new partner. If danger
and novelty are normal aspects of women's sexuality, then seeing the
waning of desire in contexts of safety and monogamy as dysfunctional
would be a prime example of the social control of women's sexuality.

Emily Nagoski offers an alternative view, arguing that the kind of
"craving" and pleasure people feel in contexts of unpredictability may be
more related to fear and relief than to good and healthy sexual

relationships. Love is about attachment. And when our attachment object – the person who makes us feel safe and whole and grounded – is only variably present to us, we crave their presence and engage in behaviors – like sex – that we think will bind them to us. The craving is partly related to fear and separation anxiety and wanting those to end, and the pleasure we feel in the sex is more like relief. You know how people talk about women who crave sex with unpredictable and commitment-phobic partners while lacking desire for the long-term domestic partner they love and adore? Nagoski calls this "solace sex" – "sex that's motivated by your desire to prove that you are loved" (2015: 135); she says it's like the pleasure when you really have to pee, and then you get to pee. Huge relief! Feels great! But only because it's a relief from something. What's so great about craving in the first place?

In safe and committed and good relationships, we never get the urgency of "yikes!" and so the feeling of eagerness can wane. Nagoski says the solution to this problem does not require us to give up closeness, commitment, or monogamy; instead, we might acknowledge the good of enjoying. In our culture, we tend to prioritize "eagerness" – that is, we think it's best when you feel the power and excitement of yearning. But there's nothing wrong with "enjoying." The dysfunction point of view asks us to see the lack of spontaneous desire as a dysfunction and a problem to be solved. But maybe this is just a bias in favor of "eagerness" that makes us see it this way. Again, not a "dysfunction," just different. Furthermore, Nagoski says that even people who want eagerness can get it in other ways – by what she calls "advancing the plot." This means experimenting with contexts to change the dynamic with your partner and to create the sense of eagerness in other ways.

The advantage of "advancing the plot" with a committed loving person over leaving them to chase thrills are obvious. But, at the same time, I think there is something to be said in defense of sexual thrill-seeking. Some people aren't in committed relationships, and some might be willing to put up with a bit of emotional chaos to feel the intensity of sexual desire and that "eagerness" feeling. Nagoski agrees that different things are good for different people. It might even be possible to combine the safety and value of commitment with the intensity of uncertainty – by simply having sex with people other than our primary partner. We'll discuss this idea of "ethical nonmonogamy" in depth in Chapter 14, but it's worth noting here as a different response to the problems of waning sexual desire.

Again, one conclusion we can draw from our discussion of waning desire is that seemingly "biological" matters often have deeply social dimensions, in ways that give a concrete illustration to Tiefer and Bancroft's ideas about social control and what counts as a "dysfunction." People vary, and this variation is normal. What seems like a "problem" is embedded in complex webs of social and cultural attitudes – about what it makes sense to want, about what people should want, about how they should interpret their various yearnings and urges and what they should do with them. In writing about the "female Viagra," for the *New York Times*, Bergner (2013a) describes discussions about industry insiders who fear the effects of increasing women's sexual desire in ways that might upset the existing social order. One researcher said that in dealing with pharmaceutical industry people there was a certain fear of "turning women into nymphomaniacs" and a certain bias against "creating the sexually aggressive woman."

There are thus reasons to heed Bancroft's call for "caution" and to be wary of labeling certain patterns as "dysfunctions" when they may be simply parts of our human experience. At the same time, we must not forget that there are also powerful reasons on the other side – for men and for women. People who experience sexual side effects, people who have health problems, people who are just unhappy with the way they experience their sexuality, can all be made much better off with the right drugs. It is a not an either–or thing but more a very complicated balancing act.

Medicalization of love?

It might seem bizarre or futuristic to worry about medicalizing love, but we already have various mood-altering drugs, and maybe one day there will be pharmaceuticals that affect whether we feel in love or out of love. Such drugs might appeal to people in a wide range of circumstances. What if you promised to love and care for your spouse for ever but you find yourself bored, antsy, and flirting with others? What if you are in love with a self-obsessed narcissist with poor impulse control, and another person, someone nice and caring but maybe a bit dull, wants to marry you? What if you're suffering from a horrible break-up and would give anything to stop feeling in love? Taking chemical control of love might be a tempting way to impose order on a chaotic set of emotions.

There's something creepy about the idea of love drugs, but it is difficult to pin down exactly what it is. In 2010, the author George Saunders published a short story that explores this creepiness in a vivid way. The story takes places in a future world in which new drugs are tested on convicted criminals, and the narrator is forced to become a kind of designer-drug guinea pig. One of the drugs they test makes you feel like you're in love: the drug makers' plan is to market the drug to people who can't love enough, or who love the wrong person, or who love too much, to make sure they love in just the right way. Whoever you're with when you take it, you feel super-connected to them and also like you really want to have sex with them.

In the story, the narrator takes the drug, sees one woman, falls madly in love with her, then, when the drug wears off a few minutes later, goes completely back to baseline human indifference. Then he takes the drug again, sees another woman, falls madly in love with her, then when the drug wears off goes completely back to baseline human indifference. To confirm the absence of love, the people conducting the experiment force the narrator to witness his recent loves experience horrible pain and suffering. They justify this by explaining that while it's just a few minutes' unpleasantness for the woman, it's "years of relief for literally tens of thousands of underloving or overloving folks" (Saunders 2010). The benefits are enormous. No longer would we be emotional ships adrift. If we see a person careening into misery because of too much love, not enough love, or the wrong kind of love, we could take action and take control.

The story is disturbing along multiple dimensions, but part of what makes it so frightening is that the love it describes does not seem authentic or real: it feels less like love and more like manipulation. Given that taking drugs like Viagra for sex enhancement has become common, it's interesting to consider whether love enhancement poses a special challenge with respect to authenticity. One reason love might be different from sex has to do with time and commitment. Love seems incompatible with changing your mind every two minutes, which is essentially what happens in Saunders' story. It's normal for sex to happen over a short period of time, people have always had sex with more than one person, and the possibility of a person having it with one partner and then another and then another, just bouncing around, has always existed. So drugs that facilitate that quick shifting around don't seem to violate the whole concept of what it is to have sex. But, as we saw in our earlier chapters, we tend to think of love as something that develops over time, something that has to do with commitments and who you are as a person. Sure, you can love more than one person at a time. But the bouncing around from person to person? Loving one person at 3:00 and then not loving them at 3:30 and loving another at 4:00? It seems a violation of the whole idea of love. This is one way that medicalizing sex and medicalizing love would be fundamentally different.

In response, it might be said that proper use of love drugs would not be like this: these drugs could be used, instead, to nudge us toward becoming the loving and committed people we want to be. In a series of writings about love drugs and family life, Brian Earp, Julian Savulescu, and Anders Sandberg have argued that because our biology sometimes makes us ill suited to long-term love and commitment in marriage, people should not only have the option to take such drugs, should they become available, but may also be ethically obligated to take them (Earp et al. 2012, 2015, 2016; see also Anderson 2013). They emphasize that love drugs need not be all-or-nothing magic pills that make us bounce from one person to another. Instead, they might gently affect levels of hormones like oxytocin to facilitate certain feelings in certain circumstances, leading to feelings of warmth and understanding, and facilitating the feeling of love.

For example, suppose a married couple is in counseling, and they can be given an option of pharmaceutical nudging to buttress their feelings of closeness and openness. A principle of "marital autonomy" means that people who want to give their mutual love a "helping hand" through neurochemical intervention should have the right to do so (Earp et al. 2012). More contentiously, they suggest that couples – especially those with children – might have a moral obligation to do so. Monogamous commitment has long been seen as a social good, and we know that divorce is difficult and bad for children; if you can save your marriage through love drugs, shouldn't you? With respect to the problem of manipulation, if you took a love drug because you wanted to fall in love with someone, then taking the drug could plausibly make you more authentically yourself (Earp et al. 2015). If you decide you ought to love your longtime spouse, and you take the drug, and it works and you love them, then in a sense you have become a true version of yourself. In fact, you might say that if you *didn't* take the drug, you'd be allowing yourself to be manipulated by your biology. Supporting that theory, lots of people have said that drugs like Prozac make them feel more themselves (Kramer 1993).

Responses to this proposal suggest that a lot of people still find the idea of love drugs troubling in one way or another. Many critiques relate to issues we've already discussed, about medicalization and social control. Medicalization can take otherwise normal parts of human life and make them seem like problems; medicalization can have the effect of increasing social control over behaviors that are different and not socially sanctioned; medicalization can draw attention away from psychological and social factors toward biochemical ones (Earp et al. 2015: 326). People in bad or oppressive relationships should obviously not be encouraged to take pills to feel better about those relationships: that there are abusive spouses is a moral and social problem, not a medical one.

Furthermore, echoing concerns from earlier in this chapter, Kristina Gupta (2012) points out that norms about monogamy might lead to stigmatizing nonmonogamous relationships and create social pressure to use neurochemicals to conform to social expectations. What if you are falling out of love and you want to break up or change your relationship, and your friends think you're crazy – or unethical – when there's a pill you could just take to make everything better? Critics like Carrie Jenkins point out that encouraging the widespread use of such drugs risks "papering over symptoms while the real issues go unaddressed" (2017: 162). If people find it difficult to have one love or sex partner for their entire lives, then maybe it's the social structures and norms that should change. As we saw in Chapter 9, we might rethink the nature of the love commitment to be more flexible with respect to what exactly we are promising to the other person. As we'll discuss in Chapter 14, maybe monogamy is part of the problem, and loving commitment should be rethought so that it is compatible with nonmonogamy. Or maybe, Nagoski suggests, it's not monogamy that's the problem, but rather "the way people *do* monogamy" (2015: 239): with better understanding of our sexuality and how it relates to our emotions and relationships, we can keep monogamy without love drugs.

In response to some of these concerns, Earp et al. (2015) point out that not all medicalization is linked to pathologization: increasingly, medical treatments can be seen as offering a range of options to people who are basically well rather than targeting dysfunctions. What matters is not whether the drugs are available to use but rather how they are used. Regulation and education could ensure they are used responsibly, alongside social and political interventions when necessary. Also, we do many actions to feel better that work biochemically: go running, eat chocolate, take a nap. What's the difference between these and drugs? What matters isn't the nature of the intervention but rather whether your well-being is increased. Finally, they say, love drugs could be useful not only in nudging us toward monogamy but also in allowing us to realize whatever relationship conception we want for ourselves. People who embrace polyamory may find jealousy getting in the way; love drugs might allow them to better realize their commitment to openness and nonexclusivity.

Whether love drugs could be used in such constructive and personalized ways depends partly on our social ability to put into practice policies that are both nuanced and flexible and partly on our personal abilities to judge accurately when we should trust our immediate emotions and when we should seek to transcend them. On the one hand, our experience with other mood-altering drugs might be cause for optimism about these matters, since these have been used to help many people with depression and anxiety. On the other hand, we've seen with the Viagra narrative how the possibility of enhancement can go hand in hand with new understandings of what is and isn't a problem. It is unclear whether drugs can be used for enhancement without creating social pressure to adopt those enhancements: even if waning love is not labeled a medical dysfunction the existence of such drugs in a culture that values monogamous lifelong commitment might make them very difficult to turn down. Imagine telling your spouse that not only have you fallen out of love you're also unwilling to take the drugs that might make you fall for them again.

This discussion of love shows again how medicalization highlights the question of who we want ourselves to be, a question that is not biological but rather social and ethical. To judge when and how love drugs should be used, we need opinions about the value of monogamy, the situations in which commitment is worth preserving versus those in which it is better for a relationship to end, when it makes sense to change ourselves to fit our ideals, and when it makes sense to change our ideals to fit ourselves.

Conclusion

We sometimes think the difference between being healthy and having a health problem is biological and straightforward, but this chapter shows that what counts as a dysfunction is deeply social and culturally embedded. While there is no question that pharmaceuticals can benefit specific people enormously, it's also the case that adding a pharmaceutical option to what's available to us can profoundly affect how we think about things as a society. As the analysis of the Viagra narrative suggests, the availability of new treatments can shift our sense of what is normal and what is not. As the discussion of women's sexuality shows, social, gendered expectations about desire shape what seems like a problem and what seems like an appropriate treatment. If love drugs become available, we will face delicate questions about how and when they should be used. Medicalization forces us to consider whether and how the emotions, desires, and responses we have are not the emotions, desires, and responses we want, thus forcing us to reflect on one of the most difficult problems of all: what kind of people do we want to be?

13 The economics of sex and love

Introduction

It might seem oxymoronic to speak of the "economics of sex and love."
Economics, we think, deals with money and markets, while love and sex are
personal and nonquantitative. But economic methods are increasingly used
to study social domains like family life and sexual decision-making, and
some policy matters – such as the gender wage gap – are thought to involve
causes that bring domestic and financial factors together. Marriage typically
involves some degree of economic partnership, and economic factors shape
marital choices and the decisions families make in spending and apportion-
ing resources. So economics and sex and love are already intertwined.

When economists apply their methods to the domains of sex and love,
various philosophical questions arise. For example, economics typically
models people as rational, self-interested maximizers of their own well-
being who make contractual exchanges to get what they want. But, as
we've seen, love and sex do not fit neatly into this paradigm: being completely self-interested seems to be inconsistent with love, and it's often
thought that sex is best when it is mutually pleasurable and not a tit-for-tat
contractual exchange. Can sex and love be aptly interpreted in terms of
the self-interested exchange of commodities?

In this chapter, we start by looking at economic analysis of love, then
move to economic analysis of sex, then consider some methodological
reflections. I'll argue that the challenges associated with applying economics to sex and love force difficult and contentious decisions about how
these should be understood and valued, not only with respect to self-
interest but also with respect to gender and the role that sex and love play
in our lives.

Economics and love: what is the problem?

Let's start with love. On the face of it, there seems to be an incompatibility
between the economic view of people as self-interested and the idea of love
as essentially other-regarding. Typical economic reasoning in our era is

"neoclassical," and central to the modern neoclassical conception of economics is the model of people as rational maximizers of their own utility. Utility is a tricky concept that can be defined in a number of ways, but "increased utility" basically refers to a person getting what they want or being made better off in some way. In contemporary approaches, "utility" is often theorized in terms of preference-satisfaction: your utility is increased when your personal preferences are satisfied. A person is rational when they choose their most preferred option, where preferences are assumed to satisfy certain formal properties – like if you prefer A to B and B to C then you prefer A to C. Beyond these formal relations, the theory doesn't say anything about which things it makes sense to prefer.

In this way of looking at things, if what you want most is to eat doughnuts, and you don't care about your health, and then you go on to eat many doughnuts every day, you have behaved rationally because you've satisfied your preferences. Likewise, if what you want most is to make money, and you don't care about other people, and you go on to focus your whole life on money-making, you have behaved rationally. It doesn't matter if your preferences seem weird or bad to others. It's about effectively getting what you want most. There are various kind of economic models, but for our purposes a model is a theoretical construct that specifies certain variables and the logical relations among them. Models typically function as idealized or simplified representations of reality. So when we say that contemporary economics "models people as rational maximizers of their own utility," this means that economic reasoning processes include a simplifying assumption that people are self-interested, concerned only with satisfying their own personal preferences, and effective at doing so.

As we've seen, though, love is often thought to be essentially not self-interested. The most obvious example of this kind of thinking is the caring-concern theory we discussed in Chapter 6, where love is characterized through volitions and reasons to act to bring about the well-being of the other person. The union theory is less straightforward – and we'll discuss some of its intricacies below – but Nozick also says that forming a "we" means giving up some of your personal autonomy and the power to make decisions based only on how they will affect you personally. Although we encountered challenges to the union and caring theories, the modifications we discussed in Chapter 7, which make love more like friendship, retain the connection between love and other-regardingness. Balancing and shared deliberation involve some care for the other person, even if it is mixed with self-interest. In his attempt to find something so basic about love that everyone will agree, Eric Cave, whose theories about marriage we discussed in Chapter 9, proposes "concern for shared agency" (2003: 333–334) in which you are motivated to act by some concern because it is one you share with the person you love or because it is something they care about. If the economic view of persons is based on self-interest and love is based on other-regardingness, then the two things seem incompatible: you can be a rational person economically, or you can love other people, but you can't do both.

Historically, this question of the compatibility of economics and love didn't really arise, because the economic domain and the caring domain were thought to be separate. As we've seen, in the history of Western culture of the past few centuries, only heterosexual romantic love was thought to be appropriate. In addition, economics was thought to study domains related to money and wealth. In the nineteenth century, women were not typically part of the public sphere; only men were seen as engaging in economic activity. When it came to "caring labor" – activities like childcare and looking after others' needs that can be both "work" and motivated by caring attitudes – feminist economist Michèle Pujol (2003) says that economists of the nineteenth century classified these activities as "women's work," and denied that women were economic agents at all. As wives and mothers, women were dependent on men, and they were thought to be essentially and naturally suited for reproduction and caring. And, as we've seen, marriage was understood to subsume a woman's identity and autonomy into that of her husband so that she would generally not be a decision-maker. So, in a sense, economics and love were understood to be completely different spheres.

But over the twentieth century various shifts occurred. For one thing, economists' ideas of what they were studying changed so that instead of being specifically about money, wealth, and commodities, economics came to be understood as a methodology or style of reasoning that could be applied to decision-making generally. In the early twentieth century, Lionel Robbins defined economics as "the science which studies human behavior as a relationship between ends and scarce means which have alternative uses" (1932: 15) – a definition that roughly captures what many people think today and allows for economic study of a wide range of phenomena. Furthermore, women came to be seen as employees, employers, owners, buyers, and participants in public life, and the idea of marriage shifted away from male dominance and toward a model of equal partnership. If economics is about applying a certain methodology to all human decision-making, then why not apply that methodology to intimate contexts?

In the twentieth century, this is just what economists did, starting with Gary Becker's ground-breaking analysis of family life, which culminated in his 1981 book *A Treatise on the Family* (expanded edition, 1991). In the next section, we discuss Becker's theories of caring and family life and what they might mean for understanding the tension between love and self-interestedness.

Altruism and the possibility of "self-interested" love

As we've seen above, a challenge of applying economics to caring relationships and family life is that economics models people as self-interested while love seems paradigmatically other-regarding. The most obvious way to address this challenge is to say that self-interest and other-regardingness are not really incompatible after all, since the person who cares about someone else and acts on that basis is, in some sense, doing what they most want to do, and thus satisfying their own preferences. As is often pointed out, self-interested need not mean "selfish": people often give to charity and make personal sacrifices for others "because they derive pleasure from doing so" (McConnell et al. 2013: 4).

Becker's model of family life dissolves the tension between self-interest and other-regardingness by using the concept of "altruism." He bases his definition of the concept on the idea of one person getting utility from someone else's getting what they want: if your well-being is dependent on someone else's, that means you are altruistic. For example, if your partner wants a cup of coffee, and you want to bring them one, because your love for them means that seeing them happy makes you happy, then you are being altruistic. Caring about another person, then, reflects a fact about you and what makes you better off. In this set-up, when an altruist acts to benefit the person they care about, both people are made better off: the loved one gets what they want and need, and the altruist gets what Becker calls "psychic income" (Becker 1991: 299–300).

Becker uses this framework to extensively analyze family life, deriving many theorems and predictions. Some of this work shows how a rational and altruistic head of a household would create incentives for other people in the family to act appropriately, for the good of the other family members. For instance, Becker's "Rotten Kid Theorem" says that a rational and altruistic parent will reward and punish dependents to make them act to benefit and not harm other dependents. For example, suppose you have a parent who can decide how much money to give each of their various kids. Suppose one kid is a cruel kid who would derive pleasure from harming his sibling – a "rotten kid." The parent can then decide to incentivize good behavior, by telling him that if he does harm his nicer sibling he will be financially punished while the nicer sibling is financially rewarded. This will cause the rotten kid to refrain from acting badly. The decision is caused by "altruism" on the part of the parent, who cares about the nice kid and does not want them to suffer.

We can see immediately one way that Becker's idea of altruism seems incompatible with Frankfurt's idea of love. In Becker's framework, the ultimate aim of an altruistic action is still self-interested: you do things for the other person because it makes you better off. But Frankfurt says that love must be "disinterested": loving actions should aim at the well-being of the beloved and not at one's own. In this sense, adopting a caring-concern theory of love might lead to the conclusion that while altruism is all well and good, it isn't love; since altruism is ultimately self-interested, the loving person could not be an economically rational one.

On the other hand, perhaps things are not so simple. Frankfurt also says that love gives the lover a reason to act to further the well-being of the beloved, and, as we saw in Chapters 6 and 7, this has the effect of collapsing the whole distinction between self-interestedness and other-regardingness. If you really love someone then when you act to benefit them you are acting to benefit yourself. This is similar to Becker's theory of altruism. In this sense, to love someone in the caring-concern way might cause you to be altruistic toward them in just Becker's sense. Interpreting love as this form of altruism would resolve any tension between love and self-interest.

Would interpreting love as self-interested altruism be a good way of resolving that tension? I am skeptical. Essentially, this resolution collapses the distinction between self-interestedness and the other-interestedness of love: they come, in the end, to the same thing. But in our chapters on love we saw reasons to keep the two things distinct and separate. Most importantly, when we understand love this way, it becomes impossible to distinguish between actions you do for other people and actions you do for yourself; this obscures, and even prevents us from framing, any questions of fairness in relationships. Remember Morgan and Nico, where Nico gets a new job far from home and Morgan wants to stay put? Intuitively, it seems like if they move Morgan has given up something important for Nico, and if they stay put Nico has given up something important for Morgan. And then whoever has made the sacrifice should be recognized as having done so, perhaps with the thought that next time the sacrifice could go the other way. But, as we saw before, when self-interestedness and other-regardingness are the same, we cannot articulate the sense that one of them has sacrificed something for the other, so there is no way to explain this sense of obligation for reciprocity.

In our discussion of Frankfurt, we also showed that if one person is domineering and strong-willed and the other is deferential, the first person will tend to always get their way. When self-interestedness and other-regardingness are collapsed, it is impossible to even articulate the fact that one person is always getting their way, so it is impossible to address it as a problem. In Chapters 6 and 7, we related these questions about sacrifice and self-interest to larger questions of fairness in relationships among equals. If there is no way to distinguish between the acts we do for other people and the acts we do for ourselves, then there is no way to express why it seems like a problem when one person always acts for the other and the other is always looking out for themselves. How, then, could we conceptualize the ideal of fair and reciprocal caring among equals?

Strikingly, in the model Becker developed most extensively, there is only one altruist in any given family, so this question does not arise. As we saw with the "Rotten Kid Theorem", the main idea is to examine how one altruistic head of household would relate to an array of selfish children. The assumption of a single altruist is made partly because when you have two reciprocal altruists – two adults who care about one another – the model becomes very complicated; the simplifying assumption of one altruist per family allows for the use of simpler and more familiar mathematics (England 1989: 16). Of course, in practice, this means the model never fits a case in which there are two or more people each of whom cares about the other. When it came to applying his theory to real life, Becker assumed that families would consist in two heterosexual parents and their children, and, for simplicity and consistency, that the patriarch would be the altruist. He then added that to fit the model to real life, the wife could be modeled as if she is one of the selfish children. This shows one other way in which Becker's idea of altruism echoes Frankfurt's theory of love: the paradigmatic case for caring is based on a parent–child relationship rather than on reciprocal caring among adults.

Though Becker didn't apply the model in this way, it's worth exploring the implications of seeing love as self-interested altruism in the context of asymmetrically selfish and non-selfish preferences. Suppose we have a situation of two adults in a domestic partnership, both working and contributing the same amount of financial resources to the partnership, and imagine that one person, Lane, has deep and wide-ranging altruistic preferences while Kerry has almost none. Lane worries when Kerry doesn't eat healthy food and suffers when Kerry is sad or unwell. Because Lane is altruistic toward Kerry, Lane engages in a lot of caring work for Kerry: cooking food, keeping the house nice, sympathizing and encouraging Kerry when Kerry is down. Imagine Kerry is not altruistic. Kerry's preferences are mostly for things involving Kerry: that Kerry gets enough to eat and a comfy chair and quiet in the house when their favorite TV show is on.

In this case, as in Frankfurt's theory of love, it seems that Lane and Kerry are both getting what they want: Lane's preferences are satisfied by Kerry's well-being, and Kerry's preferences are satisfied by Kerry's well-being. This means that, furthermore, when Kerry and Lane engage in self-interested rational behavior, Lane will take care of Kerry and Kerry will take care of themselves. This behavior will be rational for Kerry for obvious reasons, but will be rational for Lane as well because they are getting what they want.

In the model, the interaction between Lane and Kerry is seen as a rational voluntary exchange. But if you encountered such a household in real life, it might well seem unfair and exploitative. This possibility is especially salient when we consider the way that women are socialized to be more caring than men. If women are raised with social messaging that they should be altruistic, more caring, and more interested in doing the kind of labor that altruism entails – like taking care of other people because you care about them – then women – especially when they are in heterosexual relationships – are more likely to be like Lane. And, indeed, doing a greater share of caring labor is one of several standard explanations for the gender wage gap seen in many contemporary societies; men consistently earn more than women. Consistently with this, some studies suggest that same-sex partnerships involve more equality when it comes to distribution of caring labor like cooking and cleaning (Solomon et al.

2005: 562, 572). There might seem to be a disconnect between the intuitive judgment that the gender wage gap is unjust and the way the model encourages us to see the exchanges in question as rational and voluntary, benefiting everyone.

Should these considerations be understood to reflect problems with the economic models proposed? Or are they best understood in some other way? These are subtle and difficult questions. On the one hand, Becker's approach has been criticized for its seeming mismatch with reality. As we've seen with Lane and Kerry, what seems intuitively exploitative and unfair is interpreted in the model as a rational, mutually beneficial, exchange. Furthermore, the model is often applied in ways that assume the patriarch will care for all the selfish children equally, but one of the main problems in families is that parents do not care equally for all children (Nussbaum 1997; Marino 2017). Critics also point out that seeing the household as a unit, structured by altruism, is unrealistic, since households are themselves often sites of conflict and negotiation (Nussbaum 1997; Agarwal 1997).

On the other hand, it could be said that attributing these concerns to problems with Becker's model reflects a misunderstanding. The model says nothing about fairness or what is appropriate and good; it just gives formal definitions, which can then be used in a range of ways. All models simplify and idealize the complexity of the world and thus don't fully reflect reality; to present such a mismatch as an objection is to misunderstand how models work. With respect to the assumption of equal altruism, Robert Pollak (2003) says that this assumption is not part of Becker's model: the model rests on definitions and logical relationships and does not depend on facts about how altruism works in practice. In fact, Pollak suggests that calling the preferences in question "altruistic" may be misguided because they do not track what we typically associate with the concept of altruism in everyday language. Finally, why should we see problems of inequality and injustice as problems with the model rather than problems with reality (Pollak 2003; Cudd 2001)? If there are gendered asymmetries of altruism, and if these contribute to the gender wage gap, isn't this a problem with the way the world is rather than with how we are representing it?

In response to the points about simplification and idealization, though, we might challenge the usefulness of a model that elides, rather than centering, factors central to the phenomena we are trying to understand. While all models simplify and idealize, it makes a difference what they include and what they leave out. Amartya Sen has frequently commented on the ways that economic models, focused as they are on self-interest and rationality, are generally inadequate to theorizing relationships and inequality (1981, 1987). Bina Agarwal (1997) argues that seeing the household as a unit leaves aside many crucial questions related to inequalities both inside and outside the home. Agarwal says that appreciating conflict inside families, we see the salience of a number of important questions. What factors affect intrafamilial bargaining power? How do social norms affect the bargaining and negotiation family members engage in? What are the implications for bargaining power outside the household?

In response to the idea that the problem is with the world rather than with the model, we might also ask which models help us most effectively understand and change what we want to change. Here, Ann Cudd says that some economic models are, in fact, very useful, because they can teach us strategies for reducing gender-based asymmetries and thus help address the gender wage gap. We've seen the possibility that these asymmetries could be traced to women performing more caring labor, in part because of socialized preferences that are more altruistic and less selfish. Cudd suggests using economic models to figure out incentives for others to do their fair share. One way to do this would be to intentionally withhold caring labor to get other people to do it. For example, in our example of Lane and Kerry, if Lane is doing a disproportionate share of cooking and cleaning, Lane might decide to stop – to go on a kind of domestic strike – until Kerry steps up and starts doing more. If everyone in a relationship wants these tasks to be done, and women stop performing them, this will create pressure for others to do them, thus lessening the inequalities in question.

In one way, this is an ingenious and pragmatic way of putting theory to use in practice. By focusing first on our goals – such as gender equality – we then use economic theory to figure out how to achieve those goals. But I think that using economic theory this way could result in some strange consequences and unappealing dilemmas. If we're talking about a family with children, and if one adult parent does less than their share of caring work, what should the other do? Take less care of the children? Take care of children but not adults in the home? Suppose two people trade off making dinner for a family. If one adult in the home always makes a healthy dinner with fresh food, protein and vegetables and the other always orders pizza, what is the first person to do? Stop making healthy food? Make it only for the children? What if the more selfish person just doubles down and does less caring work themselves? Taken far enough, it feels like this strategy could become an arms race to the bottom of less and less caring.

That these questions seem awkward and difficult does not show that conceptualizing family life in terms of incentives and bargaining is wrong. But it does highlight how certain ways of seeing love as self-interested can lead us to see certain actions rather than others as sensible and rational in potentially contentious ways.

Since we've talked about Becker's definition of altruism and the caring-concern theory, let's consider how the economic approach and the union theory fit together. Because of the problems of selfhood and identity and their relation to the "we," it's unclear how exactly to bring the two together, but here are a few possibilities. As we noted in Chapters 5–7, Nozick pays close attention to the idea of love and rationality. The union theory may seem to address the potential incompatibility between self-interestedness and other-interestedness in a different way: instead of bringing the two attitudes together in two separate individuals, the other's interests become your interests in the merger. The "we" might then become an economic agent of its own: it has its own interests and can pursue those interests with rational self-interest – now referring not to the interest of the individuals but to the interests of the "we." Also, we saw Nozick's idea of a risk pool in Chapter 5: it's rational to team up in this way partly because bad things won't be so bad. This is a good fit with an economic approach since it implies that forming a "we" can be in the rational self-interest of an individual. Finally, in our critical discussion, we noted that one motivation for merger theories might be to carve out a space in which negotiation and bargaining aren't necessary, and we can use love and care instead. The union theory would then offer a way in which the negotiation characteristic of economic approaches would be applicable in the public sphere and inapplicable in the domestic sphere: because people in love are joined, they relate to one another in a fundamentally different way than they relate to other people in public life.

This perspective has some appealing aspects. Seeing love as union avoids the specific problem of an altruist being exploited or misused by a non-altruist. Since a "we" is necessarily reciprocal, each person takes on the interests of the other; asymmetry doesn't arise. Each person has to be part of the "we" equally. In our example, love would require Lane and Kerry to each take on one another's preferences and thus for Kerry to care for Lane getting what Lane wants and needs.

But, as I see it, using the union theory to make self-interest compatible with love leads to the same kind of ultimate problems with fairness that we've already seen. This is because, as we saw in Chapter 5, in the merger we can't distinguish different people's interests. In our example of Lane and Kerry above, if we merged Lane's and Kerry's interests, that merger would include preferences for Lane to do caring labor and make Kerry happy, since this is Lane's preference, and for Kerry to be selfish and make Kerry happy, since this is Kerry's preference. For Lane to take on Kerry's interests would be for Lane to take on Kerry's preferences for Kerry's happiness. If the "we," as a rational economic agent of its own, has its preferences satisfied overall, Lane will, again, end up doing all the caring labor.

Also, this perspective inherits the problems that Agarwal noted about Becker's model, of treating the family as a site of harmony when in reality families are often sites of conflict and bargaining. Using the union theory in this context elides the possibility of love with incompatible interests. Finally, as we saw before, the union theory leads to an understanding of love in which love is essentially something among two – or a small number – of super-committed people. It's not a theory that would allow us

198 The economics of sex and love

to love a large group of friends. This means that bringing the union theory into the economic framework might lead to conclusions in which the most rational behavior is to form small stable families in which interests are merged and to regard everyone else without the other-regarding attitudes characteristic of love – an implication with potentially interesting political ramifications.

Once we abandon the patriarchal perspective, in which only the public lives of men are in the economic domain, seeing love through the lens of self-interested rationality requires making difficult conceptual decisions. Is love, like Becker's altruism, self-interested as well as other-regarding, or does this framing inappropriately elide questions of familial conflict and fairness? Should love be seen as harmonious, as in Becker's model or the union view, or are intimate relationships essentially sites of conflict and negotiation? If the latter, does interpreting love in terms of self-interested bargaining lead to useful strategies for responding to gender-based inequalities? As we've seen in our discussion of idealization and modeling, answering these questions requires not only reflecting on which theories work best but also making judgments about what matters about love and why.

Economics and sex

Similar issues arise in the application of economic reasoning to sex. Our discussion will focus on the work of Richard Posner, a judge and legal theorist whose 1992 book *Sex and Reason* tries to explain patterns of sexual activity in economic terms to inform legal judgment and the crafting of laws. To conceptualize sex in terms of a market with exchangeable goods, and to present a unifying account that will support broad, generalizing conclusions, Posner interprets the sex drive through the kind of sociobiological account we encountered briefly in Chapter 12. Central to his analysis are a few basic and gendered assumptions: that men have a strong drive for sex and women do not; that women's decisions about whether to have sex are based on factors other than sex drive itself; that men make situational trade-offs to satisfy their preferences as best they can. From this, it follows that the patterns and diversity we observe in sexual behavior can be explained through differences in the options available to men in their particular circumstances. For example, Posner says that when it comes to choosing women or men as sexual partners, men are biologically either gay or straight, but straight men may be "opportunistically" gay – having sex with men when there are no women available. Since in this framework men have a strong drive for sex and women do not, sex is largely something that men make trade-offs to get and women use in trade-offs to get other things.

Scholars have noted some difficulties with Posner's analysis. Economist and legal theorist Gillian Hadfield points out that women's role in the theory is largely relegated to that of provider of sexual pleasure: "Posner's biology," she says, "sets the stage for an economic theory in which men are economic actors and women are economic objects; in which men are rational and women are, essentially, rationed" (1992: 491). Because of this, women's sexual desires do not exist in the model and are thus seen as irrelevant to understanding and responding to sexual behavior. Among other things, it follows that lesbians are "essentially invisible": if women do not make sexual decisions based on sexual desire but merely acquiesce to having sex with men for other reasons, then women would never have sex with other women.

In her work on the limits of markets, Debra Satz (1995) challenges the application of economics to sexuality on grounds similar to the anti-commodification arguments we saw in Chapter 4. Our relationships with our bodies are not the same as our relationships with the goods we own, and the economic approach does not respect this distinction. For example, in Posner's framework, because sexual pleasure is theorized as a good that women provide in exchanges, a rapist is essentially a "sex thief": the difference between consensual sex and rape would be like the difference between paying for something and stealing it. But this not only fails to acknowledge the way that rape is a crime of violence and assault, it is also inconsistent with a wide range of scholarship linking rape to male hostility and desire for domination. As Satz points out, if we apply standard economic approaches like cost–benefit analysis using the framework Posner has set up, it looks like we would have to count the "benefit" to the rapist against the cost to the victim (Satz 1995: 69), which just seems wrong.

Another interesting point to consider has to do with sexual orientations. In Posner's framework, there is a biological distinction between men who are "really" gay and men who have sex with men only because they are making a situational trade-off when no women are available. But this is incompatible with the Foucauldian ideas we discussed in Chapter 8, that orientations are socially constructed. If people are not biologically sorted into "gay" and "straight," and if these are social categories, then it makes more sense to talk about people making sexual choices for a range of different reasons: just because you make a certain set of choices doesn't make you a certain sort of person. As William Eskridge (1992) points out, the framework is also incompatible with the possibility of fluid desires and with the idea we saw in Chapter 8 that orientations might be partly a matter of choice after all. Eskridge notes this implication could hamper certain strategies for political progress toward social respect and equality for LGBTQ+ people.

Posner also gives some analysis that draws on the facts about race that we discussed in Chapter 10. Drawing on an implicit assumption that straight Black men will want to have sex with and marry Black women, Posner notes that because of the high rates of imprisonment and premature death among Black men, there are more available Black women than available white women, relatively speaking. From the economic point of view, we can conclude that this will keep search costs and the "price of each woman" low (Posner 1992: 136–139; see Hadfield 1992: 492 for discussion). Because of this surplus of availability, Black men will be less likely than white men to rape and patronize prostitutes but more likely to "have multiple sex partners, to be initiated into sex early, and to father illegitimate children" (Posner 1992: 136–139). But, as Hadfield (1992) notes, the text does not present a hypothesis about whether race-based preference would be due to biological factors, cultural norms, or something else. And, as we saw in Chapter 10, there are reasons to think the assumption that Black men will only want to date Black women is inaccurate in ways that would render these conclusions flawed.

As in our discussion of love, it's not always clear how to understand these challenges. Since all models make some simplifications and idealizations, the fact that Posner starts from a set of broad assumptions that are not always true does not necessarily undermine his analysis. But, as we discussed with love, not all simplifying assumptions are equally apt. Of her criticisms of Posner, Hadfield says that her objection isn't that applying economics to sex is wrong: rather, she says, the problem is the male-centric perspective from which the analysis proceeds. This perspective not only leads to the problems above but also deflects our attention away from some of the most important questions related to economics and sex, such as those concerning "the impact of sex and its regulation on women" and how "sexual practices and regulation determine the economic status of women" (Hadfield 1992: 482). Again, as we saw in our discussion of love, interpreting sex through a lens of self-interested exchange requires making certain interpretive choices; in Posner's case, these include seeing sexual pleasure as a good that men desire and that women provide. As our discussion shows, whether we see those choices are as apt depends on evaluative judgments about what role sex plays in our lives and why some aspects of sex matter more than others.

Sex, love, and economic methodology

Is there a problem applying economics to the domains of love and sex? It's interesting to consider the extent to which the various challenges and difficulties we've seen have to do with applying economics to sex and love generally versus the extent to which they have to do with the way specific theories and models are set up. Maybe there's nothing wrong with applying economics to sex and love, it's just important to do it in the right way. For example, in her discussion of Posner, Hadfield says the problem isn't that economics has been taken "too far" but rather that it hasn't been taken "far enough": the male focus of the book precludes us from what would otherwise seem to be central economic questions about sex (Hadfield 1992: 482).

In support of this general idea, we might say that economic methodology does not make assumptions about what people want and prefer; it deals with the decision-making and the trade-offs people make to get what they want, and, in principle, this should be applicable to any domain. Furthermore, economic analysis may produce especially innovative and interesting theorizing in domains of sex and love because it is free from attitudes of praise, blame, and moral condemnation that often cloud our thinking on these issues. With love, the economic point of view reminds us that negotiation and bargaining are common within families and that struggling to get what you want for yourself can go hand in hand with love – something you might not be attuned to if your theory of love is too starry-eyed. And Posner's theorizing about sex has been widely praised for the way it theorizes same-sex sexual activity, pointing out that the lack of harms associated with it did not support the cultural and legal condemnation it had been subject to (especially when the book was written in 1992 and gay sex was against the law in many US states). Because it looks cooly at preferences, costs, and benefits, the economic perspective can bring us new insights in areas we have strong and varying attitudes about.

However, there are reasons to be careful when applying economic reasoning to social phenomena. For one thing, economic analysis has a lot to say about what happens given certain preferences but not much to say about how preferences get formed in the first place or why they are the way they are. But often when we want to understand complex social domains like sex and love, the "why" is just what we want to know: we care not only what people prefer but also what factors are causing them to have the preferences they do.

Typical neoclassical methodology often assumes stable preferences that are "exogenous" – given by factors outside the domain being studied – rather than "endogenous" – affected by factors in the domain being studied and therefore variable. But sex and love are areas where our behavior is highly affected by our social surroundings, norms, cultural factors, and so on. As we've seen, Becker simplifies by framing the issue in terms of assuming an altruistic patriarch and selfish others, but, as we've also seen, the degree of altruism someone has is often a product of social forces. As with the gender wage gap, it is often the sources of those differences that we want to understand. Posner deals with the problem of preferences by the appeal to sociobiology, attributing variation to situational trade-offs. But, as we've discussed, social, cultural, and moral norms play a large role in why we want and choose as we do sexually. This doesn't mean that applying economics to sex and love is wrong. It just means you have to be careful because, as with any specific unidimensional disciplinary perspective, some of what you're looking for might be obscured from view.

Let's look at two examples where assuming people are self-interested rational actors and taking preferences as exogenous can lead to questionable conclusions. The first concerns Paula England's (1989) analysis of "marital power." Various studies have shown that in heterosexual couples where divorce is possible, husbands get their way more often than wives, and that the imbalance is more pronounced the greater the earning disparity between a higher-earning husband and a lower-earning wife. Again, economic analysis tends to assume that preferences are given, and in this context economic analysis – including England's own earlier work – has tended to proceed by using a model that focuses on resources. What high-earning husbands put into a relationship results in outcomes, like high earnings, that are easily portable to a new relationship should this one end. But the resources a lower-earning wife puts in, like learning her husband's tastes and forging relationships with her in-laws, are not easily portable. The woman therefore has more to lose than her husband, and, relatively speaking, the greater the financial disparity the greater the difference in their rational responses to conflict. It would follow that, generally speaking, "because the partner with more earnings would lose less if the marriage dissolves she or he (usually he) has greater bargaining power within the relationship" (England 1989: 24). England points out that a different explanation arises if we shift our assumptions about self-interest, resources, and preferences. What if, instead of equally self-interested actors, we think of women as more likely than men to have caring preferences? In that case, "marriage would feature men pressing their bargaining harder and getting more of what they wanted as a function of the amount of their earnings relative to their wives' earnings" (England 1989: 25). The asymmetrical caring in preferences would be the cause of the disparity not the resources involved. With this alternative explanation, it would follow that "[t]he extent to which wives pushed for their own way at the expense of a partner's would be uncorrelated with their earnings" (England 1989: 25). This could apply to same-sex partners as well, wherever there is a difference in degree of selfishness relative to caring preferences. The explanation in terms of resources and the explanation in terms of asymmetrical caring are different and potentially competing. To know which explanation is correct – or whether the difference is due to a mix or range of factors – we would have to investigate what specific preferences people have. England's conclusion is that assuming economic agents are self-interested and taking preferences as exogenous could lead us to adopt the first explanation over the second, even if it were inaccurate.

A different example related to sex has to do with casual sex. It's been observed that on many college campuses in the United States, there is more hooking up when there is a greater proportion of women relative to men. One economic analysis starts from the observation that men prefer "sex with strangers" more than women and theorizes that, among straight people, a greater proportion of women means stiffer competition for the available men, and thus women are in a weaker bargaining position: they cannot negotiate for the relationships they want because the man can more easily find another partner. As Marina Adshade puts it, "a woman's ability to bargain with her sexual partners over both the timing and the nature of sex acts has been eroded on university campuses in the face of increased competition for men among relatively abundant women" (2013: 45).

Let's take a moment to look at this idea that men prefer casual sex with strangers more than women. One frequently cited study on this topic involved good-looking strangers walking up to people on campuses and asking them to (1) have dinner with them, (2) come to their apartment tonight, or (3) have sex tonight. More than 50 percent of men and women said "yes" to dinner, but while 75 percent of men said yes to sex (way more men than agreed to dinner!) no women did (Clark and Hatfield 1989). The obvious conclusion is that men prefer sex with strangers way more than women do.

But there are many reasons a woman might say no to sex with a male stranger that wouldn't apply in the same way to men considering women. Most obviously, a woman might be afraid of a guy she doesn't know: afraid that he won't take no for an answer when it comes to things like condom use and contraception, afraid he might not leave when it's over, afraid he might become a stalker. What if he agrees to use a condom and then nonconsensually and secretly removes it, as in the recent trend of "stealthing"? Furthermore, as we've discussed, for many reasons women are less likely to get sexual pleasure from a casual encounter. A man is likely to get pleasure from having sex with any partner he finds attractive. But a woman is not, especially when her partner is a man and it's a casual encounter, because men are less likely to engage in activities like oral and manual stimulation of the clitoris that will lead to a woman's orgasm. Psychologist Terri Conley says that "when women are presented with proposers who are equivalent in terms of safety and sexual prowess, they will be equally likely as men to engage in casual sex" (2011: 321). Tweaking the original study, Conley asked men and women whether they would have sex with attractive celebrities like Johnny Depp and Angelina Jolie. Men and women responded "yes" equally often. Not only that but even with non-celebrities women were more likely to say yes to an encounter with another woman than with a man – supporting the idea that fear of men and skepticism about their pleasure-giving abilities were factors in the original results. We have to be careful about relying on generalities like "men prefer sex with strangers more than women do" when crafting background assumptions about what preferences people do and do not have.

In principle, the alternative explanations of women's choices in both examples – not in terms of preferences for more financial resources but rather instead of emotions, and not in terms of a stable, deep, or biological preference not to have sex with strangers but rather in terms of social and other factors – are consistent with economic theory. We've seen how caring preferences can be modeled as "self-interested" if not selfish so people making choices about divorce because of this could fit the model. And with sex, the women who said "no" to strange men and "yes" to

204 The economics of sex and love

Johnny Depp are making familiar trade-offs among things they want and things they want to avoid: they want sexual pleasure, they do not want sexual harm, and they make calculations about how to best get those things. That's all a good fit with the economic approach.

But because of its methodology, the economic approach when used by itself can give us an incomplete or misleading picture of what is going on. Often what we want to know is why people prefer what they prefer. Are differences in choices due to situational factors like money or differences in preferences due to complex social factors? To what extent? To get a full picture of why people do what they do, and thus to have good information about what they would do in other circumstances, we need a multifaceted approach, either adding to economic methodology a role for under-standing where preferences come from or supplementing economics with perspectives from other disciplines like sociology and anthropology (Hausman 2012).

I think a second reason to be careful applying economics to sex and love is that simplifying assumptions that seem innocuous when applied in one domain might lead to problems when applied in others. As we said at the start of this section, economics models people as self-inter-ested rational maximizers of utility. This way of seeing people might work better in some domains than in others. Originally, economics was the study of wealth, markets, and commodities. When you're working, negotiating, and shopping, it makes sense to think of yourself as self-interested, looking out for yourself only, trying to get as much as you want at as little cost to yourself.

Later definitions expanded the scope, but even here the fit might be odd. We saw at the start of the chapter Robbins' definition of economics as studying "human behavior as a relationship between ends and scarce means which have alternative uses" (Robbins 1931: 15). But love and sex might resist description as "scarce means" that can be used for other ends. Love and caring are not fixed in amount. How much love and sex there are in the world just depends on us and our feelings for one another. As is often pointed out with parenting, having more children does not decrease the amount of love one feels for each one, and, as we'll see in our discus-sion of polyamory later, many people think something similar applies to romantic relationships, so that loving one person need not restrict our potential for loving another. As we've seen, love is thought to be essen-tially particular, involving a relation between you and the person you love so that trading up would be wrong: love is thus ill suited to "serving a variety of alternative ends." Once we move away from Posner's framing of women as providers of sexual pleasure and thus as "resources," we see that sex is not a "scarce resource" that can be used for something else: as we've seen, it is often thought that mutuality, in which sexual desire and pleasure are mutually interdependent and increasing together, is a kind of ideal for sexuality. Unlike other commodities, sex and love do not take place within any zero-sum game: people can have more and better sex without anyone else having less or worse sex. While it is true that choosing to pursue love and sex can entail trade-offs with other activities, so love and sex are not exactly unlimited, there is a sense in which we determine how much of each is available. It's really up to us. In this sense, love and sex are not fixed in the sense of the Robbins' idea of "scarce resources."

Conclusion

We've seen in this chapter various ways that economics can be applied to love and sex and various complexities associated with each. I've argued that conceptualizing sex and love in terms of rational self-interest requires making difficult choices about how sex and love should be understood. Is self-interested altruism a good way of understanding love? Should our models be sensitive to power dynamics and fairness? Can sexual pleasure be understood as a commodity? These choices rest on value judgments about the role sex and love play in our lives and can lead to potentially contentious implications; one reason is that sex and love may resist interpretation as scarce resources that can be used for other ends.

In a sense, our discussion exemplifies the difference between the values we typically associate with public life – where rational self-interest may seem to be the norm – and the values we typically associate with sex and love – where caring, generosity, and mutuality are thought to be important. From an economic point of view, in our patriarchal and heteronormative past, this difference was finessed through a social system in which women were seen as naturally caring, only men were rational and self-interested, and sex was appropriate only in heterosexual marriage. In modern contexts of equality, gender-neutrality, and sexual autonomy, we need different solutions. Economic theories aim to bridge the gap by interpreting sex and love through the lens of self-interest, but our discussion shows how bridging that gap in different ways requires making theoretical choices about what it is about sex and love that matter to us and why – matters about which different people may make different judgments.

14 Ethical nonmonogamy

Introduction

Like several of the other practices we've considered in this book, ethical nonmonogamy – that is, the open and consensual experience of loving or sexual relationships with more than one person at a time – is a minority choice. In North America and in many other societies, there is considerable cultural resistance to it, and laws in many places reinforce that resistance, ensuring that ideals of monogamy remain predominant. Yet, as we'll see in this chapter, both the practice of ethical nonmonogamy and societies' resistance to it raise wider philosophical issues, with implications for understanding other forms of sex and love. Ethical nonmonogamy offers the possibility of expanding the quantity and diversity of love and sex that individuals experience; it thus raises questions about why this does not seem self-evidently desirable to most people in our society. Likewise, thinking about ethical nonmonogamy draws attention to the values associated with it and raises questions about how these might be better integrated into mainstream relationships; as we'll see, ethical nonmonogamy implies high levels of honesty and open communication, and it also entails considerable tolerance of our partners' desires and limits.

At the same time, I'll argue that examining ethical nonmonogamy points to some problems that widening its practice might present. For one thing, difficulties about pressure, coercion, and consent could be exacerbated by multiplicity, if for instance, one member of a couple finds nonmonogamy more appealing than the other; and not everyone can muster the trust and openness that nonmonogamous relationships require. Likewise, the social acceptance of nonmonogamy may pose problems for equality, exacerbating the problem that we've encountered previously of the "haves" and the "have-nots" of sex and love. As we'll see, resistance to nonmonogamy raises important questions about how people experience monogamy itself. Resistance may spring from the idea that the nature of love requires exclusivity and is antithetical to sharing.

We'll start here by considering definitions, motivations, and practices, then turn to exploring the values associated with ethical nonmonogamy. In the later sections of this chapter, we'll consider resistance to non-monogamy in North American society, considering both its effects and its sources. Finally, we'll explore challenges, ways in which the potential benefits of nonmonogamy may be bound up with potential losses, or at least difficulties.

What is ethical nonmonogamy?

As we've discussed, in Western history sex and romantic love used to be part of heterosexual marriage only. Over time, norms have shifted so that these have come to be understood also as expressions of individual autonomy; sex and love are things each person makes their own decisions about. In that case, there's no obvious reason why sex and romantic love have to involve couples and exclusivity.

Ethical nonmonogamy comes in many different forms, some centering primarily on sex, others on loving commitment; sometimes it's about people who continue to have a primary relationship with one other person but engage in sex or romance with others as well, and sometimes it can involve more complex arrangements such as more than two people in a committed loving relationship. Participants understand this situation as distinct from cheating, since honesty and openness are crucial, and everyone has to agree to what is happening. Openness and honesty don't mean each person has to know all the details; rather, they simply mean that everyone has to agree to what is going on. For example, people might agree not to disclose: "go ahead and have sex with other people, but don't tell me about it." In his popular sex-advice column, Dan Savage describes relationships that are "monogamish": two people are in a committed loving romantic relationship, and they're not actively looking, but they agree that they are permitted to have sex with people other than their primary partner should the situation arise.

The motivation for a couple to open up a relationship in this way might have to do with changing or preserving their relationship and what is good about it. As we saw in Chapter 12, over time with a single partner sexual desire waxes and wanes, and sometimes diminishes; a person might develop a crush or an intense desire to have sex with someone else. In a conventional framework, the typical response to this would be splitting up – finding what you want with a new partner – or, in a futuristic new world, taking the love drugs mentioned at the end of Chapter 12. But nonmonogamy offers other options. In a discussion of emotional complexity, Aaron Ben-Ze'ev and Luke Brunning (2017) point out that non-monogamous relationships are well suited to accommodating individual and interpersonal changes and discoveries over time.

While it's commonly thought that men are more likely to want the freedom to have sex with multiple partners, some evidence challenges this line of thought. As we saw in Chapter 12, in his 2013 book *What Do*

Women Want, Daniel Bergner cites studies showing that long-term monogamy dampens a woman's libido more than a man's. We saw also that one target for desire-enhancing drugs is women who want to recapture a sense of lust and longing. In a recent *New York Times* article on polyamory, the author says that of the twenty-five straight couples she encountered, a majority of relationships were opened at the initiation of women, and only in six cases at the initiation of men (Dominus 2017). Some couples say that their desire for and sexual interactions with each other improve when the partners are having sex outside the partnership. It's difficult to gather data on these questions, but, as we saw in Chapter 12, one possibility is that trust and comfort get in the way of sexual passion; nonmonogamy means seeing your partner in a new light and rekindles the sense of them as a separate person from yourself. Another is that you see yourself differently.

Other motivations for nonmonogamy have to do with actively resisting the restrictive and often patriarchal traditions that underlie monogamy. In *The Ethical Slut* (Easton and Hardy 2009), co-author Dossie Easton talks about how she had a relationship with a man who was extremely possessive and jealous and wanted control over her, especially with respect to her sexuality. She says that at the time she found the possessiveness intoxicating: if he was so jealous, he must be passionately and intensely in love. But over time she came to feel dominated and that her partner viewed her as a piece of property, something to be controlled. Self-ownership, she decided, meant she would determine her own sexual choices, and this meant rejecting monogamy. Just as promiscuity in general is socially punished for women, transgressing monogamy has historically been treated as much more of a violation for women than for men. So resisting monogamy is a way of reclaiming sexual autonomy for oneself in the face of problematic or oppressive social pressures.

Polyamory typically involves more than two people joined together in longer-term committed relationships. People in North America might be most familiar with this kind of polyamory in the context of religions like Mormonism, in which one man can marry multiple wives. Polygyny (from the Greek words for multiple wives) is often seen as sexist and oppressive to women and also bad for men. Typically, a married man in a polygynous society may marry multiple times, without the consent of his existing wife or wives, so women and men have unequal rights and marital power. Statistically, polygyny is also associated with women's lower self-esteem and increased risk of depression (Brooks 2009). Polygyny can be bad for men because if some individuals have multiple wives, in the nature of things others will be unable to find partners. Outside of religious contexts, however, ethical nonmonogamy embraces gender-neutrality and equality.

The values of ethical nonmonogamy

In a 2004 article, legal theorist Elizabeth Emens examines social resistance to nonmonogamy; through examples and an exploration of the values associated with ethical nonmonogamy, she counters this resistance and gives a strong positive defense of nonmonogamous practices. One example is a polyamorous four-partner family that started with a couple, Amber and Adam (see Emens 2004: 312; names have been changed). Adam was bisexual and hoped to have relationships with men as well as women; in time, Amber and Adam invited Eddie to join their family. Later, the three of them met and fell in love with Mike, and invited him to join their family as well. In an interview, Eddie explains that the difficult aspect of their family isn't so much jealousy or other negative emotions but rather scheduling and time-management. It's important that everyone feels included and respected, and that everyone feels they are getting a chance to spend time with others in the way they want. Eddie says their family works in part because the participants are a bit older and more self-aware, and thus willing to spend time and energy talking over about how things should work.

When it comes to multiple partners who all love one another, it might seem puzzling at first to think that people can romantically love more than one other person in some equal ways. There's a temptation to think each person will have one other primary person, the most important, the most loved. But I think this reflects our cultural preoccupations about romantic love. If you think about parents with more than one child, they usually love each child with specificity and particularity, and also love all their children in something like the same way. In fact, a brief consideration of our theories of love seems, on the face of it, to support the idea that romantic love can involve more than two people. From our discussion of Nozick and "shared agency" in Chapters 5 and 7, nothing seems to rule out the possibility that more than two people could form unions and share their agency. Why not a merger of three, four, or more instead of two? And if love is understood as caring concern, it's not too hard see how one could love more than one adult that way, especially since people often love more than one child in something like this way.

The example of the four-partner family highlights the ways in which ethical nonmonogamy requires a lot of mutual decision-making. There is no formula for how to make it work – no set of expectations embedded in social norms, no cultural script like those that surround monogamy; instead, the people involved have to communicate with one another and define their expectations. In these situations, ethical reflection becomes especially important. In a discussion of the values associated with ethical nonmonogamy, Emens analyzes five: self-knowledge; radical honesty; consent; self-possession; and privileging love and sex.

With respect to self-knowledge, Emens says that in addition to the obvious sense in which you have to know that you are questioning monogamy, you also need a good sense of your own feelings to make it work. Because nonmonogamy involves a lot of open possibilities, the first step is to know what you yourself feel and want. Since this is not always obvious, it can require introspection and experience. She quotes the writer Deborah

Anapol (1997) as saying that in polyamory you should "Let jealousy be your teacher." Through experience, you can learn about your own feelings so that you can communicate your wishes and your limits to others (Emens 2004: 321). For example, it might be that knowing that someone you love is having sex with other people occasionally doesn't bother you so much, but having them form extended emotional relationships with other sex partners does. Ethical nonmonogamy works only if you can know this about yourself and communicate it to others.

The second value is "radical honesty." Primarily, this means honesty with your partners. Typically, in our culture the desire to have sex and love in ways that transcend monogamy is regarded as something to lie about, but embracing ethical nonmonogamy means openness and honesty about these desires. Honesty is also required about feelings: decisions that are mutually agreeable can be made only if everyone is honest about their emotions, including negative ones. As we will see below, many people cannot be publicly honest about nonmonogamy because they may risk losing their jobs, child custody, or social standing. But the idea of social acceptance for ethical nonmonogamy includes the value that we could all be more open about monogamy's failures.

Crucially, consent is not only a practice but also a value. Getting verbal approval to go ahead with something isn't enough; it's about making sure everyone involved wants to move forward. If someone feels pushed into what's happening, it's not right; they should participate on their own terms.

A fourth value is self-possession: declaring your own rights to your own romantic and sexual identity. In one line of thought, monogamy has its roots in patriarchal thinking: women were viewed as possessions, used for barter, with legitimacy related to paternity – fatherhood – rather than maternity (Emens 2004: 325). It's often noted that when a woman gives birth, it's immediately obvious who the child's mother is, but it may not be obvious who the child's father is. If a society hopes to function in a patriarchal style in which land, money, and goods are passed down from father to son, knowledge of fatherhood becomes essential. The only way to guarantee paternity is to have a system of monogamy – at least, monogamy for women, in which each woman has sex with only one man. Thus, pushing back against monogamy as social control can be done, in part, by asserting one's rights to nonmonogamy, which thus becomes a feminist activity.

The fifth and final value Emens mentions is privileging love and sex. This refers to the idea that more love and more sex are deeply good things, which bring joy, warm feelings, and a sense of community. From this point of view, jealousy and exclusivity seem pathological, and definitely not a natural part of love. As we mentioned in the discussion of economics in Chapter 13, love and sex are not "scarce resources," and they are not zero-sum games. Loving one person doesn't take away your ability to love another; experiencing sexual pleasure goes along with giving sexual pleasure; and there is no limit on these things except time. Isn't having more love and sex better than having less?

Seeing these as values shows how ethical nonmonogamy is more than just people doing whatever they want. It is a practice that is not only open but also mutually respectful and in some ways committed to avoiding the troubling association between love and owning or controlling another person.

The "paradox of prevalence" and changing the law

As we've seen, there is widespread social resistance to nonmonogamy. In the early twenty-first century, as the United States was debating same-sex marriage, critics of marriage equality used a "slippery slope" argumentative strategy: they said that if same-sex marriage were allowed, then so would all kinds of other bad things, and these might include "polygamy" – that is, marriages involving more than two people at a time. Strikingly, the response was often not "Well – and so what?" but rather efforts to show how polygamy and same-sex marriage are different. This suggests how deep and widespread is resistance to the idea of more than two people being in intimate relationships at one time.

Hostility to nonmonogamy has very real and practical consequences. In general, in the United States and Canada, being married to more than one person is a crime. There are also adultery laws: in some states in the United States adultery is technically punishable by fine or jail time, and adultery is generally regarded as grounds for divorce. This is significant because it means that, depending on divorce laws in the jurisdiction, if two people are engaging in consensual, ethical nonmonogamy, one person could potentially unilaterally divorce the other on the grounds of these consensual activities, which might legally speaking constitute "adultery." Immigration laws also appeal to marriage; while marriage typically allows people to immigrate in order to live together, the United States and Canada limit this to one spouse. Zoning laws specify how many unrelated adults can live together in a home, and people living nonmonogamous lives can be discriminated against at work with no legal protections. In Chapter 9, we talked about the many legal and structural benefits of marriage, and these include various rights: to visit a person who is in the hospital, to determine what happens after their death, not to testify against them in court, immigration rights. These rights are weakened or disappear altogether for some participants in nonmonogamous relationships.

There are also serious child-custody issues. In the late twentieth century, a US woman named April Divilbiss had a child removed from her home because she lived with two men. Ms. Divilbiss had a child with a man who had left her; she then later married a man named Shane. After that, she fell in love with a man named Chris. Having talked it over, they decided the best solution would be to all live together, with April having sexual relationships with Shane and Chris separately. The child's biological paternal grandmother objected, and a judge removed April's child from her care on grounds of April's immoral lifestyle. The judge in the case found it objectionable in itself that April was living with two men at the same time; the fact that it was a mutually consensual and happy arrangement did not matter. The child was removed from April's home and placed with the Department of Children's services (Emens 2004: 310–312).

This resistance to nonmonogamy is striking in view of the multiple problems that are thought to confront monogamy itself. While precise numbers are difficult to measure, adultery is common enough that in one 1994 survey, 20 percent of married women and 35 percent of married men admitted to adulterous sex; given people's reluctance to admit to culturally sanctioned behavior in surveys, the real number may well be much higher. Even people who never practice nonmonogamy may feel the desire for sex and love with others: being romantically faithful to one person for a lifetime is famously challenging. The intensity of resistance to nonmonogamy is striking for another, more general reason: in most domains of life we admire and encourage sharing, and we usually want our loved ones to be happy and get the things they want. Yet with romantic love and sex we tend to insist on exclusivity and to be suspicious of sharing; and our cultural norms, social lives, and marriage laws still reflect that suspicion.

Given these complications surrounding resistance to nonmonogamy, it's worth examining the reasons for that resistance in more detail. One is that people are culturally invested in monogamy, despite its visible problems. Romance is typically assumed to require exclusivity and to preclude giving comparable attention to anyone outside the couple. But why? There's no reason why intensity of love must be correlated with possessiveness or exclusivity. In fact, what if they're attracted to someone else and want to flirt with them, or go on a date, or have sex? Wouldn't real love mean hoping those things can happen rather than preventing them? Jealousy might reflect a creepy kind of "ownership" rather than love.

A related issue has to do with children and family life. We have a belief that children are best served by two parents. But, as Emens points out, in a society that allows divorce, children are already experiencing a form of polyamory. Parents might feel they are experiencing serial monogamy – one spouse at a time. But for children, remarriage often means getting more parents. Children stay in touch with ex-spouses, some who are their biological parents and others who have helped raise them. A child might have two biological parents, then also step-parents who married their biological parents at some point, and also spouses of step-parents, who might be among their caregivers over time as well. The more remarriage, the more this web spins out. The point here is just that remarriage, while it is in one sense monogamous, introduces into children's lives a condition very like polyamory. Children already have multiple caregivers and parental figures.

Furthermore, maybe more caregivers for children would be better. Discussing her life as one of nine wives in a Mormon community in the late twentieth century, Elizabeth Joseph says that modern polygyny helps women balance marriage, careers, and motherhood. Since everyone lives in a physically interconnected space and the wives raise children as part of the same family, the wives, who often become emotionally close, can divide up responsibilities. Instead of compromising on childcare and domestic tasks, some women take care of kids while others go off to work.

In contemporary life, many parents find it really challenging to do for their kids all the things that they want to do. Polyamory – especially where there are multiple people sharing loving commitment – raises the possibility that families might do better with more than two parents. Modern mixed families, with step-parents and their spouses and so on, are already like this. Maybe in a future with more polyamory it will become common for families with children to have more than two adults. It's funny to imagine people looking back at our era and saying to one another, "Raising kids with only TWO parents! How did they ever do it?!"

To explain the depth of resistance to nonmonogamy, Emens proposes the "paradox of prevalence": it's partly because people generally find monogamy difficult that they find the universalizing of nonmonogamy to be threatening. That is, if nonmonogamy were understood to be something a few people just happened to find appealing while everyone else was happily monogamous, it might be easy for the happily monogamous adopt a tolerant attitude toward the nonmonogamous. Monogamous people and nonmonogamous ones could live side by side, each happily doing their own thing. But monogamy is not easy. Many people who promise to be monogamous cheat, and thus fail. Even people who succeed in monogamous relationships often feel powerful desires to have sex with other people – desires they must struggle with in order to stay monogamous. If staying monogamous is difficult, then the normalization of the practice of nonmonogamy might make it harder still. The normalization of nonmonogamy would be threatening; for those who want to be monogamous but struggle with it, there could be resistance on these grounds. Emens calls this a "paradox" because usually we think that if an idea is potentially widely shared, or "prevalent," it's easier for that idea to gain acceptance, but paradoxically, in this case, it's partly because the possibility of nonmonogamy is so widespread that there is such widespread resistance to its normalization.

Let's take a moment to consider in more detail why, exactly, the potential universality of nonmonogamous desires means that legitimizing nonmonogamous lifestyles for some people could be a problem for those who want to be monogamous. Suppose a person has a personal ideal of monogamy and wants to be monogamous and live a monogamous life.

And suppose that even though they have this as an ideal, they acknowledge that monogamy is difficult and recognize that they and their partner will find monogamy challenging and will be tempted to have loving and sexual relationships with other people.

In this case, it's worth noting how broad social norms function to aid or undermine us in keeping our resolutions. If you are going to attempt something challenging, it is much easier to do it if the people around you also view it as valuable and important. If others think your goal is pointless or irrelevant, it might be harder to keep your goal. For example, suppose you form the goal of quitting smoking. If you live in contemporary North America, there are many social conditions that will help you keep your goal. People are always talking about how bad and unhealthy smoking is, and how it's unappealing in others. There are many places you are not allowed to smoke at all. When you say you're trying to quit, a lot of people will say, "That's great!" and encourage you to stick with it. But if you're trying to give up something widely enjoyed, like eating sugar or drinking alcohol, it could be much more difficult. Even if you are doing it for serious health reasons, people who don't know that might treat your goal as silly or excessive. People who never drink alcohol say they're often challenged on their choice, with people pressuring them to drink and even mocking them for being nondrinkers. People who don't eat sweets are criticized for being "no fun" or excessively rigid or health conscious. These social effects might make it much more difficult. So keeping a commitment of monogamy might be more difficult the more socially accepted nonmonogamy is.

Emens says that breaking down the social resistance to nonmonogamy might be more successful with a "minoritizing" strategy than a "universalizing" one. A "universalizing" strategy is one that portrays nonmonogamy as something that is potentially good for and open to everyone. Even if we believe monogamy to be unnatural or an unreasonable expectation, the "paradox of prevalence" may cause social resistance, backlash, making this an ineffective strategy for achieving social change. Instead, those seeking recognition and legal rights might be better off portraying nonmonogamy as something that only a minority of people will ever want to pursue, something unlikely to affect those with an ideal of monogamy. This strategy might move us more toward a live-and-let-live society.

With respect to changing laws, Elizabeth Brake (2012) and others argue that restricting marriage to couples discriminates against people who want multiple partnerships, like the four-member family mentioned above. The rights associated with marriage should be enjoyed not only by people who have multiple romantic relationships but also by people who have other, non-romantic relationships. After all, why shouldn't a best friend be able to share legal protections? A close relationship is a close relationship, regardless of whether it is romantic or sexual. Brake proposes a concept of "minimal marriage," which would support rights (but not economic benefits), without restrictions as to sex or the number of people involved.

In analyzing the law, Emens imagines several possibilities for how marriage might be changed to allow for the fact that ethical, consensual nonmonogamy does not constitute adultery and is thus not a legal – or ethical – ground for complaint, from the partners or from anyone else. For example, instead of saying that marriage directly entails exclusivity, we might say that "a married person who has sex with a person not his or her spouse is subject to prosecution unless the married person's spouse has consented to the extramarital sex." Or we might allow people to enter into marriages that are by default open to sex outside of marriage, with a clause saying that people can opt to include exclusivity as part of their legal commitment.

Challenges for ethical nonmonogamy

In discussing "universalizing" and "minoritizing," Emens focuses mainly on political strategy; her primary concern is with how a group that faces significant cultural and legal discrimination might gain legal rights. But her discussion also raises questions about the practice of ethical nonmonogamy itself. In particular, it's worth considering whether ethical nonmonogamy would only ever work for a minority of people, or whether it is the kind of thing that could be a good way of life for many, or most, people. This leads to questions about the challenges we might face putting into practice both the values of nonmonogamy and the legal changes that Emens proposes.

With respect to values, nonmonogamy might exacerbate difficulties that (as we've seen throughout this book) arise in all forms of love and sex. As we've seen in Chapter 3, consent and coercion can be complicated by many background factors; the pressures of relationships with multiple people may make those difficulties more difficult to address. What if one person in a committed couple decides that nonmonogamy is something they need to be happy, but the other person wants to be monogamous? No matter what decision they come to, it may be that mutual satisfaction is impossible and that one person feels pressured.

With respect to the proposed legal changes discussed in the previous section, the clauses referring to "consent" and "non-consent" to the individual acts of nonmonogamy might cause difficulty in practice. We've seen how complicated issues of consent can be when feelings are strong, even in the simpler case where there are only two people and only their consent is relevant. Since consent seems to be the kind of thing that must be in force at the time of the act, it might be difficult, legally, to prove consent or an absence of consent. What if one person is married to another nonexclusively, and consents for that person to have sex with a third on some occasion, and then between the time of consenting and the time of sex happening, changes their mind? What if the first person consents to some range of activities for their nonexclusive spouse to engage in, but they engage in a different set of activities? Would this be grounds for legal complaint?

It's also interesting to think about the way trust and intimacy work in nonmonogamous versus monogamous relationships. Nonmonogamy requires a great level of trust, which in turn requires that people be trustworthy. One reason for skepticism that nonmonogamy could be widespread might have to do with whether people are generally trustworthy enough to make it work. After all, we know from the discussion of monogamy that many people cheat. Isn't it possible that the same people would cheat in "ethically nonmonogamous" contexts, when their desires are for things their loved ones do not want? For example, we've seen that if an activity makes one person feel bad, it's not a good activity to pursue. But what if two people are in a nonmonogamous commitment, and one really wants to do something that makes the other feel bad? It seems the risk of cheating – of going ahead and doing that thing, without the other person's consent – might be similar to the risk of cheating in contexts of monogamy. More generally, there is no reason why challenges of boredom and habituation that attach to monogamy would not recur in nonmonogamous contexts.

With respect to love and sharing, we might wonder about the limits of nonexclusivity. As Justin Clardy (2013) points out, we often desire to feel special in our romantic relationships – valued above others – and, in addition, there are practical limits to the time and attention we can pay to others. Above, we discussed the analogy between nonmonogamous and parental love and noted that parents normally love all their children, but parents also sometimes confess to loving some children more than others, and children often feel this inequality and resent it. These challenges might be more difficult specifically for polyamory – multiple loves – than for sexual nonmonogamy, which often combines involve a single love commitment with sexual multiplicity.

Another issue has to do with the honesty and communication aspect of nonmonogamy. As we saw with the "four-partner family," there is a lot of work to be done to make sure things go smoothly, to make sure everyone feels OK with how things are going, to make sure everyone feels included. Even in the case of the Mormon wife, where tradition would settle many questions, Joseph says that sex is typically scheduled by appointment; many potentially conflicting preferences must be considered. In cases of couples who have sex and love with others, there are a lot of questions to consider: What are the appropriate boundaries? What happens if someone starts to feel uncomfortable? What if one person feels jealous and wants more restrictions, and their partner starts to feel resentful? Perhaps another source of skepticism would come from the possibility that many people would be unable – or just unwilling – to put the time and emotional energy into nonmonogamy needed to make it work.

There could also be difficult issues concerning possible children. Emens discusses how polyamorous families could be good for raising children, when it's a cooperative endeavor. But what if a person consents for their spouse to have sex with others but only if pregnancy is impossible or they use contraception? Contraception can fail. Would the first person be required to help raise the resulting child?

A really committed universalizing defender of nonmonogamy might point out in response that there's no moral requirement that people only raise their own biological children. If our culture changed so that people were more willing to raise children not biologically related to them, perhaps accidental pregnancy outside of the couple would be regarded similarly to accidental pregnancy within a couple – which, of course, happens a lot. From this point of view, we can imagine that future people might regard our own widespread preferences for biological offspring as an unsavory prejudice. A truly open-minded society would be one in which adults contribute to raising the children who come their way, without special regard for genetics. This open-minded society could be a positive benefit of more nonmonogamy and more nonmonogamous reproduction.

A final challenge may be related to the ways in which, as we've seen in other chapters, increased liberty in matters of sex and love might lead to less equality of sex and love, in the sense that some people are going to have way more, and way more of the kind they want, than other people. As we've seen in our discussions of objectification, sexual racism, disability, and economics, we already have a problem with inequality between the "haves" and the "have-nots" of sex and love. People who fit social ideas of attractiveness and success have more opportunities for sex, and more people want to form romantic relationships with them.

To a certain extent, in societies where monogamy is the social norm, these inequalities of sex and love are mitigated. If everyone has to pair off, this removes the more statistically desired people from the pool of partners. So, if you're one of the people less likely to be desired, there will be others around of your preferred sex/gender who might want to pair off with you. But in contexts where the social norm of monogamy is relaxed, people who have found partners are not removed from the pool. The "haves" of sex and love can partner up with one another indefinitely, while those statistically less likely to be desired may fail to find any sex and love partners. As we've seen, this idea is familiar from criticisms of patriarchal heterosexual nonmonogamy: in a society where each man can marry more than one woman, some men will marry many women and some will never marry. Adopting a sex/gender-neutral and nonheteronormative nonmonogamy doesn't get rid of this problem and may extend it.

Crucially, to take inequalities of sex and love as important and worth our consideration is not to recommend any system of sexual or romantic entitlement and not to say that we should reduce anyone's sexual liberty. The framing of our discussion of inequalities of sex and love can and should be egalitarian in other respects: nonsexist, nondiscriminatory, applicable in the same way to people of all sexes, genders, and preferences. We can, and must, reject the idea that sex and love are things that women owe to men while retaining the idea that a world in which some people never have any of either – or have very little of them – is a world that is deficient in important respects. Once we recognize sex and love as important parts of the good life, we become sensitized in a different way to the regrettable character of the state of affairs in which some people cannot access them.

Conclusion

The many forms of ethical nonmonogamy exemplify the wide range of ways of living that become possible when sex and love are detached from traditional meanings of monogamy and marriage, and are seen rather through the lens of personal autonomy and freedom of expression. As we've seen, possibilities that open up include not only the inclusion of more than two people but also many different ways of living, from intimacy and love among multiple people to long-term couples who have sex with others alongside their primary partnership. Once we let go of the idea that romantic love somehow requires jealousy or possessiveness, new perspectives emerge.

One potential benefit of widespread polyamory is obvious: love is a good thing, so wouldn't more love be an even better thing? Love causes us to care for others, to take their needs into account, to think and worry about them. Perhaps the more we do this for others, the better our world will be. Romantic love is an unconventional route to more universal love, but it is a possible one. Even with sexual nonmonogamy, sex with multiple partners can be a way of exchanging intimacy and a kind of affection. And, as we've seen, the kinds of interaction required for successful nonmonogamous ways of life rest on values like honesty and trust that are regarded as valuable by pretty much everybody.

However, we've also seen that the widespread adoption of ethical nonmonogamy could be complex. The values of nonmonogamy may be difficult for some people to practice, and some of what we want out of love may be linked to our feeling special or specially valued.

I've also suggested that increased liberty can lead to greater inequality in the distribution of sex and love. These problems are especially pressing in contemporary societies, in which many people have come to view sex and love as among the best things in life. Why is it OK if some people live lives full of romance and pleasure and others have none? Ethical nonmonogamy certainly doesn't create this problem, but it may in certain ways exacerbate it.

Conclusion

In one form or another, philosophies of sex and love are needed in every society, for everywhere people have to find answers to the basic questions that sex and love present. They need ways of deciding on appropriate partners and activities, and ways of defining the obligations that sex and love entail. Perhaps most important, they need ways of understanding how sex and love fit with our other life commitments, to our families and communities, and to ourselves. Philosophies of sex and love provide both principles and modes of reasoning for dealing with questions like these.

But if all societies need to think about these issues, not all do so in the same ways, and what count as useful, relevant answers differ as well. Hence this book has focused on the specific questions that we confront in contemporary North American societies, and on the kinds of philosophical reasoning that seem to me most helpful for addressing them. Two background realities seem to me to define what's special about our contemporary circumstances and thus set the terms for this exploration. First, most of us today view sex and love as matters of free choice, and we make our choices as autonomous individuals, with limited reference to the dictates of families, states, churches, or other institutions. Of course that degree of freedom doesn't prevail everywhere in contemporary societies. Governments continue to set some of the basic rules regulating sex and marriage, members of many religious groups still follow the teachings of their faith in these matters, and homophobia and discrimination are still widespread. Nonetheless, as we've seen in our discussions of pornography, sex work, orientations, marriage, and non-monogamy, our expectations about individuals' rights to arrange their intimate lives as they wish have risen dramatically even within the last generation. For example, before the Supreme Court ruled in *Lawrence* v. *Texas* that intimate consensual sexual conduct is part of the liberty protected by substantive due process, same-sex sexual relations between consenting adults were still illegal in several US states (USA Today 2014); today, same-sex marriages are legal across the United States and Canada and widely, though not universally, accepted.

The second background reality confronting the philosophy of sex and love today is closely related: we live in what I've called here a liberal capitalist society, in which market relations are expected to govern much of our public life. In these domains, we take for granted a particular model of what people are like, namely, independent, rational individuals with personal needs and preferences, who make implicit or explicit contracts with others to get those needs and preferences met. If we need something, we'll negotiate an exchange for it with someone else. Since we assume that others are equally rational and equally individualistic, we expect them to negotiate in the same way, so as to maximize the satisfaction of their own needs and preferences.

It might seem that these two sets of values – our belief that we get to freely govern our personal lives, and our belief in the legitimacy of self-interested exchange – resolve many of the most basic problems that surround sex and love. As the example of same-sex relations indicates, our contemporary belief in freedom and autonomy certainly helps us resolve some long-standing issues. A form of sexuality that was recently outlawed – and that is still condemned by some religious authorities – now seems unproblematic to most Americans, provided only that all participants are freely-consenting adults. But a central argument of this book is that theorizing sex and love through the lens of personal freedom and autonomy raises important difficulties of its own. In sorting out these difficulties, I've suggested, we need to pay particular attention to the social contexts in which sex and love take place. Reasoning only in terms of individuals' rights and obligations doesn't allow us to understand fully the issues we face. We need to ask how social contexts function in shaping individual choices and about the cumulative effects of those choices. Indeed, we need to ask how autonomy itself should be understood.

Many of these difficulties stem from the fact that our beliefs about both sex and love often seem to challenge the individualistic values that are central to liberal capitalist societies. In the domains of sex and love, mutuality, generosity, and caring are thought to be crucial, but these expectations directly contradict the liberal model of people as self-interested, utility-maximizing individuals. For example, in our discussions of objectification, sex work, sexual surrogacy, and sexual racism, we've seen how widely it's assumed that mutuality is somehow required for sex to be ethical. But once we're in a more individualistic frame of mind, it's hard to see why. There are cases where a person may forgo their own pleasure to focus on another's, out of excitement or from a desire to make the other person happy. There seems to be no reason that sexual pleasure must be repaid in the coin of sexual pleasure, when other pleasures – gustatory, intellectual, comedic – needn't be. Given that it is natural to exchange one kind of sexual pleasure for another, especially when people enjoy different activities, there would seem to be nothing wrong with exchanging sexual pleasures for other things altogether. And yet the broader effects of such exchanges can be troubling. Women's sexual pleasure is often not prioritized, leading to effects like the "orgasm gap." The gendered aspect of much sex work can support gender norms in which men are expected to be dominant and women passive, and that make sex an accomplishment for a man and sullying for a woman. Sexual racism means that people racialized in certain ways can end up with less bargaining power to get what they want out of sexual interactions. These effects mean that sexual autonomy may look different from a social perspective than it does from an individual one. This leads us to ask, what are the demands of sexual mutuality and generosity, and how do they arise?

A similar set of concerns arises in the context of love and family life. Love even more than sex seems to require a concern for the other and a disregard for one's own interests: if you're in it for yourself, that hardly seems like love. As we've seen, however, at least two attempts to resolve the conflict between self-interest in public life and other-regardingness at home lead to problems. Both the idea of love as union and the idea of love as caring concern fit awkwardly with defining adult relationships in terms of equality. In considering the idea of love as union, I suggested that it's only by tracking individuals that we can see and understand the potentially conflicting interests of different people in a relationship. As for the idea of caring concern, I suggested, the conflation of self-interest with other-regardingness also leaves us unable to determine when one person does something for another rather than for themselves. As a result, these theories of love obscure questions of fairness; they offer few ways of understanding how one participant in a love relationship might exploit the other or what would constitute a good balance between looking out for the other person and looking out for yourself.

And, as we've seen in our discussions of family life, sex, marriage, economics, and nonmonogamy, people in intimate relationships in fact often do conceptualize the intimate sphere in terms of negotiation and contractual exchange. The questions of equality and fairness in relationships arise in a pressing way when we consider who will do the caring labor that family life requires. In the individualistic framing, the answer seems to come down to personal preferences, but, as we've seen, when women are socialized to be more caring and nurturing, then the burdens fall disproportionately on them. Finding an approach to love that honors its requirement of taking up the other person's needs and interests, while preserving our individuality, is not as easy as it seems.

The complexities of looking out both for ourselves and for our loved ones leave us puzzled about how much we owe to one another in caring relationships, when we should be doing more for one another, and when we should insist on our own needs and preferences being met. Some of the most heartbreaking conditions of modern life have to do with the way home can become a battleground over who is cleaning up, who is feeding the kids and changing the diapers, who takes off work when someone has to go to the doctor, and what happens when new needs arise that existing, fragile, agreements don't cover. This shows the need for new theories – not theories of love, necessarily, but new theories of the intimate sphere that would put the focus on how love can combine caring with fairness.

I've argued here that we have underappreciated the extent to which our old solutions to these problems rested on a discriminatory framework of exclusively heterosexual, patriarchal marriage. Historically, love, sex, and family life were thought to be protected from norms of self-interest, negotiation, and competition. As we've seen, if sex is only appropriate as part of marriage, and if marriage is thought to unite the wills of two people, then family life seems to create a context free of the rougher trappings of individualism. Domestic life could then serve as a refuge where the caring and other-regardingness naturally associated with love and the generosity and mutuality often associated with sex would make sense. Children could be part of a family unit in which caring and altruism are the norm rather than the exception, so the work of caring for them would not be competing for our attention with all the other demands of public life.

But, as we've seen, this system rested on heterosexual marriage and hierarchical gender roles. Moving away from gendered conceptualizations means that intimacy and family life can be subject to the same norms of individualism relevant everywhere else. This undercuts the mechanisms that once assigned individuals their roles within the family, by revealing how the old frameworks required discriminatory social norms in order to achieve their effects. Of course, the fact that fairness and equality in sex and love have been rendered potentially difficult in no way recommends a return to the bad old days of sexism. But it does suggest the importance of theorizing that starts from the specific realities of our own social world, rather than attempting to construct general and universal theories about how love and sex ought to be.

I've also argued that in matters of sex and love there are conflicts among liberty, justice, and equality. In our discussion of racialized sexual preferences, we saw how patterns of individual choice can lead not only to sexual racism but also to the hypersexualization of specific groups, and to inequalities in their marriage prospects. In our discussion of objectification, we saw how the tendency to more often regard women as sex objects and men as subjects can lead to gender inequality and a reduction in women's social autonomy, even if there's nothing inherently wrong with objectification itself. In our discussion of disability, we saw how social attitudes affect someone's prospects as dating and sex partners. In our discussion of nonmonogamy, we saw the possibility that when the structures that arise from monogamy's imposition are lessened, the difference between the "haves" and the "have-nots" of intimacy can be increased.

The question of sexual inequality is distinct and separable from the system of male entitlement in which it is sometimes embedded. In a perceptive essay (2018), Amia Srinivasan talks about the uncomfortable tension between the fact that we regard our right to our own sexual preferences as inviolable and the patterns of inclusion and exclusion that those preferences can lead to. Using a metaphor, she points out that while no one is obliged to share their sandwich with you, and you don't have a right to demand a share of someone's sandwich, it is still the case that if your child came home and said they were the only one others would not share a sandwich with at school you may find the language of "rights" and "obligation" insufficient in response. This is especially so, she says, if "your child is brown, or fat, or disabled, or doesn't speak English very well" and you suspect this is the reason for their exclusion. She concludes her essay by asking how we can dwell in the "ambivalent place" where "no one is obligated to desire anyone else," and no one "has a right to be desired," while also acknowledging honestly that "who is desired and who isn't" is a political question (Srinivasan 2018). The discussions in this book give texture to understanding this tension: while everyone has a right to their own preferences and choices, we have to acknowledge that those preferences and choices create the sexual and romantic landscape in which we live.

Taken together, these ideas show how understanding philosophical issues related to sex and love requires taking up a perspective that transcends the question of what individuals have a right or obligation to do and what they owe to other individuals. As we've seen throughout this book, preferences, choices, and their effects have to be understood with reference to context: with reference, that is, to background norms, family life, patterns of inclusion and exclusion. Understanding sex and love is always contextual. Instead of asking only one what person owes to another, as individuals we should also be asking what kind of world do we want to live in.

References

Adshade, M. (2013) *Dollars and Sex: How Economics Influences Sex and Love*, San Francisco, Calif.: Chronicle Books.

Agarwal, B. (1997) "'Bargaining' and Gender Relations: Within and Beyond the Household," *Feminist Economics*, 3 (1): 1–51.

American Association on Intellectual and Developmental Disabilities (2017) "Definition of Intellectual Disability." Available at http://aaidd.org/intellectual-disability/definition#.WcvHY2Xw9E4 (accessed September 27, 2017).

Amnesty International (2016) "Amnesty International Policy on State Obligations to Respect, Protect, and Fulfil the Human Rights of Sex Workers," May 26. Available at www.amnesty.org/en/documents/pol30/4062/2016/en/ (accessed September 26, 2017).

Anapol, D. (1997) *Polyamory: The New Love without Limits*, San Rafael, Calif.: IntiNet Resource Center.

Anderson, M. J. (2005) "Negotiating Sex," *Southern California Law Review*, 78 (6): 1401–1573.

Anderson, R. (2013) "The Case for Using Drugs to Enhance Our Relationships (and Our Break Ups)," *The Atlantic*, January 31. Available at www.theatlantic.com/technology/archive/2013/01/the-case-for-using-drugs-to-enhance-our-relationships-and-our-break-ups/272615/ (accessed June 17, 2018).

Anderson, S. A. (2002) "Prostitution and Sexual Autonomy: Making Sense of the Prohibition of Prostitution," *Ethics*, 112 (4): 748–780.

Appel, J. M. (2010) "Sex Rights for the Disabled?" *Journal of Medical Ethics*, 36 (3): 152–154.

Appiah, A. (1985) "The Uncompleted Argument: Du Bois and the Illusion of Race," *Critical Inquiry*, 12 (1): 21–37.

Baglia, J. (2005) *The Viagra Ad Venture: Masculinity, Marketing, and the Performance of Sexual Health*, New York: Peter Lang.

Bancroft, J. (2002) "The Medicalization of Female Sexual Dysfunction: The Need for Caution," *Archives of Sexual Behavior*, 31 (5): 451–455.

Basson, R. (2010) "The Female Sexual Response: A Different Model," *Journal of Sex and Marital Therapy*, 26 (1): 51–65.

Bauer, N. (2007) "Pornutopia," *n+1*, 5 (winter): 63–73.

Becker, G. (1991) *A Treatise on the Family*, enlarged edn, Cambridge, Mass.: Harvard University Press. First published 1981.

Benedet, J. and I. Grant (2014) "Sexual Assault and the Meaning of Power and Authority for Women with Mental Disabilities," *Feminist Legal Studies*, 2 (22): 131–154.

Ben-Ze'ev, A. and L. Brunning (2017) "How Complex Is Your Love? The Case of Romantic Compromises and Polyamory," *Journal for the Theory of Social Behaviour*, 48 (1): 98–116.

Bergner, D. (2009) "What Do Women Want?" *New York Times Magazine*, January 22: 26–33. Available at www.nytimes.com/2009/01/25/magazine/25desire-t.html (accessed September 28, 2017).

Bergner, D. (2013a) "Unexcited? There May Be a Pill for That," *New York Times Magazine*, May 22. Available at www.nytimes.com/2013/05/26/magazine/unexcited-there-may-be-a-pill-for-that.html (accessed June 16, 2018).

Bergner, D. (2013b) *What Do Women Want? Adventures in the Science of Female Desire*, New York: Harper Collins.

Berlin, I. (1969) *Four Essays on Liberty*, Oxford: Oxford University Press.

Bianchi, A. (2016) "Autonomy, Sexuality, and Intellectual Disability," *Social Philosophy Today*, 32: 107–121.

Boni-Saenz, A. (2015) "Sexuality and Incapacity," *Ohio State Law Journal*, 76 (6): 1201–1253.

Brake, E. (2011) "Is Divorce Promise-Breaking?" *Ethical Theory and Moral Practice*, 14 (1): 23–39.

Brake, E. (2012) *Minimizing Marriage: Marriage, Morality, and the Law*, Oxford: Oxford University Press.

Brooks, T. (2009) "The Problem with Polygamy," *Philosophical Topics*, 37 (2): 109–122.

Brown, C. (2011) *Paying for It: A Comic-Strip Memoir about Being a John*, Montreal: Drawn and Quarterly.

Brown, W. III (2003) "Discrimination Dot Com: Racially Biased Interaction in the Online Gay Male Community," *The McNair Scholars Journal of the University of California, Davis*, 6: 22–29.

Butler, D. and F. L. Geis (1990) "Nonverbal Affect Responses to Male and Female Leaders," *Journal of Personality and Social Psychology*, 58 (1): 48–59.

Cahill, A. J. (2012) *Overcoming Objectification: A Carnal Ethics*, London and New York: Routledge.

Cahill, A. J. (2014) "Recognition, Desire, and Unjust Sex," *Hypatia*, 29 (2): 303–319.

Card, C. (1996) "Against Marriage and Motherhood," *Hypatia*, 11 (3): 1–23.

Cave, E. M. (2003) "Marital Pluralism: Making Marriage Safer for Love," *Journal of Social Philosophy*, 34 (3): 331–347.

Chideya, F. (2010) "John Mayer's Playboy Interview: A 'Tweachable Moment' in Race, Gender," *Huffington Post*, April 13. Available at www.huffingtonpost.com/farai-chideya/john-mayers-playboy-inter_b_458097.html (accessed September 27, 2017).

Clardy, J. L. (2013) "Love, Reason, and Romantic Relationships," Master's Dissertation, University of Arkansas. Available at http://scholarworks.uark.edu/etd/1016 (accessed June 25, 2018).

Clark, R. D. and E. Hatfield (1989) "Gender Differences in Receptivity to Sexual Offers," *Journal of Psychology and Human Sexuality*, 2 (1): 39–55.

Cohen-Greene, C. T. (2012) *An Intimate Life: Sex, Love, and My Journey as a Surrogate Partner*, Berkeley, Calif.: Soft Skull Press.

Coleman, N. A. T. (2011) "What? What? In the (Black) Butt," *The Newsletter on Philosophy and Lesbian, Gay, Bisexual, and Transgender Issues*, 11 (1): 12–15.

Conley, T. D. (2011) "Perceived Proposer Personality Characteristics and Gender Differences in Acceptance of Casual Sex Offers," *Journal of Personality and Social Psychology*, 100 (2): 309–329.

Conly, S. (2004) "Seduction, Rape, and Coercion," *Ethics*, 115 (1): 96–121.

Coontz, S. (2006) *Marriage, a History: How Love Conquered Marriage*, New York: Penguin.

Crenshaw, K. (1989) "Demarginalizing the Intersection of Race and Sex: A Black Feminist Critique of Antidiscrimination Doctrine, Feminist Theory and Anti-racist Politics," *University of Chicago Legal Forum*, 1: 139–167.

Cudd, A. E. (1994) "Oppression by Choice," *Journal of Social Philosophy*, 25: 22–44.

Cudd, A. E. (2001) "Rational Choice Theory and the Lessons of Feminism," in L. Antony and C. Witt (eds.), *A Mind of One's Own: Feminist Essays on Reason and Objectivity*, Boulder, Col.: Westview Press, pp. 398–417.

Daniels, N. (1985) *Just Health Care*, Cambridge: Cambridge University Press.

Dargis, M. (2016) "Sundance Fights Tide with Films Like 'The Birth of a Nation'," *New York Times*, January 30. Available at www.nytimes.com/2016/01/30/movies/sundance-fights-tide-with-films-like-the-birth-of-a-nation.html?_r=0 (accessed September 27, 2017).

Davy, L. (2015) "Philosophical Inclusive Design: Intellectual Disability and the Limits of Individual Autonomy in Moral and Political Theory," *Hypatia*, 30 (1): 132–148.

de Boer, T. (2015) "Disability and Sexual Inclusion," *Hypatia*, 30 (1): 66–81.

de la Baume, M. (2013) "Disabled People Say They, Too, Want a Sex Life, and Seek Help in Attaining It," *New York Times*, July 5. Available at www.nytimes.com/2013/07/05/world/europe/disabled-people-say-they-too-want-a-sex-life-and-seek-help-in-attaining-it.html (accessed September 27, 2017).

Delaney, N. (1996) "Romantic Love and Loving Commitment: Articulating a Modern Ideal," *American Philosophical Quarterly*, 33 (4): 339–356.

Dembroff, R. A. (2016) "What Is Sexual Orientation?" *Philosopher's Imprint*, 16 (3): 1–27.

DeVidi, D. (2012) "Advocacy, Autism and Autonomy," in J. Anderson and S. Cushing (eds.), *The Philosophy of Autism*, Lanham, Md.: Rowman & Littlefield, pp. 187–200.

Dewan, A. (2017) "Britain Posthumously Pardons Thousands of Gay Men in 'Turing Law'," *CNN*, January 31. Available at www.cnn.com/2017/01/31/europe/britain-gay-pardon-turing-law/index.html (accessed September 28, 2017).

Díaz-León, E. (2017) "Sexual Orientation as Interpretation? Sexual Desires, Concepts, and Choice," *Journal of Social Ontology*, 3 (2): 231–248.

Digby, T. (2014) *Love and War: How Militarism Shapes Sexuality and Romance*, New York: Columbia University Press.

Dominus, S. (2017) "Is an Open Marriage a Happier Marriage?" *New York Times Magazine*, May 11. Available at www.nytimes.com/2017/05/11/magazine/is-an-open-marriage-a-happier-marriage.html?_r=0 (accessed September 29, 2017).

Earp, B. D., A. Sandberg, and J. Savulescu (2012) "Natural Selection, Child-rearing, and the Ethics of Marriage (and Divorce): Building a Case for the Neuroenhancement of Human Relationships," *Philosophy and Technology*, 25 (4): 561–587.

Earp, B. D., A. Sandberg, and J. Savulescu (2015) "The Medicalization of Love," *Cambridge Quarterly of Healthcare Ethics*, 24 (3): 323–336.

Earp, B. D., A. Sandberg, and J. Savulescu (2016) "The Medicalization of Love: Response to Critics," *Cambridge Quarterly of Healthcare Ethics*, 25 (4): 759–771.

Easton, D. and J. Hardy (2009) *The Ethical Slut: A Practical Guide to Polyamory, Open Relationships, and Other Adventures*, Berkeley, Calif.: Celestial Arts.

Ebels-Duggan, K. (2008) "Against Beneficence: A Normative Account of Love," *Ethics*, 119 (1): 142–170.

Elster, J. (1985) *Sour Grapes: Studies in the Subversion of Rationality*, Cambridge: Cambridge University Press.

Emens, E. F. (2004) "Monogamy's Law: Compulsory Monogamy and Poly-amorous Existence," *NYU Review of Law and Social Change*, 29: 277–376.

Emens, E. F. (2009) "Intimate Discrimination: The State's Role in the Accidents of Sex and Love," *Harvard Law Review*, 122 (5): 1307–1402.

England, P. (1989) "A Feminist Critique of Rational-Choice Theories: Implications for Sociology," *American Sociologist*, 20 (1): 14–28.

Ericsson, L. O. (1980) "Charges against Prostitution: An Attempt at a Philoso-phical Assessment," *Ethics*, 90 (3): 335–366.

Eskridge, W. N.Jr (1992) "A Social Constructionist Critique of Posner's Sex and Reason: Steps toward a Gaylegal Agenda," *Yale Law Journal*, 102 (1): 333–386.

Estes, Y. (2001) "Moral Reflections on Prostitution," *Essays in Philosophy*, 2 (2). Available at http://commons.pacificu.edu/eip/vol2/iss2/10 (accessed December 16, 2018).

Estes, Y. (2008) "Prostitution: A Subjective Position," in A. Soble and N. Power (eds.), *The Philosophy of Sex: Contemporary Readings*, 5th edn, pp. 353–365.

Fehr, C. (2011) "Feminist Philosophy of Biology," in E. N. Zalta (ed.), *The Stan-ford Encyclopedia of Philosophy* (fall 2011 edition). Available online at https://plato.stanford.edu/archives/fall2011/entries/feminist-philosophy-biology/ (accessed December 10, 2018).

Firestone, S. (1970) *The Dialetic of Sex: The Case for Feminist Revolution*, New York: Bantam Books.

Fortunata, J. (1980) "Masturbation and Women's Sexuality," in A. Soble (ed.), *The Philosophy of Sex: Collected Readings*, Totawa, NJ: Rowman & Littlefield, pp. 389–408.

Foster, G. (2009) "Bestowal without Appraisal: Problems in Frankfurt's Char-acterization of Love and Personal Identity," *Ethical Theory and Moral Practice*, 12 (2): 153–168.

Fox, M. (2013) "Patients with Benefits," *Elle*, January 4. Available at www.elle.com/life-love/sex-relationships/advice/a12548/sex-surrogacy/ (accessed September 27, 2017).

France 24 (2016) "Hollande Mocked for Calling Sexual Orientation a 'Choice'," June 15. Available at www.france24.com/en/20160614-french-president-mocked-gay-gaffe (accessed September 28, 2017).

Frankfurt, H. G. (1971) "Freedom of the Will and the Concept of a Person," *Journal of Philosophy*, 68 (1): 5–20.

Frankfurt, H. G. (1999) *Necessity, Volition, and Love*, Cambridge: Cambridge University Press.

Frankfurt, H. G. (2004) *The Reasons of Love*, Princeton, NJ: Princeton University Press.

Friedman, M. A (1985) "Moral Integrity and the Deferential Wife," *Philosophical Studies*, 47 (1): 141–150.

Galupo, M. P., R. C. Mitchell, A. L. Grynkiewicz, and K. S. Davis (2014). "Sexual Minority Reflections on the Kinsey Scale and the Klein Sexual Orientation Grid: Conceptualization and Measurement," *Journal of Bisexuality*, 14 (3–4): 404–432.

Garcia, J. L. A (1996) "The Heart of Racism," *Journal of Social Philosophy*, 27 (1): 5–45.

Garry, A. (2002) "Sex, Lies, and Pornography," in H. LaFollette (ed.), *Ethics in Practice: An Anthology*, 2nd edn, Oxford: Blackwell, pp. 344–355.

Gill, M. (2015) *Already Doing It: Intellectual Disability and Sexual Agency*, Minneapolis, Minn.: University of Minnesota Press.

Grant, M. G. (2014) *Playing the Whore: The Work of Sex Work*, London: Verso Books.

Greenberg, A. S. and J. M. Bailey (2001) "Parental Selection of Children's Sexual Orientation," *Archives of Sexual Behavior*, 30 (4): 423–437.

Grindley, L. (2012) "Cynthia Nixon: Being Bisexual 'Is Not a Choice.'" *The Advocate*, January 30. Available at www.advocate.com/news/daily-news/2012/01/30/cynthia-nixon-being-bisexual-not-choice (accessed September 28, 2017).

Gupta, K. (2012) "Protecting Sexual Diversity: Rethinking the Use of Neurotechnological Interventions to Alter Sexuality," *AJOB Neuroscience*, 3 (3): 24–28.

Hacking, I. (1999) *The Social Construction of What?* Cambridge, Mass.: Harvard University Press.

Hadfield, G. (1992) "Flirting with Science: Richard Posner on the Bioeconomics of Sexual Man," *Harvard Law Review*, 106 (2): 479–503.

Halley, J. (2016) "The Move to Affirmative Consent," *Signs: Journal of Women in Culture and Society*, 42 (1): 257–279.

Halwani, R. (2017) "Racial Sexual Desires," in R. Halwani, A. Soble, S. Hoffman, and J. M. Held (eds.), *The Philosophy of Sex: Contemporary Readings*, 7th edn, Lanham, Md.: Rowman & Littlefield, pp. 181–198.

Hausman, D. M. (2012) *Preference, Value, Choice, and Welfare*, Cambridge: Cambridge University Press.

Heldman, C. and L. Wade (2010) "Hook-Up Culture: Setting a New Research Agenda," *Sexuality Research and Social Policy*, 7 (4): 323–333.

Herman, B. (1993) "Could It Be Worth Thinking about Kant on Sex and Marriage?" in L. Antony and C. Witt (eds.), *A Mind of One's Own: Feminist Essays on Reason and Objectivity*, Boulder, Col.: Westview Press, pp. 53–72.

Hess, A. (2013) "Women Want Sex," *Slate*, June 4. Available at www.slate.com/articles/double_x/doublex/2013/06/what_do_women_want_sex_according_to_daniel_bergner_s_new_book_on_female.html?via=gdpr-consent (accessed June 25, 2018).

Hill, T. E. (1973) "Servility and Self-Respect," *The Monist*, 57 (1): 87–104.

hooks, b. (2000) *All about Love: New Visions*, New York: William Morrow.

hooks, b. (2015) "Eating the Other," in *Black Looks: Race and Representation*, London and New York: Routledge, pp. 21–39. First published 1992.

Huang, E. (2013) *Fresh Off the Boat: A Memoir*, New York: Random House.

Huffington Post (2012) "Cameron Diaz: 'Every Woman Wants To Be Objectified,'" *Huffington Post*. Available at www.huffingtonpost.com/2012/11/20/cameron-dia

z-every-woman-wants-to-be-objectified_n_2164965.html (accessed September 25, 2017).

International Professional Surrogates Association (2017) "What is Surrogate Partner Therapy?" Available at www.surrogatetherapy.org/what-is-surrogate-partner-therapy/ (accessed September 27, 2017).

Jagose, A. (1996) *Queer Theory: An Introduction*, New York: NYU Press.

Jeffreys, S. (2008) "Disability and the Male Sex Right," *Women's Studies International Forum*, 31 (5): 327–335.

Jenkins, C. (2017) *What Love Is: And What It Could Be*, New York: Basic Books.

Jones, M. (2018) "What Teenagers Are Learning from Online Porn," *The New York Times Magazine*, February 7. Available at www.nytimes.com/2018/02/07/magazine/teenagers-learning-online-porn-literacy-sex-education.html (accessed December 13, 2018).

Kant, I. (1997) *Lectures on Ethics*, trans. Peter Heath and ed. J. B. Schneewind, Cambridge: Cambridge University Press.

Kittay, E. F. (2011) "The Ethics of Care, Dependence, and Disability," *Ratio Juris*, 24 (1): 49–58.

Kramer, P. D. (1993) *Listening to Prozac: A Psychiatrist Explores Antidepressant Drugs and the Remaking of the Self*, New York: Viking.

Langton, R. (2009) *Sexual Solipsism: Philosophical Essays on Pornography and Objectification*, Oxford: Oxford University Press.

Lasch, C. (1979) *Haven in a Heartless World: The Family Besieged*, New York: Basic Books.

Lazenby, H. and I. Gabriel (2018) "Permissible Secrets," *The Philosophical Quarterly*, 68 (271): 265–285.

Lee, J. Y. (1996) "Why Suzie Wong Is Not a Lesbian: Asian and Asian American Lesbian and Bisexual Women and Femme/Butch/Gender Identities," in B. Beemyn and M. Eliason (eds.), *Queer Studies: A Lesbian, Gay, Bisexual and Transgender Anthology*, New York: New York University Press, pp. 115–132.

Liberman, A. (2018) "Disability, Sex Rights and the Scope of Sexual Exclusion," *Journal of Medical Ethics*, 44 (4): 253–256.

Lloyd, E. A. (2009) *The Case of the Female Orgasm: Bias in the Science of Evolution*, Cambridge, Mass.: Harvard University Press.

MacKinnon, C. A. (1989) *Toward a Feminist Theory of the State*, Cambridge, Mass.: Harvard University Press.

Mappes, T. (2002) "Sexual Morality and the Concept of Using Another Person," in *Philosophy of Sex*, 4th edn, Lanham, Md.: Rowman & Littlefield, pp. 207–223.

Marino, P. (2008) "The Ethics of Sexual Objectification: Autonomy and Consent," *Inquiry*, 51 (4): 345–364.

Marino, P. (2017) "Love and Economics," in C. Grau and A. Smuts (eds.), *Oxford Handbook of the Philosophy of Love*, Oxford: Oxford University Press. Available at http://www.oxfordhandbooks.com/view/10.1093/oxfordhb/9780199395729.001.0001/oxfordhb-9780199395729-e-20 (accessed December 16, 2018).

McConnell, C., S. Brue, S. Flynn, and T. Barbiero (2013) *Microeconomics*, 13th Canadian edn, Toronto: McGraw-Hill Ryerson.

McRuer, R. and A. Mollow (2012) *Sex and Disability*, Durham, NC: Duke University Press.

Mendus, S. (1984) "Marital Faithfulness," *Philosophy*, 59 (228): 243–252.

Merino, N. (2004) "The Problem with 'We': Rethinking Joint Identity in Romantic Love," *Journal of Social Philosophy*, 35 (1): 123–132.

Miller-Young, M. (2013) "Interventions: The Deviant and Defiant Art of Black Women Porn Directors," in T. Taormino, C. Parreñas Shimizu, C. Penley, and M. Miller-Young (eds.), *The Feminist Porn Book: The Politics of Producing Pleasure*, New York: The Feminist Press at CUNY, pp. 105–120.

Miller-Young, M. (2014) *A Taste for Brown Sugar: Black Women in Pornography*, Durham, NC: Duke University Press.

Mills, C. W. (1994) "Do Black Men Have a Moral Duty to Marry Black Women?" *Journal of Social Philosophy*, 25 (s1): 131–153.

Mintz, K. T. (2014) "Sexual Intimacy, Social Justice, and Severe Disabilities: Should Fair Equality of Opportunity in Health Extend to Surrogate Partner Therapy?" *Journal of Philosophy, Science and Law*, 14 (3): 4–15.

Mintz, K. T. (2017a) "Ableism, Ambiguity, and the Anna Stubblefield Case," *Disability and Society*, 32 (10): 1666–1670.

Mintz, K. T. (2017b) Personal correspondence, quoted with permission.

Mintz, L. (2018) "Orgasm Gap: Picking Up Where the Sex Revolution Left Off," *Psychology Today Blog*, May 20. Available at www.psychologytoday.com/us/blog/stress-and-sex/201805/orgasm-gap-picking-where-the-sex-revolution-left (accessed December 16, 2018).

Mohr, R. D. (1992) *Gay Ideas: Outing and Other Controversies*, Boston, Mass.: Beacon Press.

Moss-Racusin, C. A., J. F. Dovidio, V. L. Brescoll, M. J. Graham, and J. Handelsman (2012) "Science Faculty's Subtle Gender Biases Favor Male Students," *Proceedings of the National Academy of Sciences*, 109 (41): 16474–16479.

Muehlenhard, C., T. Humphreys, K. Jozkowski, and Z. Peterson (2016) "The Complexities of Sexual Consent among College Students: A Conceptual and Empirical Review," *Journal of Sex Research*, 53 (4–5): 457–487.

Murphy, G. H., and A. L. I. O'Callaghan (2004). "Capacity of Adults with Intellectual Disabilities to Consent to Sexual Relationships," *Psychological Medicine*, 34 (7): 1347–1357.

Nagoski, E. (2015) *Come as You Are: The Surprising New Science That Will Transform Your Sex Life*, New York: Simon & Schuster.

Newman, G. E., P. Bloom, and J. Knobe (2014) "Value Judgments and the True Self," *Personality and Social Psychology Bulletin*, 40 (2): 203–216.

Nozick, R. (1989) "Love's Bond," in *The Examined Life: Philosophical Meditations*, New York: Simon & Schuster, pp. 68–86.

Nussbaum, M. C. (1995) "Objectification," *Philosophy and Public Affairs*, 24 (4): 249–291.

Nussbaum, M. C. (1997) "Flawed Foundations: The Philosophical Critique of (A Particular Type of) Economics," *University of Chicago Law Review*, 64 (4): 1197–1214.

O'Brien, M. (1990) "On Seeing a Sex Surrogate," *The Sun*, 174. Available at www.thesunmagazine.org/issues/174/on-seeing-a-sex-surrogate (accessed September 26, 2017).

O'Brien, S. A. (2015) "78 Cents on the Dollar: The Facts about the Gender Wage Gap," *CNN*, April 14. Available at http://money.cnn.com/2015/04/13/news/economy/equal-pay-day-2015/index.html (accessed September 29, 2017).

Oklahoma State University (2018) "What Is Consent?" Available at https://1is2many.okstate.edu/consent (accessed December 13, 2018).

Organization Intersex International (2017) "Welcome." Available at http://oiiinternational.com/2533/welcome/ (accessed September 28, 2017).

Pascoe, J. (2012) "Kant and Kinky Sex," in S. Kaye (ed.), *What Philosophy Can Tell You about Your Lover*, Chicago, Ill.: Open Court Publishing, pp. 25–36.

Pateman, C. (1988) *The Sexual Contract*, Stanford, Calif.: Stanford University Press.

Perel, E. (2006) *Mating in Captivity*, New York: Harper Collins.

Perlin, M. L. (1992) "On Sanism," *SMU Law Review*, 46 (2): 373–407.

Perlin, M. L. and A. Lynch (2016) *Sexuality, Disability, and the Law: Beyond the Last Frontier?* New York: Palgrave Macmillan.

Petner-Arrey, J. and S. R. Copeland (2015) "'You Have to Care": Perceptions of Promoting Autonomy in Support Settings for Adults with Intellectual Disability," *British Journal of Learning Disabilities*, 43 (1): 38–48.

Pineau, L. (1989) "Date Rape: A Feminist Analysis," *Law and Philosophy*, 8 (2): 217–243.

Pollak, R. A. (2003) "Gary Becker's Contributions to Family and Household Economics," *Review of Economics of the Household*, 1 (1): 111–141.

Posner, R. A. (1992) *Sex and Reason*, Cambridge, Mass.: Harvard University Press.

Project Respect (2017) "Consent." Available at www.yesmeansyes.com/consent (accessed September 26, 2017).

Pujol, M. (2003) "Into the Margin!" in D. Barker and E. Kuiper (eds.), *Toward a Feminist Philosophy of Economics*, London and New York: Routledge, pp. 21–37.

Rich, A. (1980) "Compulsory Heterosexuality and Lesbian Existence," *Signs*, 5 (4): 631–660.

Richardson, B. (2016) "American Law Institute Rejects Affirmative Consent Standard in Defining Sexual Assault," *The Washington Times*, May 17. Available at www.washingtontimes.com/news/2016/may/17/american-law-institute-rejects-affirmative-consent/ (accessed September 26, 2017).

Robbins, L. (1932) *An Essay on the Nature and Significance of Economic Science*, London: Macmillan.

Ryan, R. M. (1995) "The Sex Right: A Legal History of the Marital Rape Exemption," *Law and Social Inquiry*, 20 (4): 941–1001.

Satz, D. (1995) "Markets in Women's Sexual Labor," *Ethics*, 106 (1): 63–85.

Saunders, G. (2010) "Escape from Spiderhead," *The New Yorker*, December 20 and 27. Available at www.newyorker.com/magazine/2010/12/20/escape-from-spiderhead (accessed September 29, 2017).

Savage, D. (2006) *The Commitment: Love, Sex, Marriage, and My Family*, New York: Plume.

Savulescu, J. and A. Sandberg (2008) "Neuroenhancement of Love and Marriage: The Chemicals between Us," *Neuroethics*, 1 (1): 31–44.

Schulhofer, S. J. (1992) "Taking Sexual Autonomy Seriously: Rape Law and Beyond," *Law and Philosophy*, 11 (1/2): 35–94.

Sen, A. (1981) "Plural Utility," *Proceedings of the Aristotelian Society*, 81 (1): 193–216.

Sen, A. (1987) *On Ethics and Economics*, New York: Basil Blackwell.

Shakespeare, T. (2006) *Disability Rights and Wrongs*, London and New York: Routledge.

Shakespeare, T., K. Gillespie-Sells, and D. Davies (1996) *Sexual Politics of Disability: Untold Desires*, London: Cassell.

Shelby, T. (2002) "Is Racism in the 'Heart'?" *Journal of Social Philosophy*, 33 (3): 411–420.

Shrage, L. (1989) "Should Feminists Oppose Prostitution," *Ethics*, 99 (2): 347–361.

Soble, A. (1997a) "Antioch's 'Sexual Offense Policy': A Philosophical Exploration," *Journal of Social Philosophy*, 28 (1): 22–36.

Soble, A. (1997b) "Union, Autonomy, and Concern," in R. Lamb (ed.), *Love Analyzed*, Boulder, Col.: Westview Press, pp. 65–92.

Solomon, S. E., E. D. Rothblum, and K. F. Balsam (2005) "Money, Housework, Sex, and Conflict: Same-Sex Couples in Civil Unions, Those Not in Civil Unions, and Heterosexual Married Siblings," *Sex Roles*, 52 (9): 561–575.

Srinivasan, A. (2018) "Does Anyone Have the Right to Sex?" *London Review of Books*, 40 (6): 5–10.

State University of New York (2018) "Definition of Affirmative Consent." Available at https://system.suny.edu/sexual-violence-prevention-workgroup/policies/affirmative-consent (accessed December 13, 2018).

Stein, E. (2011) "Sexual Orientations, Rights, and the Body: Immutability, Essentialism, and Nativism," *Social Research*, 78 (2): 633–658.

Stoljar, N. (2015) "Feminist Perspectives on Autonomy," in E. N. Zalta (ed.), *The Stanford Encyclopedia of Philosophy* (fall 2015 edition). Available at https://plato.stanford.edu/archives/fall2015/entries/feminism-autonomy/ (accessed December 10, 2018).

Suschinsky, K. D. and M. L. Lalumière (2011) "Prepared for Anything? An Investigation of Female Genital Arousal in Response to Rape Cues," *Psychological Science*, 22 (2): 159–165.

Taylor, P. C. (2013) *Race: A Philosophical Introduction*, 2nd edn, Cambridge: Polity.

Teunis, N. (2007) "Sexual Objectification and the Construction of Whiteness in the Gay Male Community," *Culture, Health and Sexuality*, 9 (3): 263–275.

Teunis, N. and G. Herdt (2007) *Sexual Inequalities and Social Justice*, Berkeley, CA: University of California Press.

Tiefer, L. (2006a) "Female Sexual Dysfunction: A Case Study of Disease Mongering and Activist Resistance," *PLoS Medicine*, 3 (4): 436–440.

Tiefer, L. (2006b) "The Viagra Phenomenon," *Sexualities*, 9 (3): 273–294.

Tsang, D. C. (1992) "M. Butterfly Meets the Great White Hope," *Informasian*, 6 (3): 3–4.

USA Today (2014) "12 States Still Ban Sodomy a Decade after Court Ruling." Available at https://eu.usatoday.com/story/news/nation/2014/04/21/12-states-ban-sodomy-a-decade-after-court-ruling/7981025/ (accessed June 22, 2018).

Varden, H. (2006) "A Kantian Conception of Rightful Sexual Relations: Sex, (Gay) Marriage, and Prostitution," *Social Philosophy Today*, 22: 199–218.

Warner, M. (2000) *The Trouble with Normal: Sex, Politics, and the Ethics of Queer Life*, Cambridge, Mass.: Harvard University Press.

West, R. (2010) "Sex, Law, and Consent," in F. Miller and A. Wertheimer (eds.), *The Ethics of Consent: Theory and Practice*, Oxford: Oxford University Press, pp. 221–250.

Westlund, A. C. (2003) "Selflessness and Responsibility for Self: Is Deference Compatible with Autonomy?" *The Philosophical Review*, 112 (4): 483–523.

Westlund, A. C. (2008) "The Reunion of Marriage," *The Monist*, 91 (3/4): 558–577.

Wilkerson, W. S. (2009) "Is It a Choice? Sexual Orientation as Interpretation," *Journal of Social Philosophy*, 40 (1): 97–116.

Wonderly, M. (2017) "Love and Attachment," *American Philosophical Quarterly*, 54 (3): 235–250.

Zembaty, J. S. and T. A. Mappes (1987) *Social Ethics: Morality and Social Policy*, 3rd edn, New York: McGraw-Hill.

Zheng, R. (2016) "Why Yellow Fever Isn't Flattering: A Case against Racial Fetishes," *Journal of the American Philosophical Association*, 2 (3): 400–419.

Zheng, R. (2017) "Race and Pornography: The Dilemma of the (Un)Desirable," in M. Mikkola (ed.), *Beyond Speech: Pornography and Analytic Feminist Philosophy*, Oxford: Oxford University Press, pp. 177–196.

Index

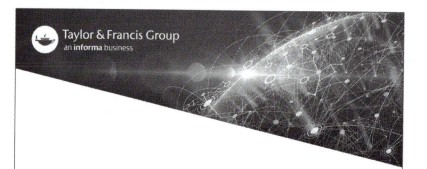